GRACE IN EVERY SEASON

Grace
in Every Season

Through the Year with Catherine Doherty

Daily Reflections Selected
by Mary Bazzett

MADONNA HOUSE
Combermere, Ontario

PUBLICATIONS
Canada   K0J 1L0

Cover design: Micheal Andaloro
Cover photo illustration: Martin Soo Hoo

Canadian Cataloguing in Publication Data
Doherty, Catherine de Hueck, 1896-1985

Grace in every Season

ISBN 0-921440-31-6
  1.Devotional calendars. 2. Meditations
     I Title
BX2182.2.D64   1992   242'.2   C92-090169-7

second printing 1996
Madonna House Publications
Combermere, Ontario
K0J 1L0

Printed in Canada

Dedication

To Catherine's beloved readers,
many of whom she never met in this life.
We know she will be walking with you
through this year of grace and
holding you before the face of the Father.

Contents

April / 95
> *Major Themes:* Lenten and Easter meditations with emphasis on prayer and the virtue of hope.

> *Fixed Solemnities, Feasts, and Other Special Occasions:*
> April 25: St. Mark, the Evangelist
> April 29: St. Catherine of Siena, Doctor of the Church

May / 119
> *Major Themes:* Marian focus, springtime, new life, prayer, and farming.

> *Fixed Solemnities, Feasts, and Other Special Occasions:*
> May 1: St. Joseph, the Worker
> May 3: Sts. Philip and James, Apostles
> May 4 : Anniversary of Fr. Eddie Doherty's Death
> May 15: St. Isidore, Patron of Farmers
> May 17: Foundation Day for Madonna House
> May 26: St. Philip Neri
> May 31: The Visitation

June / 143
> *Major Themes:* month of the Sacred Heart of Jesus, Christian recreation, God as Father, and practical tips for supervisors.

> *Fixed Solemnities, Feasts, and Other Special Occasions:*
> June 8: Our Lady of Combermere
> June 21: First Day of Summer
> June 24 : Birth of St. John the Baptist
> June 29: Sts. Peter and Paul, Apostles

July / 167
> *Major Themes:* month of the Precious Blood of Jesus, the Ten Commandments, vacation, and prayer.

> *Fixed Solemnities, Feasts, and Other Special Occasions:*
> July 3: St. Thomas, the Apostle
> July 16: Our Lady of Mount Carmel
> July 31: St. Ignatius of Loyola

August / 193

Major Themes: summertime stories, the beatitudes, prayer and silence, superficial communication, boredom, and just anger.

Fixed Solemnities, Feasts, and Other Special Occasions:
August 4: St. John Vianney, Patron of Parish Priests
August 6: The Transfiguration
August 10: St. Lawrence, Deacon
August 15: The Assumption of Mary into Heaven
August 28: St. Augustine, Doctor of the Church

September / 217

Major Themes: back-to-school emphasis on learning and teaching, work including production mentality and "workaholism," conformity and diversity, the nature of the church.

Fixed Solemnities, Feasts, and Other Special Occasions:
September 8: Birth of Mary
September 9: St. Peter Claver
September 13: St. John Chrysostom, Doctor of the Church
September 14: Triumph of the Cross
September 15: Our Lady of Sorrows
September 21: First Day of Autumn
September 29: The Archangels
September 30: St. Jerome, Doctor of the Church

October / 241

Major Themes: prayer, love, pain, spiritual growth, dealing with fear, and Christian manners.

Fixed Solemnities, Feasts, and Other Special Occasions:
October 1: St. Thérèse of the Child Jesus
October 2: Guardian Angels
October 4: St. Francis of Assisi
October 7: Our Lady of the Rosary
October 15: St. Teresa of Avila, Doctor of the Church
October 18 : St. Luke, the Evangelist
October 19: Sts. Isaac Jogues and John de Brebeuf, Martyrs

November / 265

Major Themes: thanksgiving and the virtue of gratitude, handling doubts, managing time well, and the beginning of Advent.

Fixed Solemnities, Feasts, and Other Special Occasions:
November 1: All Saints' Day
November 2: All Souls' Day
November 3: St. Martin de Porres
November 22: St. Cecilia, Patroness of Music

December / 289

Major Themes: Advent and Christmas

Fixed *Solemnities, Feasts, and Other Special Occasions:*
December 6: St. Nicholas, Bishop
December 8: The Immaculate Conception
December 12: Our Lady of Guadalupe
December 13: St. Lucy, Martyr
December 14: St. John of the Cross and Anniversary of the Death of Catherine Doherty
December 21: First Day of Winter
December 24: Christmas Eve
December 25: Christmas Day
December 26: St. Stephen, First Martyr
December 27: St. John the Beloved, Apostle
December 28: Holy Innocents, Martyrs
December 31: New Year's Eve

Introduction

If there is anyone in our modern age who can show us how to apply the Gospel to daily life, it is Catherine Doherty.

By her personal example and her work with the poor, by her lectures and writings, and through the community that she founded—the Madonna House Apostolate—she offers many concrete examples of how to bring Christ into the marketplace of today's world. Her rich spirituality forms a blueprint for living the Gospel today, for persons in all walks of life, in every segment of the church.

Her way of living Christ's teachings is little and simple and humble like Nazareth. It is agonizing and public and courageous like Calvary. But always it has the mark of Bethlehem—*God existing in our human flesh.* Catherine tells us that the task of every Christian is to *incarnate* the Gospel, to "put human flesh on it" each day, whatever our situations may be.

Indeed, the genius of her spirituality is its "portability" to any locale, and the way it applies to any life situation. Although her writings were often directed to her own staff, they are capable of speaking to many others, from the most learned theologian to the school child. Their rich variety ranges from practical down-to-earth advice, to mystical spiritual poetry; from her cogent explanations of the faith and forceful admonitions to live the Gospel without compromise to tales about her idyllic childhood in old Russia.

Catherine's extensive collection of writings are found in numerous published articles and books, as well as personal correspondence and other unpublished materials. This book draws from all these sources, to provide an introductory "sampler" of her spirituality for readers unfamiliar with her, as well as selected gems for readers who already know her. The themes of this book—poverty and humility, sacrifice and service, prayer and silence, faith, hope, and love—are woven into the very fabric of Catherine's personality. Their threads run through every season of her life and every part of this book.

Whatever page you turn to, you will be met by her voice, speaking out with authority and clarity. Her words may be instructive, inspiring, or consoling. They are sometimes humorous, and often prophetic, with a message that rings resoundingly true today. Hers was a voice that spoke fearlessly and clearly. Thomas Merton, after he first heard Catherine speak in public, wrote, "She had a strong voice, and strong convictions, and strong things to say, and she was saying them in the simplest, most unvarnished, bluntest possible kind of talk, and with such uncompromising directness that it stunned."

A PASSIONATE LOVE AFFAIR WITH GOD

Whenever Catherine spoke, on whatever topic, her words ultimately reflected one thing: her passionate love affair with God. It was a love affair that understood the cross as a marriage bed and pain as the kiss of Christ. It was a love affair that Catherine lived to the hilt, never counting the cost. It was a love affair into which she dove head-first every day, on good days and bad days, in all the seasons of the year, and all the seasons of her life. This book reflects those seasons.

Catherine loved God not just politely, not just reverently, but deeply, totally, passionately—in everything that she did. Her whole life, in fact, was a big, passionate love affair with God.

This love story sprang from Russian roots, beginning with

her birth on the feast of the Assumption, August 15, 1896, in Nizhni-Novgorod (later called Gorki) in Russia. She was raised by wise and devout Christian parents who owned an extensive estate where Catherine learned numerous practical skills in an Old World atmosphere. Her father was a businessman who often acted in a diplomatic capacity, so she was exposed to many cultures. She traveled extensively, learned many languages, and first attended school in Egypt.

Catherine's life contained enough adventure for an epic film, including her marriage at age fifteen to her cousin, the wealthy Russian Baron Boris de Hueck; her involvement in World War I, during which she served as a nurse to the Czar's troops at the German front and was decorated for bravery under fire; and her firsthand witness of the Bolshevik takeover of her beloved city of St. Petersburg.

Catherine and Boris escaped Communist Russia, fleeing first to a family summer house in Finland, where they nearly starved to death at the hands of Communists. Then they were liberated by White Russian soldiers. In late 1919, they left from Murmansk for Scotland, then England. In 1921, the couple, by then penniless, traveled to Canada, where their son, George, was born.

Catherine worked as a sales clerk, a laundress, a maid, and a waitress to support her infant son and her husband, who was in frail health. After a time, she found well-paying work in the lecture field, criss-crossing North America to give lectures and working out of New York City as an executive with a literary agency there. Meanwhile Boris, who had been trained as an architectural engineer in Russia, managed to form his own company in Montreal.

Their journey had been one from riches to rags, and back to riches again. But it did not end there. Though outwardly successful, they had endured deep inner pain. They had struggled through war and revolution. They had experienced refugee status as stateless persons, with a total loss of their cultural heritage. This aristocratic couple had endured emigration to a foreign shore and menial jobs, suffering the long miles and long separations, as each sought ways to pull the family out of the mire of poverty. Seemingly, they had survived the ordeal, but at great damage to their married life. Finally, they had the chance to be reunited again. Catherine quit her job in New York and moved to Montreal, continuing to act as literary agent for some of her former clients. But the Great Depression shattered all their hopes: Boris' firm went bankrupt; Catherine's income declined; the fabric of their family life totally unraveled. Aware that their honest attempt at reconciliation had failed, Boris and Catherine decided to go their separate ways.

As the economic decline deepened and became worldwide, Catherine found herself pulled in two conflicting directions. She realized she was a single parent with a small child to support. Yet she felt hounded by Christ's words to the rich young man in the Scripture verse, "Sell all you possess, give it to the poor, and come—follow me!"

Eventually, she did exactly that, giving away her wealth and possessions to the poor, keeping only enough to provide for her son. Then, with the blessing of her bishop, Neil McNeil of Toronto, she went to live and work with the poor in the slums of Toronto, where she founded Friendship House. Her passionate love of Christ in the poor and her sacrificial service to them in small, humble ways led to the establishment of Friendship Houses in New York City's Harlem section, in Chicago, and other cities in the 1930s and 1940s.

She became well-known for her social justice work with the poor and minorities and was a friend of Dorothy Day and Thomas Merton. For her words and her work, she received honorary degrees, awards and accolades, as well as persecution, threats, hatred, and heckling. But always her words, like her actions, were strong, clear, and uncompromising, solidly based on the Gospel of Christ.

Catherine's son George finished college in Canada, went off to war in Europe, and eventually became a successful businessman in Alabama. Catherine's first marriage had been annulled by the church, and Boris had gone on to start a new career and to form a new family. Catherine continued her work with the poor, and met Edward J. Doherty, a famous Chicago newspaper reporter who interviewed her in Harlem. The blue-eyed Russian baroness captured the romantic Irishman's heart. In 1943 the pair were married by Bishop Bernard Sheil of Chicago.

In 1947 she and Eddie moved to Combermere, Ontario, in the backwoods of Canada, to begin a new life and to engage in rural mission work that was close to Catherine's heart. They lived in a small wood-frame house that they called Madonna House, in honor of the Blessed Virgin Mary.

Life in the rural setting was both rustic and rigorous. Madonna House had a hand pump for water and an outdoor toilet. There was wood to chop for the cookstove and there were mountains of snow to shovel during the long, cold winters. Life there was anything but comfortable.

THE MADONNA HOUSE COMMUNITY LIFE

Although the life at Madonna House was difficult, people came to join in, much to Catherine's surprise. They prayed together, ate together, sang together, and worked together, peeling vegetables, chopping wood, cleaning and sorting—learning from Catherine how God can permeate even the smallest task when it is done out of love for him.

Catherine's friends came to visit too. Among them were psychiatrist Karl Stern, author John Howard Griffin, various bishops and archbishops, and many priests.

As time went on, the budding apostolate attracted more people and Madonna House grew and thrived. People from around the world came to the remote village to join her on a permanent basis. Today Madonna House has grown to nearly 200 single lay men and women, as well as 15 staff priests. The group also has more than 90 associate clergy (deacons, priests, bishops, and archbishops) around the world. Its members live in poverty, chastity, and obedience. According to church canon law, Madonna House is called a public association of the faithful, a group of people recognized and approved by the Holy See.

Members of Madonna House now staff 22 fieldhouses of the Apostolate, which are sprinkled across the globe, from the Yukon to Barbados, from England and France to Ghana and Brazil. Some of the houses are devoted to prayer and listening to people, while others assist people in more "active" ways, such as providing meals and clothing. The fieldhouses were established at the request of local bishops.

The main location in Combermere serves as a training center for new applicants who wish to join Madonna House. There is a working farm that produces much of the community's food. The group is supported by donations of clothing and other materials, as well as through private financial contributions. Catherine once explained to a bishop, "We beg for money when we need it—and it always comes."

Through the years, Catherine had come to live by a series of words she believed came from God. These words eventually were gathered together to form what has become known as "The Little Mandate." It expresses the Madonna House way of life in a nutshell:

> Arise! Go! Sell all you possess... give it directly, personally to the poor. Take up my cross (their cross) and follow me—going to the poor—being poor—being one with them—one with me.
> Little—be always little... simple—poor—childlike,
> Preach the Gospel WITH YOUR LIFE—WITHOUT COMPROMISE—listen to the Spirit—he will lead you.
> Do little things exceedingly well for love of me.
> Love—love—love, never counting the cost.
> Go into the marketplace and stay with me... pray... fast... pray always... fast.

Be hidden—be a light to your neighbor's feet. Go without
fears into the depth of men's hearts... I shall be with you.
Pray always. I WILL BE YOUR REST.

Over the years, Catherine continued to speak and to write.
Her extensive writings already have enriched the church,
notably her book *Poustinia,* which has been translated into
almost a dozen languages and has become something of a spiritual classic. *Poustinia,* which is the Russian word for desert,
details the need for a place of silence and prayer for every
Christian who seeks to love, and, as Dorothy Day said, "shows us
a new way of growing in the spiritual life."

Catherine was consulted by bishops and cardinals and was
encouraged in her work by several popes. In fact, it was Pope
Pius XII who suggested to her that staff workers of Madonna
House live the evangelical counsels of poverty, chastity, and
obedience. This step was taken, after which Catherine and her
husband Eddie lived as brother and sister, living apart in separate houses on the Madonna House grounds. Eddie was later
ordained a priest in the Eastern Melkite rite, which allows married clergy. He died in 1975. Catherine followed her husband
in death on December 14, 1985.

Preliminary preparations are now underway to request
church permission that Catherine Doherty may be publicly
venerated, the first step in the process of canonization as a recognized saint of the Catholic church.

Thomas Merton, after he first met her, wrote,

Catherine de Hueck is a person in every way big. And the
bigness is not merely physical: it comes from the Holy Ghost
dwelling constantly within her, and moving her in all that
she does. I never saw anyone so calm, so certain, so peaceful
in her absolute confidence in God.

She was full of the love of God; and prayer and sacrifice
and total, uncompromising poverty filled her soul. She had
tremendous spiritual vitality of grace, a vitality which

brought with it a genuine and lasting inspiration, because it put souls in contact with God as a living reality. And that reality, that contact, is something which we all need.

THE LITTLE THINGS IN LIFE

Catherine often measured her life by the span of time between two Masses. She was fond of saying, "We live our life between two Masses," and "I can endure anything between two Masses." It was typical of her inimitable way of combining the spiritually sublime with the nitty gritty of everyday life.

Whether or not you measure your "life chunks" in the time spent between daily or Sunday Masses, Catherine's reflections in this devotional have been given to you in order to make your time more fruitful. That fruit can grow from her practical approach that applies the Gospel to everyday life, found in what she often called "little things." Since most people live their lives doing endless "little things," her approach can apply to most anyone.

Your little things might be diapers to change, computers to program, parts to manufacture, lessons to learn or teach, repairs to make, or customers to serve. They might be tears to dry, meetings to attend, meals to cook, or miles to travel. Whatever your life situation, it is my hope that the words of Catherine Doherty in the following pages will help you to apply the Gospel to your daily life.

The book is arranged to complement the church year, especially the Advent and Christmas seasons, Lent and Easter time. It also reflects the changing seasons of nature, with meditations that range from the noisy racket of bullfrogs in summer to the quiet stillness of freshly fallen snow in winter. It includes the rhythms of human life as well, with thoughts about love and sin, birth and death. Its topics range from Catherine's meditations on the Ten Commandments and the Beatitudes to her thoughts about doing laundry and taking vacations.

Read a page during your lunch hour, or while the kids nap, as you ride your bus or train to work, or in the morning or evening when you take time to pray. Just leaf through the book or start reading at today's date. Mull over the words a bit. Let them penetrate. Think of how they might apply to you. And pray for understanding. As Catherine would say, "It's all so very simple." Just use her words to get you started and to guide you along your way.

I believe Catherine's reflections echo God's voice. They are words to be pondered, absorbed, and enjoyed. Above all, they are words to be lived, day by day, throughout the year. May this be a year of God's grace for you in every season.

Mary Bazzett
Editor

January

✡

1 | *Solemnity of Mary, Mother of God*
Going Forward in Faith

We should be grateful for another year that God has given us. To me, this is the year of faith. God is giving us an increased gift of this precious virtue because he knows that we shall need it. It is not easy to walk in faith, but this is the only way that is open to us this year, when one can almost hear the world cracking apart, the trembling of the church which seems at times sitting astride an earthquake zone. No, it is not easy, but God will give us that faith, and we have to continue to pray for it so that, full of hope, we might love.

It is the fruit of that faith and hope and love that the Lord bends and picks up, and with it he changes the world! He allows his church to expand because one or two or more people believe, hope, and love!

In Russia Mary, the Mother of God, is called the *Bogoroditza*, which means, "she who gave birth to God." This year the *Bogoroditza* will help us grow in faith and in love to follow her Son as she did. She will teach us how to remain people of faith. We will walk in faith, and it will grow and grow!

The new year is yours to shape, in Christ or outside of him. I know that you will do it in Christ, so it will be a good year.

2 Faith: A Gift We Can Ask For

Faith is a gift of God. It is a pure gift indeed, and God alone can bestow it. At the same time God passionately desires to give it to us. He wants us to ask for it, for he only can give it to us when we ask for it.

When we ask for faith we are turning our face toward his face, for we have to! It seems in truth that God desires this very simple action to happen so that he can face us, face to face! Yes, He wants to look at our face. He loves to see our face facing him, for so often we avoid this simple act. Even while we beg him for simple favors we somehow close not only our physical eyes but the eyes of our souls as well—strangely avoiding looking at him. Yet we know that he always looks at us, looks at us with deep love.

Faith, that God-given gift, healed so many who believed in God. There were the leper, the blind man, the woman with the issue of blood, the servant of the Roman soldier, and millions of others not recorded.

Faith is the father of love and of hope, as well as of trust and confidence. Faith sees God's face in every human face. Faith, as it slowly grows, and as we pray for it and beseech God for it, identifies us with Christ.

3 Our Key Is Faith

Faith allows us to enter peacefully into the dark night which faces every one of us at one time or another. Faith is at peace, and full of light. Faith celebrates the very warp and woof of one's existence.

Faith walks simply, childlike, between the darkness of human life and the hope of what is to come. "For eye has not seen, nor ear heard what God reserves for those who love him." Faith is fundamentally a kind of folly, I guess, the folly that belongs to God himself.

Our face is turned to God through faith, and their eyes meet, so that every day becomes more and more luminous. The veil between God and us becomes less and less until it seems that we can almost reach out and touch God. Faith breaks through barriers. Faith makes love into a bonfire. Faith holds the wind of the Holy Spirit which fans the bonfire into flame.

Faith is contagious when we show it to one another. Men and women cannot resist faith, even when they deny it and laugh at it and jeer at it and even kill the one who has faith.

Men and women of today certainly must pray for faith, especially we who desire to preach the Gospel with our lives. Without faith we cannot do it. We must believe in God.

 # 4 Be Gentle to Yourself

How important it is to be gentle with ourselves! And how often we swing in the opposite direction, getting angry with ourselves, or even angry at God! Often we flagellate ourselves, mentally speaking. We dwell upon our sins and think of ourselves as horrible people. Or we harass ourselves with the "wrong decisions" we have made or with "indecisions"... especially in regard to sin. We become exhausted.

We forget that the mercy of God is part of his gentleness. We forget that if we but turn to him when we have sinned and say "I'm sorry," the sin is erased completely. He does not remember because he does not want to. His mercy overshadows all.

Christ said to love our neighbor as ourselves; and our first neighbor is ourselves. If you can't love yourself you can't love anybody else. So be gentle with yourself! How often we are "ungentle" with ourselves. We can inflict so many wounds on ourselves. I can almost take you in my arms and say: "Rest now. Be gentle with yourselves. Be gentle."

Where do you learn how to be gentle? St. John used to recline on the breast of Christ. I think we will become gentle toward ourselves, and toward others, if we go and do likewise. Then we will hear the heartbeats of God, and we will be able to let others hear them. Then we will be gentle to ourselves and to everybody else.

5 | The Season of the Star

You know one of the ornaments of this Christmas season in Russia is a star. The people would make enormous stars and put them over their "isbas," which is what they called their log houses. Always stars, for the three Magi that came from afar came to follow a star.

The star is always before us. We only have to open our eyes to see the star. In fact, we can see it when we close our eyes. The star is deep and immense and profound in its significance.

Are we going to follow it or are we going to waste a lifetime catching stars that are not there?

If we really go and follow that star, that one and only star, we will become a star and others will follow us, to that immense star, which is Christ.

And then, we will become a flame, for the star is fire and flame and beauty and love, faith and hope. And at that moment we have ceased to meditate, to contemplate, to pray, for we are enveloped by the Spirit and we, ourselves, have become a prayer. Then you will walk, and I will walk, in the revelation of his infinite love that surrounds us and reveals itself wherever we go.

6 | It Was Love

Epiphany is a very profound feast day, the revelation of Christ to the Gentiles. Somewhere, very deep in their hearts, the non-Jews were awaiting him, expecting him. It was a strange affair. It always cheered me up, especially when I was lecturing on interracial justice.

Just think for a moment. Three Wise Men from the East. One was supposed to be a Negro, and the others were Persians. Three came to worship him, multicolored, in a manner of speaking.

So did I worship him. I used to worship him in a crummy little storefront, with children dancing on the garbage cans amidst all the noise of Harlem. He revealed himself to the whole world on Epiphany. Oh, I know, there are all kinds of revelations of the Lord. But the first one was Epiphany. And I was there.

I even brought gifts to him. Myrrh of my works, frankincense of my prayers, gold of compassion and understanding that he had put into my heart. And I strewed it out right in front of him. He was little, but he gathered it all up, because it was all intangible. It wasn't gold, it wasn't frankincense, it was love. Even when he was little, barely born, he would put out his little hands and gather it up. It was very simple, because he was love. Epiphany is such a beautiful feast. It brought everybody together.

7 | The Spirit of Madonna House

Today I wish to synthesize the spirit of Madonna House for you. The immensity of this simple definition will open its riches to you daily if you approach it reverently and prayerfully:

The spirit of Madonna House is the beautiful and awesome spirit of the Gospel applied to daily living, without compromise. The spirit of Madonna House is one of childlike simplicity. It recognizes that the duty of the moment is expressed in hourly and daily needs. It is the spirit of little things done extremely well, with the exclusive motivation of the love of God. The essence of this spirit is charity and peace. This love spends itself on little things, first for one's brothers and sisters, then for the world at large—little things like seeing what has to be picked up, like cleaning a stove, like being on a job with 100 percent concentration, because one loves.

This, dearly beloved, is it. It will take us a lifetime of prayer and practice to understand the height, the width, and the depth of this definition. There it is, for all of us to see, to ponder, and grow into.

8 | The Spirit Explained

Let us try to review a bit what the spirit of Madonna House means. To live by the Gospel, without compromise, means to live the life of love. But to love means to die to self and live for others. It means to follow Christ's footsteps from Bethlehem to the tomb. This means to ask oneself, perhaps a thousand times a day, "How would Christ act, think, or feel if he were in my place—if he were I?"

To be childlike means not seeking to evade Calvary. Many times in our lives God gives us the grace to catch a glimpse of his reality—someone who loved us first. We must respond to that love by *loving him back*. This is what our faith is all about. Childlike simplicity is this: not evading the cross but being crucified on it and dying to self. Only thus can we love him back.

So away with all the tortuous arguments and intellectual and spiritual rationalizations! The stark fact is that love is walking the straight line from where we stand now to the cross. Love means not deviating one iota from the direct and shortest path between myself and Calvary. *This* is childlike simplicity in its most fundamental form. Our motive can only be *caritas*, love. The fruits will be *pax*, peace.

Think about this, dearly beloved. If we live this to the hilt, there is no doubt whatsoever that we shall see God and be saints.

9 | Ordinary Daily Life

It is important to understand that the ordinariness of routine and daily life is the warp and the woof of living the Gospel without compromise. No part of the Gospel is abstract. Each part demands and cries out for an incarnation. Spirituality must be incarnate, as Jesus Christ was incarnate. Unless it is, it isn't true spirituality.

First and foremost is the love for God. Scripture tells us that we must love God with all our hearts, with all our souls, and with all our hearts and minds. And so we should. But this doesn't mean that we spend our whole day in formal prayer. It means that we go about our Father's business.

A carpenter works with wood. An electrician is concerned with all the things necessary for repairing and installing electrical equipment. In sewing, one understands that the routine of mending, patching, and sewing on buttons is in itself a prayer. Doing the laundry is clothing the naked. The kitchen routine of preparing food in its ordinariness is feeding the hungry in the reality of everyday life.

I hope and pray that you, now and in the coming tomorrows, will remember the holiness of little things done well over and over again for the love of God. Every task, routine or not, is of redeeming, supernatural value because we are united with Christ. We must be recollected and stay aware of this truth.

10 | Little Things Done with Great Love

What can a person do who tries to love God tremendously? Everything, from putting the lights off, to refraining from changing clothes every five minutes, to being indifferent to food, to going where God calls you. Once I know God's will I am going to try to do it perfectly. My heart swells and I say, "This also, Lord, for love of you." I know very well its redemptive value. Do I speak too symbolically? Another example. I have empty hands. I consider that I have to bring something to the altar to offer at my next Mass. What can I bring? I can bring a thousand buttons well-sorted with great love, understanding full well that because of my attention these buttons have redemptive value. I can bring hours of conversation or letters written with attention to details. It never occurs to me that I can possibly separate anything from love. For example, I will speak of washing dishes. If I have the attitude that this is a beautiful, little thing that I can give to God, then washing a cup becomes an adventure. Do you get the picture? Every little thing should be done perfectly, completely connected with God. Otherwise, it ceases to be interesting. It has no sense and no being. Wherever you go you will certainly have to do little things. Try to do them without love, and see what happens. But doing little things with our whole hearts is our vocation.

11 | Making Connections

This is the essence of your vocation: to connect an ordinary and seemingly boring life with its repetitious details, with Love who is God. Then boredom vanishes, and a day spent in sorting buttons is glorious. Then a day at the typewriter, when your back is aching and your mind reeling with tiredness, is a day that has redeemed many souls; how many God alone knows. We must have that awareness and make that connection. If it isn't made, it is a wasted day. What a horrible and a tragic thought that one of the most precious gifts of God—time—has been wasted.

Awareness is a terrible responsibility before God and us. You must see the connection between this awareness, thoughtfulness, recollection, and the implementation and restoration of the world to Christ. How are you going to restore the world to Christ if your workshop or clothing or dishes or the kitchen reflect the disorder of your soul? How can you be aware of the world of souls, if you are not aware of the fact that when it snows, it would be a good idea to shovel a path and clear the steps?

How are you going to restore the world to Christ, if you are doing the minimum required—the letter of the law—and never plunge into its spirit? Christ is waiting for you to become aware of him and the work he has given you, by becoming aware of the connection between brooms, dishwater, letter typing, tidiness, and the restoration of the world.

12 | Deeper Connections

Where did I learn to connect physical things with spiritual truths? My parents never let me forget that every task, however ordinary, was of redeeming, supernatural value, if done out of love. Awareness of little things, done well for the love of God, is daily living lifted up into the heart of Christ.

This awareness is an important, glorious, and holy word. Awareness means to be recollected, to be all there. Where? Before the face of God. It means that we arise in the morning, aware that this day is given to us to grow in love and grace and wisdom before the Lord. It means that we realize that once again we have been given a little piece of time between two Masses to gain or lose the Beatific Vision. It means to realize that we have one more day to spend in the school of the love of God and that if we waste it, we may not go to hell, but we will go into the painful refinery of love—purgatory. In order to enter heaven, we must be lovers. We must learn either here or there. Not to learn it at all is hell.

For instance, wash the dishes for the love of God. When you serve the family, do it quietly and efficiently. If you learn to connect serving to the supernatural order, you will grow greatly in wisdom and love, and you will be a light shining in the darkness of the world. The light of your loving service will lead people to God.

13 | Let's Stop and Notice One Another

So many of us are crying out today for recognition. We want to be noticed, not in any ostentatious way, not because we might have or not have money, but just because we are human beings, persons. But we pass by one another without noticing, without stopping, without the slightest sign of recognition. This is why we moderns daily come closer and closer to despair, and why we frantically continue to search for the one who will love us.

Our search is for God. But God isn't easily found if he isn't reflected in the eyes of men and women. It is time that we

Christians began to take notice of each person we meet. Each person is a brother or sister in Christ. Each person must be "recognized." Each person must be given a token of friendship and love, be it only a smile, a nod of the head. Sometimes it may require the total availability of one person to another if they are to fulfill a particular person's hunger for God.

Such love and recognition must always be given with deep reverence, irrespective of the "status" of the person encountered. Reverence, understanding, and hospitality of the heart —these are the immediate, intense needs of men and women today. Are we Christians going to wake up and act as Christians, incarnating the law of love into our daily lives in real depth? These meetings with our brothers and sisters are the true crossroads of time and history. When we meet there, will we act as Christians or not?

14 | Hospitality of the Heart

What the world needs most today is the hospitality of the heart. Hospitality of the heart means accepting all others as they are, allowing them to make themselves at home in one's heart.

To be at home in another person's heart means touching love, the love of a brother or sister in Christ. Touching the love of another means realizing that God loves us. For it is through the other—our neighbor, our brother, or sister—that we can begin to understand the love of God.

This is especially necessary in our strange technological loneliness that has separated us so thoroughly not only from our neighbors, but from our fathers, mothers, grandparents, in short, from our relations. Yes, our technological age has begotten a terrible loneliness! We must begin to give the hospitality of the heart. In other words, we must open ourselves to a sharing of friendship that is rooted in the very heart of Christ whom we call our friend.

We have to shed our "stiff upper lips." We have to be open to the other, share with the other, express our love for the other. This can only be done if we open the doors of our hearts. Let us do that now, before the doors of our hearts are frozen shut by some new technological achievement!

15 | Service in Simplicity

God writes straight with crooked lines, and I remember the passage from Scripture that says, "My ways are not your ways, and my thoughts are not your thoughts." What appears hopeless to us may be exceedingly hopeful to God. And there is much that appears hopeless.

Why, then, do I feel hopeful? I feel hopeful because the Lord has plowed a field, harrowed, and seeded it. I feel hopeful because green shoots of prayer are rising from the hearts of people everywhere, not only in those dedicated to religious life, but in men and women of all vocations. People are praying in their hearts, and they are taking time to go to quiet places to reflect. They are being drawn inwardly toward him who poured himself out in the service of others.

I see quiet service being rendered by one person to another in great simplicity. It isn't a frantic thing, where people rush to the ghettos to become social workers, or leave their ministries to become psychologists. No, it is a quiet service, person-to-person, and that is what Christ desired. His life was spent in prayer and service, and so must ours be. We must not only love our neighbor; we must take the time to listen, to have a personal relationship. This is possible for everyone, wherever you live. In high-rise apartment buildings, in private homes and condominiums, you can reach out to your neighbors.

16 Preaching the Gospel with Our Lives

Now we come to the question of how to preach the Gospel with our lives. We look to the Holy Family for examples, as Nazareth is our model and spiritual home. Like the Holy Family, we lead an ordinary life, filled with many monotonous jobs to be done with great love for God and neighbor. Through these little daily tasks, we become witnesses of God, to live in such a way that one's life would not make sense if God did not exist. Each day laborious work at little tasks, if performed with great love, truly preaches the Gospel loudly!

In the marketplaces of the world, we must be preachers of the Gospel with our lives as well as (when required) with words. We must be preachers without compromise. We are people called by God to give him birth in a particular Nazareth setting, namely, in the modern marketplaces of the world. We are to show him to those who dwell around us, and we do this by how we *live*.

All of this sounds so simple, but it presupposes a death to self—a death we call *kenosis*, an "emptying" that does violence to oneself. Yet, as Scripture says (Luke 16:16), "Heaven is taken by violence." Therefore we must learn to exercise a loving and gentle "violence" toward ourselves—and to do so out of love of God, with whom we want to spend this life and all eternity.

17 The Duty of the Moment

All through my childhood and early youth I was indoctrinated with the fact that the duty of the moment was the duty of God. When I was fairly little I thought God was right by my side, embroidering or whatever. Later, I still believed that the duty of the moment was the duty of God. God speaks to us, then, in the duty of every moment.

As this duty of the moment is the will of the Father, we must give our whole self to that. When we do so we can be certain that we are living in the truth, and hence in love, and hence in Christ.

Doing the duty of the moment means focusing our *whole* person—heart, soul, body, emotions, intellect, memory, imagination—on the job at hand! The duty of the moment done for God is glamorous, exciting, wondrous—if only we can see it for what it truly is! But we are human. And it takes a long time, my dearly beloved ones, to see reality through God's eyes. Unless we pray exceedingly hard, it takes a long time. But—with prayer—we see an entirely different world about us! Sorting clothes becomes a joy. Washing dishes becomes an exciting challenge. Careful, repetitious tasks of creating take on new meaning. Whatever your tasks are, they take on new meaning.

18 | We Need More Prayer

What we need today is more prayer. The people of God are weary of being classified on the right or on the left, weary of hearing about bishops and priests marrying, weary of reading about nuns who are seeking answers to questions that only God can answer.

It is this very weariness that is driving people today to pray as perhaps they have never prayed before. The ordinary, simple, "grassroots" people are seeking answers to their weariness in prayer, prayers for themselves, and prayer for others. The right, the left, bishops, priests, nuns—all are coming to realize deep down what they always knew: prayer can change things.

What we need today is prayer, prayer that is truly interior, coming from the heart, the prayer of Jesus. The human heart needs prayer, needs to listen to the Word speaking through the Gospel. It is the Word who lives, the Word who prays.

Slowly, slowly, quietly, like a tide coming in, we Christians are beginning to pray again! All across America and Canada people find time to enter into solitude, fasting, and prayer in order to meet Christ. Prayer must become an integrated part of our daily lives, the most important part. Then will our house of sanctity rise high and be well built on the rock of faith. Then will our fields be fertile in the Lord, bringing forth a good harvest.

19 | Praying for God's Will

We tend to pray with great intensity for the things we want, but do we ever think of praying for what God wants? Usually, when our desire for something "cools off," so does our prayer. It is very important, therefore, that when we pray, we move *with* the current of God's will, and not against it. This is true even when we are praying for someone we love tremendously.

When my husband Eddie was in a car accident and I was on my way to be with him, I prayed fervently that he might be well. But in my mind, every second, I forced myself to add, "If it be thy will." If God wanted to take Eddie home, for whatever reason, I had to be willing to accept it. I had to mentally pronounce words to that effect that I was ready to do God's will and to move in its stream.

The greatest act of a person is to do the will of God. You may ask me, "How do I know his will?" How do I know which ideas are mine, and which belong to God? There is only one answer. To know his will, I must learn how to listen to him. This can happen only through prayer and under the guidance of a spiritual director.

20 Prayer as Listening

To me, prayer has always been a matter of listening. When I was little, I used to run in the low hills which were covered with wild flowers. I would lie down and the wind would go through the wild flowers, and they would bend back and forth and God would speak. Of course, I was little then, and my imagination was vivid. But if you keep listening to God, one day you will see him, and this is what makes it an adventure.

Now, I get up in the morning, and I begin to listen as I move through the day. As I do so, a tremendous peace comes upon me. I dictate letters, I sort donations. I look at books, I talk with members of the community and with visitors. Sometimes people are not feeling up to par, and there is anger and irritation, and the voices become a cacophony that rolls over me like thunder. But I smile and listen, and answers come because somewhere deep, deep within, I have peace, God's peace. In the midst of the turmoil around me, this inner listening brings peace. On a human level, I might be mad as a hatter at the things that are going on. But it is like a storm over an ocean; fifty fathoms down, everything is calm. Men and women are like that. The storm can rage, but as long as there is peace beneath it, all is well. It is a way of participating in the sufferings of Christ. He too must have had some pretty stormy days, living with those twelve uneducated fishermen.

21 First Things First: Contemplative-Action

We must *be* before the Lord first and *do* for the Lord next. Our model for this is the Holy Family of Nazareth.

There is no denying the fact that Mary was a contemplative.

First and foremost, *she was always before God.* She lived in the presence of God the Father. God the Holy Spirit overshadowed her. God the Son was with her, in human flesh! Yet she *worked* for the Lord too. She worked hard, serving the needs of Jesus and Joseph and many of the villagers. She served by listening and gently advising those in trouble and sorrow, by sharing her food, by general hospitality, and in many other simple and direct ways which today we call the corporal and spiritual works of mercy.

Joseph was also a contemplative. How could he be anything else! He lived with God and with God's mother. He was a silent man, a man of deep prayer. Yet one feels sure that he too *worked* for the Lord—first by being the provider for his own family, and then surely by assisting his neighbors. He not only did things for them but probably also counseled them. In these two quiet human beings, Mary and Joseph, I see so clearly the Madonna House spirit.

As for Christ himself, *being* before the face of his Father was his very life—the very essence of it. *Doing* the will of his Father was also the essence of his existence.

22 | Being and Doing

If only we took a few minutes of time just to sit and think a few things out, we would have more peace, and the way ahead would be much clearer.

As it is, modern people, Catholics included, resemble the proverbial squirrel in a cage. Around and around they go, feverishly, from business to pleasure, and back to business. Action is their watchword. "What are we going to *do?*"

Few ever ask themselves, or their friends, the all-important question, "What are we going to *be?*" Yet in the answer to that question lies the answer to peace of mind, happiness of heart, and the ineffable joy of knowing where one is going and why.

For men and women have been made first *to be* before God, then *to do* for God.

To be before God means to remember who God is. To render him, therefore, the adoration and love that are his due from us, his creatures. It means remembering our last end, and fulfilling the obligations of a prayer-life that will lead us there. It means knowing that we are an empty cup that daily must be filled by God, and going to him to have the cup filled.

Then work, recreation, and the rest will fall into their proper places, and what we do, we will do for God. Eat, sleep, and whatsoever you do, do for the glory of God, says St. Paul. We will, if we keep straight the two things that go into the service of the Lord—the *being before God* and the *doing for God.*

23 | Doing the Works of God

Why, why, why do we put work as a measure of our worth? Why is it so difficult to understand that a sick person may be more useful before the Lord and for the church than one who runs around and produces one hundred letters a day, or a million potatoes peeled, marvelous meals, etc.?

Why is it that so many of us go to pieces when we are not working with the gang? We feel out of place, humiliated, miserable—why? What does it matter what we *do,* so long as we are listening to the silence of our mind until all is uplifted to God? The *works* that we do must be the works of God, not ours.

If we work to satisfy *ourselves,* so that we have a yardstick (today I wrote one hundred letters and yesterday ninety-eight, and tomorrow, I'll write one hundred and two) and be useful to the church, well, brother, we won't! And not to God either.

The greatest work of God on earth was not his carpentry or

his speeches; it was hanging on that cross—immobilized—unable to *do* anything. That was the moment of greatness. And his resurrection afterwards. But the greatest work he did for love was to *die*, to be crucified, nailed, incapable of *doing* anything.

24 Watching Television with a Critical Eye

One of the things I thought about last night was television. TV is an insidious influence which, if allowed to run freely, will become a hypnotizing thing that wastes time. It militates against using that time to better advantage, such as doing something more worthwhile that would help to promote the family spirit.

The usual excuse for having a TV is the good programs available—serious music, good plays, and news coverage. But that is often *not* what the family is watching when we have a TV in the house. Often there are shows based on a very superficial value of life. Be careful about programs that skirt the limits of propriety, make light of marriage vows, show disrespect for in-laws, etc. Many of these programs have been devastating enough to keep me awake the whole night wondering how it is possible for us to restore the world to Christ with that kind of entertainment penetrating every home.

One of the key factors is that many family members do not have a critical faculty to judge the programs. Typical youth are sponge-like in reception of the knowledge given them. They never analyze or criticize, but accept facts as given or read. Good programs of music or plays can be watched if they are not on too late, though perhaps you could have a critical discussion about it to enable the family to *watch critically* and develop this *ability to judge* what is good entertainment.

25 | *Conversion of the Apostle Paul*
Flu and Sickness

One January the flu descended on Madonna House in full force with all its vehemence. Forty of us went down like trees felled by a hurricane. The remainder, twenty or so, did miracles trying to run the complex of Madonna House and nurse us too.

Strange, how sickness brought us all closer together, how charity bloomed among us, how those who were a little less sick helped those who were more sick, and how everyone tried to help everyone else.

As we recovered, we thanked God for his goodness in sending us a little bout of the flu. It showed us our weakness, and in our weakness it showed us the strength that St. Paul always talks about when he lists his frailties.

Physical sickness can depress us or elevate our spirits, depending on our attitude toward it. Whatever is in our hearts and our minds will solve the present and future problems of our world. We hold the life and death of the world in our hands.

26 | Chastity and the Gospel

In many ways we have forgotten what chastity is all about. Jesus Christ set up a pattern, an ideal. There are people who are chaste in marriage, and there are others who are chaste as celibates for the kingdom of God. But to everyone the commandment of the Father was directed: Anyone who looks with lust at another person has already committed adultery in his or her heart. Christ put the whole matter of chastity in the context of the heart, not of the mind. You can rationalize things away, but the Gospel doesn't rationalize; it goes straight to the heart of the matter.

Chastity demands purity of heart, for the pure shall see God. When you see God, your respect and love for your neighbor begin to become like that of the heart of Christ. In marriage two people enter the most glorious adventure that man and woman can enter, *provided* the foundation of their coming together is not lust. Love is in the heart, not in bodily functions.

If I am pure of heart, I see God in everyone. Once I see God in them, I respect them, I love them. I will not use any person for my own end, so *I* might be satisfied physically or emotionally, and then drop the person like a rag doll when I am through fulfilling *my* needs.

If we are in love with God, we will not spoil the image of God in others. It is always out of love that we respect the gift of sex in another. It is a precious gift. It is not something to be treated lightly.

27 | Temptations against Chastity

Temptations against chastity are a normal part of the devil's equipment. Chastity is one virtue that he likes to destroy because it leads to purity of heart. Those who practice it to a high degree see God long before they are dead; they possess him long before their house of clay returns to the earth.

The devil also attacks chastity because it is a social virtue. Strange as this may seem to you, it brings the very breath of God—of purity, beauty, innocence, childlikeness—to a world surfeited with sin and sexual aberration.

So naturally, the devil is going to attack your chastity. God will allow it, so that you might grow in grace and purity while fighting this temptation, as millions of priests and nuns do—as do married people for whom continence is the only way of practicing birth control for long periods.

Chastity is a virtue that is so "social" that it astounds and amazes people in every civilization and in every age. Pagans remained chaste because chastity has been a virtue respected from time immemorial. It is the reflection of God's face. So naturally the devil wants to blot it out. Take it for granted that you will have temptations against chastity. They will come on quiet feet. They will feed on loneliness and aloneness. But you will have the graces to fight them.

28 | Loneliness and Aloneness

Loneliness is what every human being has to endure. St. Augustine put it well when he said, "Our hearts are restless until they rest in God's heart." The disappearance of loneliness will come only in the Beatific Vision. Loneliness is hunger for union with a perfect being, i.e. God. If you imagine that married people do not know this loneliness, you are mistaken. Much as I love my husband Eddie, he and I, ultimately, are lonely. We cannot penetrate each other's innermost being.

Aloneness is man-made. Some are alone because they flee from reality or withdraw from life. This is a pathological aloneness, as is also the aloneness of a shy person; but mostly aloneness stems from not knowing that God loves us, or from accepting this truth with great difficulty. Also, we don't love ourselves as we should, or our neighbor as we must. Then it is hard for us to dedicate ourselves to a cause, even to God. We spend part of our time in daydreaming and imagining an ideal partner, a friend, a lover, a husband, a wife, who will "understand" us; but we make no steps toward understanding others. Aloneness in this sense can be alleviated. The temptations against chastity will play on that aloneness through daydreams. Of these we must beware. Every time that you overcome these temptations with the grace of God, you become a pure and shining light to the world, and the church moves forward by leaps and bounds.

29 The Voice of Christ

I walk the streets of crowded cities. So few I meet who know my name.

I walk the scented fields of the country, yet not one greets me with a kind word.

I am a stranger to those for whom I died a thousand deaths one sunny afternoon.

I long to rest upon the hearts of those who are my own. But I find them too busy to stop and give me rest. They say they are busy about my business or that of my Father, but what a lie!

They waste the time of which I am the Master. They squander it so lavishly, forgetting that I shall ask account of every thing and deed, of every second, minute, hour.

Who then will open their hearts to me? For I am weary and want to rest. Isn't there somewhere just one apostle who will share loneliness and weariness once more with me?

30 Urodivoi: Fools for Christ

I want to talk about something that is not very popular. I want to talk about being a fool for Christ's sake. *Urodivoi* is Russian for "the foolish ones." This is the time in which we must become foolish. It is not a question of joining the revolutionaries somewhere in Timbuktu. No. It is a question of renewing the parish. Did it ever occur to you that perhaps the foolishness of Christ is to remain right there in the parish and rebuild it? That, my friends, is foolishness for Christ's sake.

You go and seek elsewhere, in other communities and other places, solace for yourselves. But when you leave your parish because the priest is impossible, when you leave because Sister Superior doesn't understand you, is that being a fool for Christ? When husband and wife seek a divorce, is that foolishness for Christ's sake? Or is it foolishness for Christ's sake to stay with the pastor, with the husband, with the wife, with Sister Superior?

Foolishness for Christ's sake is a change of heart, your heart and my heart, from *within*, not from without. Don't kid yourself. Nothing that you think will change you from without is going to change you. Only that which comes from the very heart of you, the very entrails of you, so to speak, will change the world. And the world *needs* to be changed. Now! Today!

31 | Littleness and Choices

We crave greatness for our lives, and God asks us to become little. To pass through the door that leads to the kingdom, we must go down on our knees. Paradoxically, if we do so, we will find ourselves growing in stature, for "eye has not seen and ear has not heard what God has reserved for those who love him."

This is a moment of choice. It is one of many such moments, for we will be called to choose every day of our lives until we die. But the fantastic thing about it is our freedom. We are utterly free to turn back from this power that draws us on. We are free to loose ourselves from the bonds of a love that demands our total surrender. Nothing prevents us from saying No. Nothing except God's love.

Thus, prayer becomes very simple. "Lord, I believe; help my unbelief. Jesus, help me." He is used to that prayer, and often it is not even voiced aloud. It's a cry of few words, a cry of agony, a cry for help, a wordless cry for clarity. But behind these short cries, accented with pain or sorrow, or sometimes even joy, lies the plea, "Help me to move on, to wherever you want to take me."

February

❄

1 | Your Daily Sacrifices

Your daily life seemingly will be very dull. You have only one moment to live at a time. One day at a time between two Masses. You have no past; your yesterdays are gone. You have no future; your tomorrows belong to him. You have only today. Only this moment to be obedient unto death. Only this moment to burn with a fire that knows neither beginning nor end. Only this moment to spill yourself out in service to neighbor. For you must prove to your beloved that you love him. Words are not enough! Words die before the Word. You can only prove your love for him by loving your neighbor, for your neighbor is Christ.

What will your love bring to your beloved? Beautiful vestments that you have sewn of finest gold? Will you bring a crown of gold, or a scepter that you've spent half your life carving out of priceless ivory? Or poetic verses to move multitudes, or music to enchant the world? Or books to make him better known?

No! At Madonna House, your life is made up of a myriad of small, humble tasks, for the most part. What you will bring him is stew well made, endless vegetables finely peeled, three-by-five cards correctly filed over and over again, floors eternally scrubbed so as to allow his feet in your neighbor to walk across, machinery kept clean and oiled, day in and day out, garbage removed, and endless trips to bring someone to the doctor or hospital. Years of this! You will bring such humble gifts as these.

2 Presentation of the Lord
Go to Jesus through Mary

He who seeks Christ without Mary seeks him in vain. Christ said, "I am the Way." But the gate to the Way is Mary. All that we do, we do through Mary. We can dedicate ourselves utterly to her Son, because it is she who shows us the Way.

You see, you go to Jesus *through* Mary. She possesses the secret of prayer and of wisdom, for she is the Mother of God. Who else can teach you to burn with the fire of love except the Mother of Fair Love? Who else can teach you to pray except the woman of prayer? Who else can teach you to go through the silence of deserts and nights, the silence of pain and sorrow, the solitude of joy and gladness, except the woman wrapped in silence? Who can span the bridge between the old and new, the "dedicated you" and the "undedicated you"? Only Mary, the bridge between the Old Testament and the New, the Jewish girl who brought forth the Messiah, the Son of the Almighty.

Without Mary, how can one speak of God the Father, who was so well-pleased with her that he made her the Mother of his Son? How can we speak of Christ (who was her Son begotten by the Holy Spirit) without speaking of Mary, the Spouse of the Spirit? Our Lady of the Trinity and Our Lady of Madonna House are one and the same.

3 | The Little Mandate

The words of the Lord which came to me over the years, and which form the heart of our way of life at Madonna House are called The Little Mandate. I would like to explain this mandate to you one part at a time in the coming days, so you can better understand it.

The Little Mandate is as follows:

Arise—go! Sell all you possess... give it directly, personally to the poor. Take up my cross (their cross) and follow me—going to the poor—being poor—being one with them—one with me.

Little—be always little... simple—poor—childlike,

Preach the Gospel WITH YOUR LIFE—WITHOUT COMPROMISE—listen to the Spirit—he will lead you.

Do little things exceedingly well for love of me.

Love—love—love, never counting the cost.

Go into the marketplace and stay with me... pray... fast... pray always... fast.

Be hidden—be a light to your neighbor's feet. Go without fears into the depth of men's hearts... I shall be with you.

Pray always. I WILL BE YOUR REST.

4 | Arise and Go!

"Arise and Go!" Those three little words mean you cannot lie down on your job. You must stand up! And, standing up, you cannot remain still (except in your soul); you must be about his business. You should be both active and contemplative, both Martha and Mary. Make no mistake; the stillness of Mary is an even bigger "action" than the action of Martha. It is important to *be* before the Lord, and then to *do* for him; we are to be contemplatives in action. And so your life is a constant "arising," and a constant "going." Both actions are concerning your Father's business and that of your tremendous Lover, Jesus Christ.

How are you going to do all this? You will do it in grace and humility, realizing your utter poverty. You will do it by depending exclusively upon God. You will do it by walking hand in hand with Mary, through whom you will always find Jesus. You will do it in utter simplicity of faith, seeing to it that you have the heart of a child. You will do it by making the Mass and Scriptures the twin lights of your life... its foundation, its very essence, its center.

You will do it by regular confession to keep your conscience as clear as a child's, and spending time before the Blessed Sacrament when possible, and by prayer and fasting, under the rigid direction of your spiritual director.

5 | Learning to Live in Poverty

Poverty, according to Paul Evdokimov, a celebrated Russian theologian, means "when the need to have becomes the need not to have." Meditate on that sentence—it belongs to the early monastic life of all peoples, but also it's very Russian.

You too are called to live poverty, as all baptized faithful are. Poverty is a way of becoming "naked" so to speak, but a few of us are called to the total nakedness of a vow of poverty, such as religious take. At Madonna House, we make a promise of poverty and give away our possessions to the poor, to become poor ourselves.

How do all of us live poverty, as all Christians are to do? Sharing the "wealth" that we have should become simplicity itself to all. Your love of Christ, the Holy Spirit, and the grace of the Father will tell your conscience how far you have to go to share the wealth. No two people are the same as to sharing the wealth, but all who believe in Jesus Christ should be "dispossessed," by not being attached to anything except the Most Holy Trinity.

I pray that you will inculcate that spirit of detachment, of *non-possession.* Let there be poverty and simplicity in the hearts of us all!

6 | Littleness, Simplicity

Our Little Mandate says, "Little—be always little... simple—poor—childlike." This eschews arrogance, the arrogance of the intellect which is so prevalent in the West. "Everything has to be according to the way I think it has to be." And so economics, politics, peace, war—all are shot around about, and divisiveness is endless everywhere.

Especially in the last decades this divisiveness has entered the heart of religious orders, both female and male, entered into the priesthood and the dioceses. It has entered into the family. It has entered into the children.

Listen. Can you hear the breakup of the world? The pollution extends not only into the earth and the river and the air, but the heart itself of humanity is in danger of being totally polluted. It ceases to be *little.* It ceases to be *childlike.* It ceases to be *simple* and *poor.*

As a result, listen again to the cacophony of voices which come falling from the lips of Satan slaying people all over the world, leaving them as dead, hungry, and cold and alone. Suicide rates mount because men and women have ceased to be little, to be simple, to be childlike.

7 Preaching the Gospel

The Little Mandate says, "Preach the Gospel *with your life— without compromise*. Listen to the Spirit—he will lead you."

We must live the Gospel without compromise, at all costs, even that of our lives. We are to witness to Christ in the market-place by loving and doing, not so much by speaking. This was summed up for us by Charles de Foucauld when he said, "We must cry the Gospel *with our lives*." (The same idea came to us both from God, I guess, in almost the same way.)

Yes, the time has come for all who believe in Jesus Christ, and all who hunger for him and for that unity which he alone can bring to bear against divisiveness. Yes, the time has come for us all to have the courage to submit our intellects to that of Jesus Christ as he operates in our families, in our personal relations, in governments, Madonna House, religious orders, everything, everywhere.

Arrogance has no place when we desire to preach the Gospel without compromise, because he who is the Gospel said, "Learn of me, for I am meek and humble of heart."

8 Little Things

The Little Mandate says, "Do little things exceedingly well for love of me." Like a whisper that ruffles the trees at night, in the same breeze the Lord comes to us and repeats this. Can you hear the voice of the leaves that gently, even as God is gentle to you, say: "I don't ask for big things. I ask for little things done well for the loved one."

Here I repeat, the incarnation comes to greet you, for isn't that what he did... little things, exceedingly well, for love of us?

Can you visualize a table or chair that was not perfect when it left his hands in Nazareth? He did everything well for the love of his Father, and for the love of us. At first his childish hammering, imitating Joseph, then later the measured hammering of a competent carpenter. Then later, the sound of leather on his back—flagellation; then the sound of hammering of nails on soft flesh. These were his love letters to us. He gave us the example: "Do little things exceedingly well for love of me."

And so he reduced love to our size. We are little people. So our housework begins to be a way of loving him. Or our typing, or driving a taxi, or changing diapers, or farming, or anything we may do! These are all little, seemingly unimportant things, but oh, how vastly important because this is part of living the Gospel without compromise.

9 Love, Love, Love

The Mandate continues with, "Love—love—love, never counting the cost." Well, there is very little that I can say about that. The world is a very cold place these days because people do not love. There is lust. There is temporary commitment to what appears to be love, but it is not lasting enough to be called love. Love is stronger than death.

Because love is God, love is stronger than death. Love is a Person. Meditate on it. Contemplate it. You will begin to understand the source of true love, the heart of God.

The heart of God calls us to give him our hearts, which means to give him ourselves. We must hold nothing back. This means if we truly love God as he wants to be loved, we assume full responsibility for our actions and are not afraid of the approval or disapproval of anyone in authority.

Having accepted responsibility, we accept both praise and censure peacefully, knowing the first is proper to God and the second proper to us sinners. It also means loving God so much in the nitty-gritty routine of our daily lives that we make up for the coldness of other hearts. So we prove our love by taking responsibility, by listening attentively to directions, and performing our duties efficiently in all we have been given. We do it with our whole being, never thinking of ourselves or how it affects us, never counting the cost.

10 | Prayer and Fasting in the Marketplace

The next paragraph of The Little Mandate says, "Go into the marketplace and stay with me... pray... fast... pray always... fast." Yes, these days what my father used to say really must take place. He used to say, "If you want to reach God you must lift two arms, fasting and prayer." In our day when everybody is catering to the appetites of the flesh, when senses rule as if they were God, it is time that we should fast as well as pray. The Lord fasted quite a bit and we should follow his footsteps. He said to his apostles when they complained that they couldn't cast the devil out from someone, "This kind can be cast out in no way except by prayer and fasting" (Mark 9:28). We who are of one mind and one heart, who have held hands to walk into the darkness of this world to restore it to Christ, we must continue to do so in the marketplace and stay in that marketplace, and fast, and pray.

Prayer is, first and foremost, standing still before God. Before we even begin to ask questions about prayer, we must stand still. No one can teach us to pray except God. When our lover is God, prayer is a secret between the King and the one he has chosen for his bride. Prayer is something like a continuous wedding night. It is stillness. It is lovemaking. Who can describe how God makes love to us and how we make love to God? Who can tell us how to stand still before the miracle of love? We have to remain still and wait. God himself will come and tell us about it.

11 | *Our Lady of Lourdes*
Be Hidden

The last sentence of The Little Mandate is the consoling one, but here we come to a strange sentence: "*Be hidden.*"

All of us have to carry the cross of the Lord. There isn't anyone among Christians who could possibly be without a cross. It's through the cross that we reach the resurrection. We should be absolutely sure of this truth, and we should keep this cross hidden and not place it on the shoulders of others. It is our cross we have to carry. It is the one God has given us to go through into his resurrection. This is the one we should keep hidden.

But there are crosses and crosses, some of our own making. These we should immediately discard. Some are permitted by God for our sanctification. These we can share for they are also for the sanctification of others. True, we can help to carry other people's crosses and they can help to carry our crosses, but the operative word is "hidden." Look up Matthew 6:16-18 about this.

Our very hiddenness becomes a light if we do not complain, if we carry our cross courageously. Then we become a light to our neighbor's feet because we become an icon of Christ— shining! But this is only possible if we are one with Christ, if there are no divisions among us, if we are of one mind. Then we are hidden, yet revealed as people of peace and unity.

12 | When All Is Said and Done

What is our spirituality when all is said and done? I see us silently, in a manner of speaking, doing little ordinary things men and women do everywhere, always with an immense, burning love, knowing that love makes every gesture, step, word, and work, redemptive. I see us loving each other, serving each other and all the world, because to our eyes of faith and truth, each is Christ to the other! That is all. The rest he will do through us. We are just lovers witnessing to love, servants reflecting the light of the Master and torchbearers of love and light in our modern darkness, by being lovers and doing ordinary daily tasks for Love's sake and with great love.

Three places are our school: Bethlehem, where we become like little children; Nazareth, where we are hidden; and Golgotha, where the world sees us stripped of all, dead to self, sharing unto death on the cross the passion of him whom our hearts love.

What is our spirituality when all is said and done? To me it is so simple. It is to shed our whole selfish self, to take up our cross, no matter how heavy, and to follow him from Bethlehem to Golgotha, follow him humbly as a servant follows his master, yet as a bride her husband. Walking in his footsteps, reflecting his light, being his little, humble apostles.

13 | Prayer: Hunger for Union with God

Prayer is that hunger for union with God which never lets go of us. It beats into our blood with the very beat of our hearts. It is a thirst that can be quenched by nothing except God. It is as if one's whole body is poised on tiptoe, our hands stretching upward as if to touch the cosmos.

The act of praying, like the act of love, involves movement and effort. You don't pray like a robot any more than you make love like one! Prayer is movement, stretching, seeking, holding, finding only to seek again, as in the Song of Songs, "I opened to my beloved, but he had turned his back and gone."

Prayer is constant movement, and strangely enough, it is movement into oneself, where the Trinity dwells. That is why dispossession has to come from within, for the obstacles that separate us from God are never outside us. "What goes into the mouth does not make a man unclean; it is what comes out of the mouth that makes him unclean." Dispossession is like taking a broom to one's inner being to clear out everything that keeps us from being united to God.

Prayer is walking up to an abyss, looking down, and being unable to see the bottom, for there is none. This is where faith comes in. You spend years balancing on the edge, almost jumping in, then retreating. Suddenly, at some given moment, the hunger becomes too great, and you jump, only to discover it's no abyss, but only God and the depth of his love for you!

14 Love, Prayer, and Self-Emptying

Prayer is such a simple thing. It has its own rhythm. First I get in touch with God, and then I get in touch with myself. Before I can love my neighbor, I have to love myself. Then I can love everyone else. God is love, and our relationship is a love affair between God and human beings. Making contact with God inevitably must lead to making contact with others. In other words, prayer is for the service of people.

In the process, *kenosis* takes place. *Kenosis* is the Greek word for emptying ourselves in order that Christ might grow in us. What does that mean? It means that the dimensions of our heart must constantly increase. Because Christ became incarnate in humanity, we too can truly take humanity into our hearts. We can serve humanity in a thousand ways, including fasting and prayer.

Fasting and prayer can never be for oneself. They are always for the other. More people today are seeking ways to empty themselves of the self-centeredness and greed which permeate our North American culture. More young people these days are turning to God in prayer and fasting and I rejoice when I see this. Just imagine what could happen with younger people, solid in their faith, going out to reflect the face of Christ and preach the Gospel with their lives!

15 Why We Need Spiritual Direction

Through the Fathers of the Church, God has made it clear to us that we need spiritual direction. All Christians, all Catholics, should make use of it. St. John of the Cross has said that "only a fool directs himself." Especially should people dedicated to God seek direction. Through this grace they realize better their poverty and their weakness. We need a spiritual guide on the narrow road that leads to heaven, for the devil delights in placing confusing signposts on our way, especially at our major crossroads. Definitely a guide is needed.

We cannot know ourselves objectively. Another can. Alone, individuals cannot develop their full spiritual and active potential. They need the help of priests God appointed for it. Pope Pius IX said, "Grace comes to men through men, and especially through men divinely appointed to bring that grace to others... priests." But before you can decide to seek such a guide, make up your mind that you must *love him as if he were Christ himself! Obey him absolutely, as you would Christ himself... and trust him completely.* Without this love, this obedience, this trust, you will only waste his time and yours.

I strongly encourage you to have a spiritual director. Not to have one is to be a foolish person, one who is guideless in a great, utterly unknown wilderness.

* See Appendix One in the back for more explanation of Catherine Doherty's views concerning spiritual direction.

16 | How to Find a Spiritual Director

My answer to the question of how to get a spiritual director is always the same. Pray for one. Pray very earnestly to God before choosing one. It is a very important relationship that you are entering into with Christ in the priest, and you must turn to him to direct you to the right person. He may do this by giving you a certain spiritual attraction to some priest. Perhaps it is through a sermon, a retreat, or a spiritual truth expressed by this priest that went straight to your heart. These can be indications that God is directing you to him.

A priest is not chosen for his personality, his intelligence, his deep knowledge of theology, or for any other such traits. He is chosen because he is the incarnation of Christ in the special moment of spiritual direction. This is a mystery of our faith.

So you pray for a spiritual director, for someone you judge to be competent and interested in you. Then you love, trust, and obey him, for he is Christ for you. His competency is self-evident: the priest is trained for spiritual direction, has the grace of the Sacrament of Holy Orders, and is obviously interested in the salvation and sanctity of souls. So when you find a priest you feel will help you get closer to God, approach him simply, and ask him to be your spiritual director.

17 | Your Relationship with Your Spiritual Director

Once the priest has accepted you, you must enter into a very childlike relationship with him. You must love him as you love God—supernaturally. You must trust him completely. You must obey him implicitly. Otherwise, you wouldn't need a spiritual director. If you try to get around him in the thousand ways that human beings try to get around even God, you will encourage Satan to trap you. One does not do such things to God.

Some of you may see a conflict between the independence you have been brought up with and the freedom of the children of God which comes through obedience to a priest. You rebel against submitting your will to that of another. This "individuality," this being your own master, is really slavery to self, to one's own judgment. In a word, it means pride. Pride is the greatest enemy of a Christian, the one sure guide to hell. But through spiritual direction, you have taken the greatest precaution a human being can take against pride.

On a practical note, at your first appointment with the priest, give him a short biographical sketch. It will help him direct you. Also give him a short list of what you think are your virtues and weaknesses. That will help him too. Don't be verbose on paper or in your interview. Say what you have to say. Listen to what he has to say. And go forth and carry his advice into your life.

18 | Christ Guides and Heals through Your Director

Your director has the charism to show you the way; he listens to the Spirit while you talk, and is silent and prayerful with his heart; then he transmits to you what the Spirit has given him. I believe, with an unshakable belief, that the Holy Spirit speaks in him. And if this not be so, then God will step in and correct whatever mistake he has made.

Even if the priest be sinful, in him resides Christ the Good Shepherd. And when you, the sheep, come for spiritual direction, even if the human shepherd is a leper, Christ can still work through him. Because that's the way Christ does things.

Because you go to a director for inner healing, you accept the word of this man as coming from the Holy Spirit. You see, you go to be healed. You go because you're wounded. So the first thing that you must know is that you *are* wounded. If you don't think you're wounded, and if you're going to argue with the guy, well, you might as well just dispense with spiritual direction. When a doctor tells you to put a poultice on your arm, and you say, "To hell with the doctor; he's a stupid old oaf," then why go to a doctor at all? The first question in obedience is to know that you have a wound that has to be healed.

19 We Do Not Live the Gospel

We do not live the Gospel of Christ, that is all there is to it. We say, "Oh, Christ doesn't mean this or that." But Christ *does* mean that and this and all the things we don't want to take in. All the things we want to discard are frightening. I was just reading the other day that 75 percent of the people disagree with the Church's teaching on abortion, sex, and what-have-you. Well, that is an awful lot of people who disagree. And all along Christ is watching this happen. Sometimes I think we make Christ cry, I really do; because he is human, he can cry. And I think we make Christ cry because we don't live by his way and his commandments.

Preaching the Gospel to the whole world means *living* it. We cannot preach unless we live. It is all very nice to talk about it; it is beautiful to sit in the evening and discuss the Holy Spirit and Our Lady, but it doesn't get us anywhere. We go to Mass. We receive the Body and Blood of Christ, a mystery beyond any mystery. A mystery of love in a cup! And a piece of bread! Things so familiar to all of us. And yet they contain within themselves God! We are receiving God, communicating with God. Now let us communicate with each other! Let us *show* that we are Christians! *Make it so that others can touch it.* We are weak, sinful and unimportant. But we must *try* to live the Gospel with our lives.

20 To Live the Gospel Is Painful

You can't live the Gospel of Christ without pain. Christ was the greatest revolutionary on earth. He calls you to the impossible.

Are you willing to be totally poor, in spirit or otherwise? Are you able to hope when every hope is gone? Can you love when you are not loved? Can you continue to have faith when all around you faith is dying?

Love those who hate you! Renew the faith of those who have lost it! Bring hope and love to everybody! For this you have been created! And you have to do it, my friends, because the time is so short.

You have to restore his church. Yes, it's the Mystical Body of Christ. Yes, it is the people of God. But far more, it is the bride of Christ. The beautiful, incredible bride of Christ! Behold the bridegroom, as it says in the Psalms, jumping over mountains coming to his bride. The church was born out of the death of Christ. He left this to us. He abides in it.

So love God and your neighbor! Love yourself! Love those who hate you! And die for everybody! And start going into the depths of your own heart. Not just superficially. Go deep into it.

21 Giving God Room: Dying to Self

How can we love if there is one-millionth of an ounce of self within us? Love is a person. Love is God. Where love is, God is. And so our vocation is to make room for God in ourselves. It is to clothe God with our flesh, to once again give him hands and lips and eyes and a voice.

But to do that we must die to self. God is immense. He needs much room—our whole being! Not one crevice must be left to ourselves. Otherwise, we maim Christ if we refuse him access to any part of us. And where is the lover who keeps back anything from the beloved? Such a person is not a true lover.

And so that is our vocation—to burn, to die, to become a flame, so as to make room for Christ to grow in us. Once the feet of Christ, through our feet, touch again this earth of ours, the earth will grow and be restored.

This dying to self to make room for God is painful. But dedication is seen in pain. There is a radiance emanating from that pain which disperses the shadows in another's face. That is the essence of our vocation—to burn with love, to be a light, to be a fire. And we cannot start a fire with green wood. The fire of love of God will not take hold in a soul that is not utterly dedicated to him.

22 | *Chair of Peter, the Apostle* Christ's Followers Will Be Crucified Too

You go forth as an apostle—with no shoes, no gold, or silver. Then, once more, you too will hear the words of Christ at the end of the journey, "Have you wanted for anything?"

Your vocation is simple, so utterly simple, that words fail to describe it. It is intangible, yet very concrete. To burn. To do the will of God in the humble duty of every moment. To die to self through obedience, poverty, love. Through chastity also. To be ready to be crucified, in the mystical sense, on the cross of the will of God. To be ready to be crucified by men and women. You will be.

You will be crucified with their words, not yet realizing that words spoken by men and women are like chaff in the wind. They will be words of disapproval, of doubt, of ridicule. You will also be crucified by gestures (the shrugging of shoulders, for example). You will be crucified by others' disbelief in your way of life.

Your cross will be very small. It will probably be in the marketplace or where you live. Yes, the cross will be small, as tall as you or I, each according to his size.

23 | The Cross Is the Answer

Oh God! When we're afraid to love, we take a course on interpersonal relationships! We take another course in psychology when we're afraid to look at our inner self. Always a fear of loving... A fear of the cross.

Remember the song, "You can't go under it; it's too deep. You can't go over it; it's too high. You can't go around it; it's too wide. You have to go through it." It's the cross!

And here we are, busy eschewing that cross with tranquilizers, and with euphoria, with LSD, with—oh well—I can name them, but I won't. Anything and everything. We eschew *any* kind of faith.

Yet, when we're discouraged, the cross is the answer!

✠ ✠ ✠

When I'm discouraged I remember that I have recourse to the only thing I know will keep me from absolute discouragement, and that is Calvary. Whenever I feel that the things of the world are too much for me, I take refuge at the foot of the cross, and even if the whole world is shrouded in darkness, and the curtains of all my temples are rent, I know that—although I cannot see, nor hear, nor understand—I am safe at the feet of my crucified Savior.

24 Lent: Spring Cleaning Your Heart

There is the deep stuff inside, where you have to go and cleanse your soul and your heart of all that accumulated junk through the years. Go into your heart and you'll see. Thousands of things: envy, jealousy—a lot of things.

So, come Lent, you make a genuflection—not so much of your knees but of your soul—and you say to yourself, well, here is where I cleanse my soul; here is where I spring-clean it; here is where I make it a place in which God can live.

Think of your soul as a room, a room that you are making ready for God, and if you knew that God was coming, you certainly would wash and clean and scrub. Do it now. Do the washing and scrubbing and cleaning. Lent is for that.

And as you come out of it, a great joy will prevail in you, and Easter will be a really beautiful time. Beautiful! If your Lent has been true and one that really cleansed your soul.

Do it now; face it. Talk to your spiritual director; talk to God himself and to Our Lady. *TALK!* So that Christ may be ready to walk into your room, your soul.

25 A Time to Plumb the Depths

Lent is a time to go into the depths of yourself, to really advance in the "journey inward" that everyone must undertake to meet the God who dwells within.

This Lent, especially for North Americans, should be the time to ask and answer one question: "What has my life contributed to the immense spiritual battle being waged across the world today?"

Strange as it may seem, today each Christian is responsible for projecting the true face of Christ to others, or for blurring it or annihilating it in the souls of other people. The voice of the church is not heard as well as it used to be in the times when the world was Christian. And it must be heard better than ever, for never have human beings been so hungry for the truth as they are today.

The way it will be heard now will be through every Christian and not so much in one's speech as in one's life. For the contrast between our beliefs and our behavior is more glaring and more noticeable against the backdrop of modern secularism, atheism, plain ignorance, and the indifference of things spiritual. We must live the Gospel and preach it by living it. It is the only language that human beings will understand today. They have been hurt, confused, wounded, and upset by the immense contradictions between the luminous teaching of the church and the incredible behavior of its members that seem to deny every tenet of that teaching.

26 | Surrender to God

What does it mean to be *totally* surrendered to God? It means to enter into his mind and his will. It means to open ourselves to his will so that, day after day, nothing matters but his will. You say, "Lord, here I am. Speak. Your servant heareth." And, "Lord, send me wherever you wish."

That to me is the totality of giving. That to me is reaching for the absolute. And we find this totality of surrender to the will of God moment by moment, day by day. It means being able to endure personal difficulties because we see Christ in each other. And he is there, there is no denying it.

It means too that we do not eternally think that the grass is greener on the other side of the fence. It isn't. It is only green when we are doing the will of God. And we don't have to change jobs, houses, this or that. No. We just trust, resting peacefully on God's breast, listening to his heartbeats, and in them we find the answer to our question, "What must I do?"

God simply answers, "The duty of the moment is *my* duty. I want you to follow in my footsteps, no matter where they lead. Do not use your normal intelligence to evaluate my footsteps. Just walk in them, that's all. Be simple, childlike, docile to my will and my wishes. Then you shall know happiness. Then you shall know freedom. Then you shall know *me.* And then you shall be like *me.* And I will call you friends, not servants any more." Yes, that exactly is a totality of surrender.

27 | On Being Misunderstood

People will not know you for who you are. They didn't understand Christ in Nazareth for who he was. They won't understand you either, and being misunderstood will be hard for you. It was hard for the God-Man to be misunderstood, too. But you will rejoice with great joy, for all this will make you more like your beloved.

All these little things are the fingers of God the Father, conforming you into the loneliness of his Son, conforming you into the misunderstanding that his Son suffered, conforming you into Christ's hiddenness, and into his pain. Slowly, the fingers of God's will and the fingers of time will become one. You will be shaped and shaped, not knowing that you are being shaped. You will enter into a great darkness, a great aridity, a great temptation. But oh, rejoice! For this is the desert where Christ spent forty days fasting! This is his hunger you are experiencing. This is the lover paying court to your soul, hiding himself, as lovers do, so that you, whom he loves, might arise and go in search of him. The hide-and-seek of love, the eternal playfulness, is now lifted to a supernatural plane.

Be at peace! This dark aridity is joyful, for this is the beginning of wisdom, for your beloved is the very Wisdom of God. He teaches you his wisdom now in the loneliness and silence of the desert, now in the quiet and darkness of the night of love. There are two nights in this world: the night of hate and the night of love. This is the night of love.

28 | To Be Like Christ

To be alone, forgotten, neglected, to have all you do accepted either as a matter of fact, or without gratitude, to suffer in silence, to be silent under injustice and provocation, pain and suffering, to feel left out of things and have your love rejected or coldly received—all of this is to be like whom?

Already the answer is on your lips—an awesome, strange, yet beautifully true answer—to be like Christ! You love him; I know you do. Then why object when in his gracious kindness and his great love, he tries—through people, events, and things—to shape you into his own likeness?

Think this over. And thinking, pray that you may understand and cooperate with his incomprehensible ways of leading you to him. Look at him today. In the words of the psalmist, he is more like a worm than a man, bruised and battered, our God. The world over, he walks like one drunk, not with wine, but with pain. Crucified again and again by those who have not the excuse that they do not know what they do, and for whom he once died naked on a cross. Neglected and forgotten by the majority, who do not care. Do you see? To walk with Christ means walking the way of pain, sacrifice, and loneliness *until the end.* How well we understand this with our minds but rebel against it in reality!

Lord, have mercy on us sinners and inconsistent creatures! Teach us to see, to think, and to do things for thy sake only.

29 A Leap in Faith

In the aftermath of Vatican II something went nutty in the church. Priests thought they had to become "relevant." Many wanted to leave the priesthood. I don't remember a pain so deep as that of meeting all those priests who wanted to leave the church, become laicized, or marry. I told them, "Be priests for us; give us the Eucharist. Why do you want to be somebody else?" Nuns shed their habits and my heart wept over nuns curling their hair, smoking, and wearing smart clothes. Everything was going overboard. Next, the hippies came—for about ten years they came to Madonna House in droves. Our staff just accepted them and took everything in stride. Quite a few became converts.

In the early 1960s the church appeared to be in chaos, to be dissolving. But I knew, with a God-given faith that nothing could shake, that the powers of hell would never prevail. I discerned in my soul that *this was the moment of faith!* But I was sorely tried. There were moments I would hang on to Our Lady's garments; she seemed to be the only one who could understand and console me. It was in the 1960s that I realized how prophetic were the words that Pope Pius XII had spoken to me years before. He said, "Madam, we need stable, dedicated lay people who will defend the church, who will restore the church, because the church is about to suffer again." He foresaw what would be needed and we at Madonna House said yes. We stood for years under the Cross of Christ and held on to Mary. She knew what it was to stand there.

March

✝

1 | The Media and Our "Noise Level"

The media today permeate our whole life. If it is not TV, it is music. Music is a kind of "background sound" instead of something we listen to. In fact, this need for constant music reveals the incapacity of modern people to enjoy silence, to understand silence not as a mere absence of sound but as the condition for all real presence.

If Christians of the past lived in great measure in a silent world, giving them ample opportunity for concentration, contemplation and the inner life, Christians of today have to make a special effort to recover this essential dimension of silence, which alone can put them in contact with God. Thus, the problem of radio and TV during Lent is not a marginal one, but in many ways is a matter of spiritual life or death.

I suggest you drastically reduce your use of TV and radio so an "addiction" to TV does not take place—transforming you into a vegetable in an armchair, glued to the screen and passively accepting anything coming from it. What is involved here is the experience of Lent as a special time for silence created by the absence of the world's noises, to be filled with positive content. We need a break from the ceaseless hammering of the media. I suggest you feed your intellect by spiritual reading and feed your soul by prayer.

2 | Faith in Darkness

"I am the light of the world," said Christ. Because he has come, we are no longer living in the shadow of death. We can live in light. But without darkness, we would not know the light. God allows us to enter the darkness because he desires intensely that we identify with him, who took on himself the darkness of sin. In the darkness, we experience our helplessness and powerlessness. In the darkness, we are blind. Now God can heal us. The act of faith takes place in darkness, in regions where intellect cannot penetrate. When we enter this darkness of faith, eventually the light bursts in. But not right away. First God says: "If you believe in me, come." But most of us are too filled with fear even to start out.

There is a story of a boy in a burning house. His father is outside, calling to him, "Jump! Jump!" The child cries, "Daddy, I can't see you!" "That's okay," the father says, "I can see *you*." We want to see, not only the Father, whose arms are poised to catch us, but the very earth beneath his feet. We want everything sorted out and in order. We are afraid to walk into what seems like chaos to us, but it is really perfect order to God. We want to say to God, "Let's get organized," and God refuses to organize himself to our standards. We cannot manipulate him—but oh, how we try!

3 | Loneliness

There are many kinds of loneliness in the world. There is the human loneliness that can be swallowed up by friendship. Unfortunately, friendship today is very hard to come by. People do not make friends any more. There is television—the mechanical friend—which, above all, promotes things to buy.

One of the most terrible kinds of loneliness is that of old people living on a meager pension, barely enough to feed them. Slowly, they decline into an abysmal state of loneliness. During their last years, none of their children come to visit them; one can see how loneliness eats them up, as cancer does. This kind of loneliness is very prevalent all over the world, especially in the Western world.

There was a time (older people can tell you) when people were neighbors. They did not sit glaring at TV with a glassy stare. No, people were neighbors and they used to visit each other, or play games together, or have other kinds of entertainment. There was a time when people painted, wrote books, and opened their souls in thousands of ways to others. People could talk and think together.

We cry for release from our loneliness and someday we will understand we are prisoners to computers and technology. Someday, we will arise and destroy their fascinating power, and we will be free again; we will be able to communicate with others. Then our natural loneliness will disappear.

 # 4 Loneliness and Communication

We are prisoners today. Prisoners of technology. We are almost unable to make friends. Between us and friendship lie miles and miles of electrical cords and electronic circuits. We have lost the joy of simple things that were so good, and along with them, the ability to laugh and really communicate.

We have lost the evenings with father and mother when little children were told fairy tales and went to sleep dreaming of beautiful ladies and the like. We have lost the time of little farms, when children grew up learning about trees and flowers and wheat and oats and how they grew. There were church suppers where everyone was friendly and knew each other, and barn dances and the thousand things that seem old but could become new any day because they are immortal, and disperse loneliness like wind disperses fog. When people communicate, loneliness is broken into tiny pieces that are scattered by the wind. One has to laugh to communicate, and communication is the enemy of loneliness.

Recently I was in a clinic for a checkup and was astonished at the kindness and constancy of everyone there. The clinic had been built with love and understanding of the sick. A little word or smile or helping hand here and there, a little conversation while waiting meant so much to the people there. How simple the ways of God are, how very simple! It is Christ who gives us power to communicate simple gestures of love: a smile, a helping hand. It is he who directs us to communicate.

5 | Prayer and Communication

There is a point which must be investigated when we discuss loneliness. If we wish to get rid of loneliness, we have to make contact with others, and also with God through prayer. But there is an even deeper contact than prayer. We have to enter the mystery of Christ's loneliness. We must enter it without understanding it, as it is impossible to understand; so, we have to make contact with God.

One of the first things in facing loneliness, especially old-age loneliness, or any kind of loneliness, is to understand that Christ calls some people to *share* his loneliness. Can you imagine the utter loneliness of Christ in Gethsemane? When his apostles fell asleep? This calling is redemptive. For if we share the loneliness of Christ, then we too, with his help, can redeem the world. Those who follow Christ will find peace, and will understand that loneliness is fruitful and not sterile, because we can share it, if we wish, with God.

The key that opens to you the true essence of loneliness is *sharing it with Christ.* If you share it with him, how is it possible to be lonely when the two lonelinesses—yours and his—blend together? You can share his loneliness at any time, in any place—and he will share yours. The result will be that there will not be any loneliness, because when you have entered into the mystery of Christ's loneliness, it ceases to be loneliness. This is a great mystery of God.

6 | Sharing the Pain of Christ

One day it was as if Christ were speaking to me, and he said, "Catherine, I want you to share my pain." I said, "How can I?" He said, "I will help you to bear my pain." And so he did; but it didn't lessen the pain. The whole thing was spiritual. It had nothing to do with other things or anybody else. It was my heart that cried out to God and said, "Lord, how can we help you?" And always the answer came, "*Bear my pain.*" So that was it.

What happened to me was like a lightning flash. It was an understanding or realization that *Christ was not loved.* Clearly, totally, obviously, I saw that the Lord was not loved. I saw that he was rejected. True, he had been rejected ever since he left his mother's home, right up to his crucifixion. Oh, he was accepted by some people, and in some places, but most of them were not very strong in their acceptance.

We have to get busy. We have to do little things *exceedingly well* for the love of God. We have to open our hearts to people, because they are still closed. So bit by bit, they must become open. For you see, Christ comes into our hearts *with each person* who comes in. Remember, we are to share his pain. That's why we will share his joy, because to those who share his pain, he will give infinite joy.

7 Common Temptations— and How to Handle Them

The devil uses common temptations on us. I have made a list of them below and I bet I'm not far from wrong. I have gathered from those who have passed through Madonna House (and myself) many of his techniques. Let's look at the list:

1. Fears.
2. Temptations about your vocation in life.
3. Discouragement.
4. Personality clashes.
5. The monotony of your job (he will hammer on that).
6. Confusion.
7. Questioning authority: Why do I have to do this and that?

Add a dash of day-dreaming (at which the old boy is past master), salt it with self-pity (he produces it out of nowhere), add a dash of paprika (which is withdrawal from your family or community) with a feeling of "no one understands me—not even God," serve it on a platter of disobedience and the desire to be left alone, and you have put together the devil's masterpiece, the old boy's stock-in-trade! I bet if you reread this, you cannot say this hasn't happened to you in one fashion or another.

Here are some of your weapons against his temptations:

1. Be open to your spiritual director.
2. Sprinkle holy water on yourself, and especially on your bed, and your place of work.
3. Use common sense, together with a sense of humor and the ability to laugh at yourself.
4. With regard to personality clashes, ask yourself, "If so-and-so is such a pill to me, maybe I'm more of a pill to him or her."

8 | Controlling Our Speech

Lent is the time to control our speech. To control speech is to recover its sacredness, to understand that sometimes the words of an innocent "joke," proffered without even thinking, can have disastrous results, can be the "last straw" that pushes a person into ultimate dispair and destruction. But our words can also be a witness. A casual conversation across the desk with a colleague can do more for communicating a vision of life, an attitude toward other people or toward work, than formal preaching. It can sow the seeds of a question, of the possibility of a different approach to life, the desire to know more. We have no idea how, in fact, we constantly influence one another by our speech, by the very "tonality" of our personality. And ultimately men and women are converted to God not because someone was able to give brilliant explanations, but because they saw in that person a light, joy, depth, seriousness, and love which alone reveal the presence and the power of God in the world.

As Matthew 12:36-37 says, we shall be judged by our words. Lent is a time when we must think about what God's words in the Bible say. And out of this thinking, we must speak words of tenderness, love, pity, compassion, and gentleness because we are men and women of faith; we are Christians.

9 | Priesthood: A Gift of Love

Do you ever wonder why at Madonna House we have this tremendous love for priests? Why do we rise when they come to the table for meals? Why do we relate to them with respectful informality? The answer is simple: it is because when a priest walks into this house, *Christ walks in.* We know that in faith. It isn't astonishing that, upon realizing this, one falls to one's knees, enveloped and absorbed in the mystery of God's love for us.

Christ didn't want to leave us orphans! He wanted to give us someone in whom we could see his resemblance. I don't mean physical resemblance, but the resemblance of that which he really is—the lover, the tender one, the forgiving one, the servant—one who would do what he did: wash the feet of humanity.

But Christ did more! He gave the priest a special power so that, when he utters a few words of absolution, Christ washes our soul and embraces us in love and reconciliation. Christ comes to us, therefore, in such tremendous simplicity of love that our breath should be taken away. He comes to us in the guise of a priest!

So then, approach a priest with the understanding that he has God in him in a special manner through his ordination. Approach him as you would approach Christ.

10 | Divine Priesthood in Human Clay

After yesterday's thoughts on priesthood, you might say, "What of the priest who is sinful and unholy, who marries without dispensation, etc.?" You ask this because, in North America, you haven't been given the full knowledge of what priesthood really is. Therefore you don't realize that the seal of priesthood has been etched in the soul of this poor, sinful man. It has been placed there by the fire of the Holy Spirit and the touch of the Father's hand, and that he can never lose that gift.

In Russia, when the last Roman Catholic priest in my city died (he was killed before my very eyes), if there had been a priest who I knew had committed every mortal sin in the book (and who was, perhaps, living in the house of his mistress), I would have *crawled on my belly* to that man to receive the divine gifts he could give me. I couldn't have cared less about his sinful ways. Because faith penetrates these things; it tears off the outer facade—which I would have seen in the physical presence of a priest in sin—and it shows me the inner reality. Suddenly, in faith, I would have seen this man transfigured in divine glory. I would know that on his ordination day, in a strange, unexplainable mystery, this man was transfigured into Christ. I would know that, whether he is a sinner or not, *Christ in him* would absolve me.

11 | We Shouldn't Judge Our Priests

You ask an awful lot of questions about priests, and a good many of them are irrelevant... why do they get married, or do this or that or the other thing. Well, that's the humanness of them. But in them is Christ—always Christ! Priests can bind him, for they are human beings just as we are. But there is one thing in the priest which is very different from anyone else's soul: Christ will unbind himself in them *if anyone else needs him.*

We have to remember that the twelve apostles weren't perfect men. One left. One denied him for a while. One stuck around for the crucifixion, but the rest just turned their backs and kept running away from Golgotha as far as their legs could carry them. They were pretty ordinary guys.

Often we judge priests by human appraisal (their winning smile, their great knowledge, their savvy about one thing or another). All this is a lot of baloney if I may say so! We should not judge a priest by his good looks, education, and so forth. We should just look at him and say to ourselves, "Thanks be to God he is here," because he is one of the greatest signs of God's love for us.

Why do you want to criticize priests? Why should we criticize anyone? Christ told us, "Judge not and you shall not be judged."

12 Priests Deserve Deep Respect

Priests deserve our deep respect. Here is a human being like you or me. But he is a special human being, someone before whom we can kneel and have our sins washed away. He is someone who can give us the Body and Blood of Christ so that we might have life everlasting.

The way to treat a priest is with *respectful* informality, and the accent is on the word respectful. I remember one time a priest arrived here at Madonna House and he was very drunk, so I put him to bed to "sleep it off." In the morning I brought him some coffee. He was bleary-eyed, and sort of "lost," but I knelt by his bed and asked him to bless me. He looked at me and said, "Do you realize who I am and what I did? Do you realize that I am a bum?" I answered, "Yes, but you are a priest also and I ask for your blessing, for *it is Christ's blessing!*" He blessed me, and then he started to cry.

So remember, priests are a gift of God and we must treat them with generosity, gentleness, and kindness, and make life simple for them, not complicated. Above all, we must pray for them because their vocation is hard and difficult. They depend very much on our prayers.

13 A True Story about a Priest

When I was ten years old, our family went to Poland for vacation. I was walking down the road when suddenly, there in the mire, I saw the village priest. Now I had been brought up from babyhood to love and reverence priests, and this just completely shattered my little heart! I ran home to my mother and said, "There's Monsignor, and he is drunk, drunk, drunk! The priest is drunk!" Mother looked at me and said,

"Is that so? Then let's go to him."

With her holding my hand, we retraced my steps in silence. When we came to the priest, still lying there in the mud, my mother said, "Catherine, you are a big girl. Help me to lift him up." Before we did so, however, she kissed his dirty hand. Then we carried him into the presbytery where, still silently, she handed him to the woman in charge.

When we got home, mother asked me to get the baby's little potty, fill it with water, and bring it to her. While I did so, she gathered a bunch of beautiful white lilies from the garden. When I arrived with the potty, she put the bouquet into the potty and said, "Look at that. The white lilies don't change, though they sit in a potty instead of in a beautiful vase. Always remember that, Catherine. The potty might be the priest. The white lily is Christ, the Christ who never changes, the Christ who is in the priest in a special way. Yes, the priest might be the potty, but the Christ in him always remains just like those lilies. Never in your life make the mistake of mixing the two together!"

14 | Pain as a Means to Holiness

What kind of a Christian would you be if there were no pain in your life? Expect it, therefore, and welcome it, because pain is like a fire sent by God to cleanse your soul, your heart, and your mind. Because of it, you can cease to be self-centered, and can go out to all your brothers and sisters. So when there is pain in your life, try to add the words, "Praise be to God for the pain!"

Pain is the path that leads higher into the mountains of the Lord. It is also the tool that helps you straighten out the path of the Lord in your own heart so that you level out its hills and fill in its valleys. Then you yourself, and your brothers and sisters too, can walk on a smooth path to the Lord—the path that you have made with the tools of love, of hope, and of pain.

The Bible says of Christ, "Son though he was, he learned the meaning of obedience through all he suffered" (Heb 5:8). Jesus came to do the will of God; and to be obedient to the will of God is to suffer. But where does that suffering lead? It certainly doesn't lead to depression. No. It leads to joy, to love, to faith. Pain is the chalice of love. I hope that we will understand *why* God gives us a share of his pain; it is so that we may imitate him and be led by him to his Father.

15 | Sources of Pain

The pain you express is the pain of hurt. Sometimes this pain might have begun in the womb, or it might have begun before the womb, for we human beings carry tribal memories in our souls. Some of these hurts may have been inflicted in babyhood, childhood, adolescence, or even in adult years.

Some person or persons of importance may have rejected you. Society also had a share in inflicting hurts and pain and sorrow and anger, creating in you the hostile symptoms of either aggressiveness or withdrawal. So there is Pain! Pain! Pain! Many of you carry this burden of pain not even knowing you do. When people are in pain, they sometimes say that pain "blinds" them.

Yes, sometimes pain does blind us to all the beauty of life in the church. Because we haven't been trusted, we don't trust others. Since people haven't been open with us, we are not open with ourselves. And so on. So, instead of being bearers of the Good News, we start singing dirges in a low and minor key!

As I prayed about this, some words came into my heart: "Tell them about the healing of memories." I think God gave these words to me because healed memories means forgiveness. And forgiveness engenders understanding, tenderness, generosity, and deep healing.

16 Remedy for Pain: Forgiveness

We must forgive the society from which we came; we must forgive the ways it has hurt us. We must have forgiveness for all the pain that we have unknowingly experienced, even in the womb before our birth. We must forgive those who may not have understood us, or have seemingly neglected us, or perhaps even rejected us. It is especially important that we forgive our parents for their human frailties. If we can generate that first impulse of forgiveness within ourselves, then—like lightning going through a darkened sky—our forgiveness will cover everything! It will flash across our memories as a lighthouse scans the sea, so that whenever its rays illuminate anything that we think has hurt us, the touch of that light will bring forgiveness into our hearts and bless those whom we forgive.

As I pondered this word forgiveness, another word suddenly came forth: reconciliation. Forgiveness will bring reconciliation; and I know there has to be reconciliation among nations, among peoples, among all of us. We have to be reconciled to God first, then to ourselves, and then to the whole world—including whoever has hurt us.

But we have to do more than that! If our forgiveness isn't accepted, we have to turn the other cheek. This is not easy, but Christ, who is the Way, found the going pretty rough too. So if we are walking with him, that is what we can expect also.

17 *St. Patrick* What Christ Asks of Us

Right on our own doorstep, and in our midst, stands Christ. If only we would listen, we could hear him! He says, "I do not even ask you to watch one hour with me in my agony; I simply ask you to get out of bed when the alarm rings. I do not ask you to be smitten on your cheeks nor to be spat upon; I just ask you to take correction (which you deserve) humbly, for love of me, with an open heart and mind and a willingness to change. I do not ask you to be bound to a post and flagellated with leaden whips. I simply ask you to do every task that is given to you with total recollection and thoughtfulness.

"I do not ask you to hang naked upon my cross; but I ask you to deepen the spirit of poverty in the care and use of my created things. I was stripped naked; why can't you strip your soul of your self-centered thoughts and begin to see things such as cups, dust cloths, food, and clothing with deep reverence? You can do this only if you strip yourself naked of self-centeredness and connect everything—work, walking, sitting, sleeping—with me.

"I haven't yet asked you to hang on the cross with me; but I will, if you prepare yourself in the way that I mentioned above. Remember, unless you hang on the other side of my cross, you cannot share heaven with me. Without the cross, there would have been no resurrection. The key to heaven is my cross; when will you understand that?"

18 | Keep Going!

Let us face the facts of life. Sometimes you will be tired, sometimes you will feel emotionally drained. We are all human, but we go on in spite of this. You can have no mental agony that will ever equal that of Christ in Gethsemane or that of his Blessed Mother under the cross. No one will ever be as tired as Christ was on that cross. So what are you getting excited about? You feel lousy? Fine. Keep going. You are an apostle—a man or woman in love with God and totally dedicated to him in the world.

Stop taking your psychiatric pulse. Stop worrying about your aches and pains, your little tensions and fatigue. Keep going! You've been told you are on your way to the cross, so set your feet at a hundred miles an hour to get there. Physically you are well taken care of. All your legitimate needs are being met. You are loved and cared for, so what's the problem? Christ is waiting.

Let's look at those personality clashes. X gets on the nerves of Y. Okay, let the person. Keep smiling. Be extra charitable to that person. Don't withdraw. This is only a tiny splinter of the cross on which you are supposed to be crucified. What are you worried about? Keep going. You have problems? The type of work you are assigned? Nagging fears? Christ must have had fears too, when he saw them preparing to flagellate him. Unite yourself with him and his passion and *keep on going!*

19 | St. Joseph, Husband of Mary
The Gentle Joseph

Out of the silence, deep and holy, the gentle Joseph comes; and every movement, every step, even his carriage, speaks of courage, understanding and of love. He is not old, but young and vital, tall, sparse, with hair as soft as silk and dark as night. His eyes are blue, reflecting a glory that is rarely seen, for it has been given to him to father the Son of God without fathering, the only man to whom the Father would entrust His Son.

The bride, the church, knows him well. It is at Joseph's feet that nightly she lays her burdens, for who better than he, who cradled in his arms the flesh of God, to deal with his Mystical Body? And her children bring to him thousands of broken dreams, sorrows, and hearts that are wounded. Who better than the man who believed the impossible, the craftsman of silence and faith, to answer the prayers of children who walk in darkness alone?

Yet, notwithstanding his glory, his beauty, his light, he is still Joseph the unknown; for silent and humble, he always stands on the side, letting the mother and child go ahead of him, for they are his only delight.

St. Joseph, spouse of the Virgin Mary and patron of the

bride of Christ, we need you! How timely your coming, O Joseph, foster-father of God and of us.

20 | Lent and Personal Relationships

Lent is a good time to measure the incredibly superficial character of our relationships with people, things, and work. The "keep smiling" and "take it easy" slogans are the great "commandments" we joyfully keep. What they *really* mean is: "don't get involved, don't question, don't deepen your relations with human beings; keep the rules of the game which combine a friendly attitude with total indifference; and always think in terms of material gains and advancement."

This Lent, search for meaning in your professional life, in terms of vocation; the meaning of your relationship with other persons; the meaning of friendship and responsibility. There is no job, no vocation, which cannot be "transformed," even if only a little, in terms not of greater efficiency or better organization but in those of human value. The same effort is needed here, but directed toward the "interiorization" of all our relations, for we are free human beings who have become prisoners of systems that progressively dehumanize the world.

If our faith has any meaning, it is to be related to life in all its complexity. For Christians, everything comes from the *inside,* from faith and life according to faith. If you take your faith seriously all the time, you can do more to change the world than a thousand printed programs and a million revolutionaries.

21 | *First Day of Spring* New Hope in Our Hearts

Soft pastel shades tint the evenings of spring and the early morning, bringing new hope, new life, especially in the hearts of those who live in the midst of nature.

So it is with the church, the people of God. Hope is like the sap rising in the trees. Easter reminds us that Christ is truly risen, and that all Christians have life in the risen Christ. Each member of the church lives in the resurrected Christ, the Lord of time and eternity. Slowly the snow of doubts, confusion, and criticism is melting away. More and more people are talking about love. More and more people begin to realize that in order to implement and incarnate Vatican II, all of us must begin with ourselves and must preach the Gospel with our lives. Unless each one of us begins to love, and to serve both his brethren and his enemies, there will be no real change in the world.

Luminous is the light of spring. Luminous is the light of the resurrected Christ. Let us enter into this light of the Lord, who brings us the spring of hope, eternally renewed. He brings us the gift of faith that can grow by leaps and bounds. He brings us the love that can change the whole world if only we incarnate it as he wishes us to.

Alleluia, spring has come to the land! Let us allow that spring of faith, hope, and love to come to our hearts as well.

22 Will You Take the Risk?

Christ does not preach liberation theology, nor is he a German philosopher. Not at all. But he asks for risk, and that is why people don't want to follow him. That's why they stay away. Yet they want to *make believe* that they're Christian.

I realize that in myself. Don't you realize that within yourself? When you stop to think about it, do *you* want to risk your whole life on the word of a man? "No," I said to myself. "It's too risky." That is the real reason why people don't want to follow the Gospel. It demands too much.

In Matthew 10:37-39 Christ says we cannot prefer our family

to him. Think about that! And that anyone who does not take up his cross and follow in his footsteps is not worthy of him. Get the picture? A cross is a heavy thing.

On top of this, in verse 35 he even says he came to set family members against one another! So you have to give up your father and mother, and brothers, and sisters, everybody!

Yes, the reason we don't follow Christ is because of *risk*. Millions of people who are supposed to be Christian *are not taking the risk* of following Christ.

It's all very well to read and write, but it's the *doing* that is difficult.

23 | What Happens When You Take the Risk

Yes, when you follow Christ, you take a risk. Every time you open your mouth you take a risk. You risk the disapproval of people, the anger of people, the dislike of people.

Just after I arrived in Canada, I was invited to lecture in a town called Timmins. I was describing the Communist Revolution and what it did to my family, when zip! A knife whizzed by me. A "pukko" it's called in Finnish. Followed by another pukko. A constable of the Royal Canadian Mounted Police jumped up in the audience, rushed to the stage, got his revolver out and sat by me. I looked at the pukkos and I looked at the audience that was somewhat stunned, and I continued to lecture. The audience applauded. I spoke about Christ and atheism, of the struggle between good and evil. There is your problem. I opened my mouth and I got pukkos. In other words, I was taking a big risk. Similar things happened to me in the South at the hands of the Ku Klux Klan, and in other circumstances.

Christ warned us: whenever you preach you take a risk. That's nothing new. "Beware of men: they will hand you over to sanhedrins and scourge you in their synagogues" (Matthew 10:17). That's what will happen to you, make no mistake about it.

So it's very risky to follow Christ, and that's why few do! Dear reader, think about that yourself, because each one of us has to face a different risk!

24 | Mary and Faith

Just imagine a fourteen-year-old girl having an angel stand before her and say, "Hail, full of grace, the Lord is with thee." How does it feel to be addressed by an angel? But she answered simply, directly, regally, without any false modesty. She said, "Let it be done to me according to his will." Incredible! Here is this little girl accepting God's will. The *world's* existence depends upon it.

I think of how she was betrothed to Joseph and his wonder at it all. Did *she* question it? As her pregnancy became more obvious, and she felt the child move within her, what did she think? It's almost incredible because she was just like you and me! She was a person, a human being; she had certain graces given to her, but she wasn't God. And she didn't understand many things. It was not understanding, but a *plunge into faith!*

When we have difficulties with faith, we should turn to her and bow low before this little girl-woman, who is truly the mother of all who believe. She showed a faith beyond our understanding. Right now, this very moment, I invite you to enter into that solitude of faith, as Mary did. Cast your mind inward, and open your heart. Do you really believe? All you have to do is enter this solitude of faith, as Mary did, and say *yes!* That's all.

25 The Annunciation
What Faith!

One day, out of nowhere, while Mary was busy with her chores, an angel spoke to her and gave her a fantastic, incredible message: she would be the mother of the long-awaited Messiah. She accepted this role with simple words, saying she was ready to do God's will. She said *fiat*... "let it be done."

That was only the first of ten-thousand *fiats* she had to say. She said *fiat* during Joseph's bewilderment. She said *fiat* when she gave birth in a miraculous fashion to her child. What must have been her thoughts when she resumed her humdrum life? Nothing happened. This child, who was to be the Messiah, was just a boy like any other. He ate and slept; his diapers had to be changed. Then he grew up and helped Joseph around the carpentry shop. He learned the trade. Then he left to preach all over Palestine. He was executed in the end, which caused her much grief.

Serenely, silently, Mary accepted all this. But she must have wondered what it was all about—even as many people today are wondering what it is all about! But we wonder without Mary's serenity, without her peace, without her love and without her faith and trust. How we need her attitudes and her endlessly repeated *fiats!* She was no ordinary woman, though she might have appeared to be to her neighbors. What courage it took to live like Mary! What faith! May she teach us how to be people of faith in our world today!

26 The Splurge of Anointing Christ

In Matthew 26:6-13 we read about something "wasteful." Christ's anointing. Read through it now. Doesn't it give you shivers? Don't you begin to realize what it's all about? The Gospel is so simple. The more your head is filled with theology and what-have-you, the less you understand the Gospel. For the Gospel has been told and written for the humiliated, which means the little ones. One must be simple and humble when one reads the Gospel. Listen. Come with me, into these verses....

Here were those future bishops of ours and they were yelling that this ointment business was a waste. I understand this perfectly. When I was at Friendship House in Harlem, I had a funny streak. When I was preparing a clothing box for a poor woman, I put in it the very best things, and I used some of our money and bought six oranges, for she was sick. Now this was a "splurge." And then I said, "She would like a little sherry, so I'll buy some." I did. And, "She's so poor, she'll never have ice cream," so I bought a brick. And then our faithful staff worker, Flewy, bawled me out! She said the money could go to those poorer than this woman! Boy did she bawl me out! So I took out my little Gospel and read her this story of the anointing at Bethany. Flewy was very holy. She said, "Sorry, Catherine. I forgot."

27 Failure

How often do we look at ourselves and feel that we are a total failure? We grow older, we look at our lives, and we don't feel there is anything in them worth recording. We feel we have been utter failures. That is the moment when we should look at Jesus on the cross. There is no greater "failure" than that.

Let us face the word failure head-on, mind-on, heart-on, because it is a devastating word in our vocabulary. What is this strange word that everybody is so worried about? This word we equate with a loss of face, that says we don't amount to much, according to the strange North American yardstick of production?

None of us are failures, dearly beloved, *unless we make ourselves so.* What we call failure in ordinary life is actually a stepping stone to success. You can't become proficient in anything unless you fail in it again and again and again. You just can't! It takes a lot of clay to make a pot. It takes many a thread to make beautiful embroidery.

Yes, failure is painful, but without pain there is no living in love. So then, go through the arches of Christ's pain and enter into the joy of his heart. In the process, there will be many times when you will fail. You will fall flat on your face—even as he did on the way to the cross. Alleluia!

28 Meeting Failure Head On

In this civilization, failure is anathema. We fail in a job, we are kicked out. We fail in university. It seems to us something shameful. Everywhere, to failure is attached shame, whereas I say failure is a stepping stone to success! I am not superhuman. I will fail someplace, somewhere, sometime. So will you. But it devastates us. It's difficult to admit that we are failures in some way. It's difficult to admit we're sinners, isn't it?

But you see, joy comes with suffering. Real inward spiritual suffering, not physical only. And we don't want suffering and we don't want to face what sin is, and we don't want to face failure.

But you see, we belong to Christ. True, he is awesome and all this, but he doesn't want to be that way or else he wouldn't have become the carpenter of Nazareth. By becoming who he was, he showed us how much he loves us and wants us to come to him just as children do. So, all we have to be is childlike and not worry about the rest. We just stick close to Christ and at the same time realize that Christ is a big shot. But to us, he is our lover, our brother, our husband, the bridegroom. He is a lot of things.

29 | The Sea of God's Mercy

Lent is a sort of sea of God's mercy, warm and quiet and inviting for us to swim in. If we did, we would be not only refreshed, but cleansed, for God's mercy cleanses as nothing else does. But we are reticent to really plunge into God's mercy. We want to be washed clean and forgiven, yes. But we say to ourselves, "If I enter into that sea of mercy and I am healed, I will be sort of bound to practice that which Christ preaches, that is, his law of love. And that law of love is so painful." And there we stand by that sea and think, "It will mean that if I seek mercy, I will have to dish out mercy; I have to be merciful to others."

What does it mean to be merciful to others? It means to open one's own heart like a little sea for people to swim in. We don't like trespassers. If strangers came to use our beaches, we might say to ourselves, "Well, what gives? What are those people doing here? Why do they come to our beach?" It's not so easy to make one's own heart a little sea of mercy for the other. So we stand there before God's mercy and drink again.

So Lent is here to remind us that the mercy of God is ours, provided we embrace that which he has given us to embrace—his law of love—provided we realize that it's going to hurt and hurt plenty, but the very hurting will be healing. That is the strangeness and paradox of God: that while you hurt, you heal. That's true healing.

30 | Rejection

Often we cannot understand why we or others are rejected. It is so simple. We are rejected because God loves us. Jesus loves us so much that he wants to give us the opportunity to share in his passion, for his passion was his supreme rejection.

If we enter into his passion, and are ready to be crucified with the nails of rejection which hurt so much, we will know the joy of Christ. As St. Paul said, we can make up what is lacking in the sufferings of Christ—do we remember that? So when we are in pain—physical, psychological, spiritual—we are capable of understanding why this pain was given to us. Then we lift our pains (and the pain of rejection is the hardest) into his cupped hands. It is like the water that is added to the wine in the sacrament of the Eucharist. The Lord takes our pain, especially the pain of rejection, and he uses it to help others across the earth.

To persevere under the constant blows of a whip of rejection can only be done when Christ and Mary are at your side. Faith alone can continue amid this immolation.

We all can say that we know what rejection is. We know because at one time or another we have experienced it in our body and in our mind, but we also can experience the tremendous joy of those who follow Christ on the cross.

31 | Mercy and Forgiveness

I remember when I was a little girl in Russia during Holy Week every member of my family—father, mother, and all the servants—lined up and, beginning with father, bowed low before one another and said to each, "Forgive me for any hurt that I might have inflicted on you." And the answer from the other was, "May the Lord forgive you as I forgive you. Amen." So everyone asked forgiveness from one another, because without forgiveness, which is the greatest sign of love, how can one receive the God of love?

We hurt people, unwillingly and even unwittingly, by the weakness of our nature, so we need forgiveness from our brothers and sisters, and we need to forgive them as well. We cannot enter Holy Week unless we forgive totally, uncompromisingly, and completely. For before our eyes will soon be Jesus Christ himself, who will cry out from the height of the cross, "Father, forgive them."

Since we are baptized into the death and life of Jesus Christ, we should not allow the night to fall on our anger. We should beg forgiveness and forgive every day. Let us pray that we may forgive, because no one forgives these days, nationally and internationally speaking, and perhaps also personally. That is why we have the mess that we have.

April

1 | Surrender Means Love

I've been thinking about that strange word—surrender. You know something? I don't want to surrender. It's a frightening word. But I know that surrender is love. How do I know that? Very simple. I look at the crucifix. Sometimes I avert my eyes from the crucifix because it is a symbol of surrender. Then I start thinking straight, instead of thinking crookedly: God became man. That was some surrender! Think about it. When doubts assail you like a thousand flies buzzing in your ears and heart and mind and all around you, think about it. As a child, he was obedient to his parents, and later obedient unto death to his Father in heaven. Think about that and lay all your doubts before that obedience; then you will understand what the word surrender means. Don't stop. Go a little further. See him being crucified. Can you hear the nails against the wood? He died for us because he loved us. So it is obvious that surrender means love.

Do we love? Now that, my friend, is the question. The answer is "very little," or we wouldn't have wars or all the tragedies we're surrounded with. Love means open arms ready to embrace you. That's what he did when he was crucified. So think again and get to the very bottom of the word surrender. You will find that it has no bottom.

2 Special Easter Foods

Traditional Russian Easter foods have great significance to the people of my country, and I want to tell you a little about them. Easter eggs are the heart of the season, for they symbolize eternal life—our new life, lived in Christ. The eggs are the symbol of our rebirth in Christ through baptism, and in Russia eggs were prayerfully dyed and decorated with age-old hallowed symbols. They were blessed by the priest and treated reverently as sacramentals, being used to break the Lenten fast at Easter. The other traditional foods used to break the Lenten fast were koolitch and paska. Koolitch is a sweet yeast bread symbolizing Christ, the Bread of Life, while paska symbolizes the lamb led to the slaughter in the Hebrew feast of the Passover, thus blending the Old Testament and the New. Two tall, round koolitches are baked to represent Christ and the church; twelve smaller ones represent his apostles. They are filled with raisins, nuts, and spices and decorated with frosting, cherries, and almonds. The koolitch is spread with a scoop of paska, which is a rich, sweet mixture of butter, sugar, eggs, cottage cheese, and raisins.

These foods are an important part of celebrating Easter, the feast of feasts, the day of days, when Russians greet one another with, "Christ is risen!," to which the other replies, "Truly he is risen!"

3 Love Is Resurrected

Easter after Easter comes, and deeper and deeper I go into myself and up to the hill of the Lord, the mountain, higher and higher, for Easter calls. Love is resurrected. And I can meet him in any place: "Where have you laid him whom my soul loves? He has disappeared from the tomb." And suddenly, you know and I know that this is not the gardener—it is Christ himself. "Rabboni!"

When I am recollected in that fantastic thing called Easter, I am immersed in an incredible time that is renewed every year symbolically and historically, but not just symbolically and historically. It touches me to the very end of myself, to the very inner core of me! And I know it is Christ himself. For I have gone recollected toward all these days of his last pain and his great joy, for he came to be crucified. And then, as I did this, I begin to know what love is. Now my identity is complete and I am fulfilled. Not by anything that can happen to me in this world, but by Christ himself.

What can the world give me when I have Christ? I can give something to the world. I, in my empty hands, can give God.

4 | Learning to Pray

Prayer is so very simple. Many people think they learn to pray only after studying theology and spirituality. But I think if Christ had wanted to talk to Ph.D.s, he would have found their equivalent in the society of his day. He didn't. He talked to Peter and John. He talked to people who couldn't read or write, and they absorbed his voice and understood his words because he spoke so simply.

If you want to know what prayer is like, listen to a child of two or three. When you address God in a child-like way, that's a prayer. When you fall in love with someone and begin slowly, shyly, to explore each other's lives as lovers do, that's prayer. When you are husband and wife, having entered into the fullness of your love in the great sacrament of matrimony, and experienced the tremendous silence of a unity that is both physical and spiritual, that silence is a prayer.

Loneliness can be prayer, for every man and woman, married or single, in every vocation, at some time, is lonely. When that terrible loneliness comes upon you, a cry wells up deep in your heart like the cry of a mute person, and rises to God. That cry is prayer.

How can you define prayer, except by saying that it is love? It is love expressed in speech, and love expressed in silence. To put it another way, prayer is the meeting of two loves: the love of God and the love of a human soul.

Our Prayer Is Simple

Our prayer is simple. Many Eastern religions repeat one word over and over, and we do too. We repeat the name of our beloved: "Jesus, Jesus, Jesus." We call this "prayer of the presence of God." When we close the intellect's window and open the heart's door, when we go into the depths of silence, we return with the name of God on our lips and in our heart. Now we go about the world repeating it, and in this way we become a prayer. A human being achieves great joy when he becomes a prayer. Wherever he goes, he radiates Christ.

Prayer will come when we fall in love with God. The way to fall in love with him is on our knees. Everything in us resists this falling in love. Who wants to fall in love with the crucified one? Who wants to climb the hill of Golgotha, eternally present to all of us? Who wants to be crucified on the other side of Christ's cross, even though this is his wedding bed?

But if we fall in love with the crucified one, we shall know something else as well. We shall know joy beyond all knowing. We shall have peace, the peace he promised. We shall be able to lift up all things; before his face. We shall make up what is wanting in the sufferings of Christ, for the Body of Christ still suffers. Are we ready?

6 | Doubts, Faith, and the Resurrection

Doubts are silenced only by prayer and faith. Then, miraculously, men and women know that they cannot doubt any more. They believe with their whole hearts in the Triune God and in Our Lady and in all the church's teaching. *They believe that in them is hidden the answer to all doubts.*

By belief we become men and women of faith, men and women of Christ. He said, "Whoever acknowledges me before men, I will acknowledge before my Father." Now is the hour. Doubts fall away and Christ is acknowledged before men and women. Now faith has spread its wings and chased away all doubts. This is the moment of joy. It doesn't matter that it might be also the moment of pain. Joy overcomes pain, because now we suddenly know that all the while we were in darkness, knocking at all kinds of doors, Christ was there. So we stopped knocking and fell prostrate before his face. Somehow we knew that he would come to us, and he did.

Those who shed their doubts through faith know the resurrection. It is only when we really doubt, and things are in the twilight zone, that we realize what the resurrection is. He rose on the third day. Because he did, I have no doubts. Nor should you, for the simple reason that, obedient to his Father, he came to us, the sign of reconciliation under the sign of the cross. He died for us, and was buried for us, and then, on the third day, he arose. When faith conquers, doubts disappear. Alleluia! Alleluia! Alleluia!

7 | Gossip

A person who is a gossip is a frustrated personality, often a mousy creature who passes unnoticed, but actually craves to be the *center of attention*, at the price of anybody's reputation. It is a pathological state. The church lashes out with knotted cords against gossipers as Christ lashed out at the vendors in the temple. It is the only sin for which the church demands public restitution. The only way to restore a reputation is to publicly announce that the gossip is untrue. It is interesting to note that in civil law, one can sue a person for defamation of character, that is for gossip. In the church, one who listens to gossip and confesses the sin is given a stiff penance. That is because *listening to gossip is participating in it.* If there were no listeners, there would be no gossip.

I presume that you will not participate in gossip, and I suggest that you do what I try to do when people gossip. I have to listen, because I cannot stop other people from talking, though I try. However, if this is impossible, then I simply say nothing. This usually acts like a cold shower. Definitely I never show any *curiosity.* I listen with a bored face which at least stems the flow of the gossip. At the end of the story I usually try in some gentle, charitable way to minimize the whole affair. I try to say something good about the person, and gently to point out the evil of gossip.

8 | The Priesthood

In 1918 in St. Petersburg, I watched the last priest in the city shot at the altar. We buried him, and then we were without a priest. The tragic, horrible fact of what it means to be without a priest I wish I could impress on many grumbling American Catholics who feel anti-clerical. Life for a Catholic without a priest is so tragic, so empty, that it has to be lived to be realized. Who of us who have lived through it would raise our voice in complaint against men whose anointed hands hold the very life of our souls? Who of us would judge or criticize their actions? We know that the humblest, the least among them, are nevertheless representatives of Christ, and that what they bind on earth is bound in heaven. We know they have the power to bring God from heaven to earth within our reach, so that we sinners can partake of his Body and Blood. In Poland the people kiss the hands of a priest because they are holy hands that touch God daily. They never allow a priest to go away from them without asking for a blessing, for they know it is the blessing of God. Yet here, in North America, there are some who talk lightly about the clergy and consider it smart. It would be better for us all if rather than criticize, we recited daily this prayer:

"Divine Savior, give to your church priests who abound in true holiness; and to me give a true spirit of faith and humble obedience, in order that in my pastor I may ever behold the representative of God. Amen."

9 Christ on the Cross

"Father, Father, why have you forsaken me?" How is it possible that Christ, the Son of the Father, could say such a tragic thing on the cross? Christ was human like us in all things except sin. Like any human being, he cried out because he was hurting. His humanity asserted itself. In his moment of stress, his humanity experienced the darkness which we all experience.

Just think. Underneath the cross of Christ was a sea of people. Many had come just to see him dying. The torture of criminals was like a sports event in those days. From his cross, Christ could see that some of those people were the ones he cured. Imagine the tremendous pain of rejection that overtook him at the sight of those he had helped. Of his apostles he saw nothing except the dust they kicked up in the wake of their flight! Only St. John remained. Could he feel anything else but rejection?

People yelled from below, "If you are the Son of God, get down from the cross and we will believe in you." This was blasphemy, of course. Obviously, there was something to cry about to his Father. And he did. In that tremendous cry of Christ from the cross, the whole of humanity's pain was found.

10 Rejection and Resurrection

The psychiatrist Karl Stern used to say to me, "When you deal with emotionally depressed people, try to show them how to unite their depression with the depression of God in Gethsemane." If your friends fell asleep when you needed them most, how would you feel about that? So it is not astonishing that Jesus cried out! So do we. And the Father listens to our cry as he listened to the cry of his Son. That Son died, but three days later, he arose. Thus the Father showed how much he loved his Son. It is the same for us.

When we are absolutely down, we cry, "Father, Father, why have you forsaken me?" The echo of our voice is in our ears. This echo is something that moves us up the mountain of the Lord very quickly. The Lord stands on the mountain and says, "Friend, come higher," and we are crying to his Father, "Why have you forsaken me?" But if, in total trust and utter faith, hope and love, we really bend close to the ground, and continue to appeal to the Father, our voice becomes lower and lower until it becomes a whisper, until we are silent. As we move up the mountain of the Lord we suddenly understand what is happening to us: we are entering into the resurrection of Christ.

11 Christ Is Risen!

Alleluia! Christ is risen! Verily he is risen! Because he has, darkness has been conquered by light, death by life, and hate by love.

Now the world lives in the resurrected Christ. Whether men and women know it or not, the world has changed; it and the cosmos are now living, existing in the Lord of history, of eternity, of time, and of love. And not only the church is on pilgrimage toward the *Parousia,* the Second Coming, but so are all men and women and all the world, and all that surrounds God's world.

The resurrection of Christ brought love among us, and it is the very principle of our existence. If we recognize this, we can transform the world. It's such a simple thing that requires only faith in the resurrected Christ. It is so simple, it is overlooked by many who write heavy treatises about abolishing poverty and stopping wars. But human beings are not satiated with bread alone. They desperately need love, almost more than the air they breathe.

Why not start the fire of love by loving—one by one—all whom we meet and deal with during the day? Then indeed the resurrection of Christ will become meaningful and our pilgrimage to him will become joyous and we will restore the world to him, and we will eat the fruit of love daily—peace and happiness, the like of which we never dreamed existed. Let's begin now.

Alleluia! Christ is risen! Verily he is risen!

12 | Easter and the Parousia

Easter—the resurrection of Christ! The feast of feasts! The final proof of Christ's divinity! Easter—the only feast of the early church, around which all the other feasts grew like stars around the sun. How clearly the early Christians understood that each Sunday was a "little Easter," that each was a *Parousia,* which means the Second Coming of Christ, for in each Sunday Mass Christ came again in the Eucharist. And, at the same time, each Sunday renewed their expectation of the *Parousia* of Christ yet to come. When this was to be, no one knew for sure, but all people should always be expecting it!

In old Russia, Easter was truly the *Alpha* of the year, its beginning, along with the hope that perhaps it might also be the *Parousia*. That feeling, that flaming hope, was deeply rooted in the Russian heart, and it made all things bearable. All pain and sorrow was endurable because the hope of the *Parousia* brought a mysterious understanding of the things the human intellect alone cannot understand. The *Parousia* was an ever-present reality to rich and poor alike. It gave buoyancy to everyone, a zest for living, while at the same time, took away the fear of dying. Russians, like the early Christians, understood Easter—its promise and its stupendous reality. Because they did, in flaming faith, they had little fear of life and death. For there was the resurrection and there was the *Parousia*—his Second Coming! All was well, even if all seemed to go wrong on earth.

13 | Spring, Easter, and Simplicity

A blade of green grass finally and triumphantly pierced the dark, heavy wet earth. The big mound of snow melted two more inches under the widespread pine tree. Spring danced madly in the golden air of a sunny day.

Down the scented country road, the bells of the little white church rang out the thousand alleluias of an Easter morning, like a choir of children unexpectedly released from school. There was joy in the world, for love had risen from the dead.

Are we part of that joy? Do we remember how to be joyous? Or have we lost joy, along with so much else? Perhaps it is because we have lost simplicity.

The virtue needed above all others today is simplicity, that holy, childlike, joyous simplicity that walks in humble, strong faith, that sees clearly, acts resolutely, and lives in love. We have become too complex to live with ourselves, or our neighbors—or even with God.

We have allowed our needs and fears to conquer us. We have become dependent on gadgets and the power that runs them. We have allowed simpicity to go out of our lives, souls, and hearts! A slightly bigger snowfall, a little less rain, an unexpected storm or two—these paralyze us and the city we live in.

We must find again the master plan of simplicity. We must find it in our spiritual lives as well.

14 Simplicity Can Return

Thousands are the paths of love. Millions are the ways to it. Yet they all meet at a hill on which stands a cross, where Love died for love of us.

Knowledge is a good thing. But the learned do not always know how to love. And to love is the true end of real knowledge.

Let us take holy simplicity for a guide. Let us rest on her breast even as a child. Let her guide our steps, our lives, our prayers. Like the blade of grass, let us pierce the dark, wet earth of our fears, and lose fear, secure in simple faith. Like the snow melting under the spring sun, let our thousand imaginary needs melt away, leaving us free from all the gadgets we think we need and yet need not.

Like the spring, let us dance on the golden days of our newfound freedom in God, and go about doing his will in our smallness and joyousness, loving the world and him with a love that asks nothing but to love more.

Let us sing the Easter alleluias all year long, even as freed school children do, running hand in hand with holy simplicity, up, up the little hill of the cross where Love died for us to rise again on the third day. Let us become small, simple, uncomplicated again, emerging thus from our labyrinthine ways into God's sun of love! Alleluia!

15 Peace

In the Gospel, Christ says, "By their fruits you shall know them." One of the basic fruits of the Christian life should be peace—a deep, inner peace in each one of us.

What is there to be unpeaceful about? Difficulties will abound. Trials will dwell with us constantly. Little pressures and big pressures will encompass us with their eternal demands. Temptations will besiege us from within. Loneliness will knock at the door of our hearts. The devil will roar all around us, not only like a lion but like underground thunder. Mental, physical, and spiritual weariness will chant their endless lullaby. The flesh will seek escape into sleep.

These things will happen, but if our soul remains in its cell of peace, dwelling at the feet of the Prince of Peace, all this will be as if it were not, for peace is the fruit of charity, and nothing can penetrate that cell unless we let it.

I was praying to Teresa of Avila, and I recalled her words: "Let nothing disturb you. Let nothing affright you. All things are passing. God alone remains."

Let us try then to dwell at the feet of the Prince of Peace. Let us work in the noonday darkness, in the many dark nights of the spiritual life, holding high the torch of peace. If we do that, then faith will become strong, the vision of our priorities will be clear, and peace and love will grow.

16 We Love Daily in the Resurrected Christ

We must be Christians who "work out" day by day, hour by hour, the life of Christ from Bethlehem to Gethsemane and the resurrection. All this adds up simply to one little word. We must *love.*

We must love with our burden of emotions, of miseries, of doubts, confusions, and temptations, because they are the door through which we are going to the *Parousia.* The door is cruciform, true, but it is bearable if we have the faith that is necessary to accept it as lived this very moment, this very day, *in the resurrected Christ.*

He is the Christ who is with us at our typewriters, our laundry, our meals, our darknesses and lights, our little hurts and our big days. It is "with him, in him, and through him" that we are going to know that elusive happiness which escapes all those who do not believe in him.

But with him it is not illusory; it is real. Go into yourself and ask yourself, "What do I see?" And the answer will inevitably be happiness. Happiness is with you, happiness is in you, happiness, love beyond understanding, yet real and touchable. It feeds you daily on itself, for the Lord is with us. So even though you may live in the midst of trials and temptations, your heart can be filled with the joy of the resurrected Christ. Alleluia! Alleluia!

17 | Charity's Essential Parts

Charity, whose other name is love, is a powerful reality that is much misunderstood among us. You cannot dissect it as you would a dead body in an autopsy. That would kill it. Yet there are some parts of charity without which it is not charity, but an illusion. Let me illustrate these essentials of charity:

- Constant watchfulness over the needs and pleasures of others.
- The desire "not to be loved, but to love; not to be understood, but to understand."
- Watchfulness over one's own little mannerisms and habits that may annoy others.
- Care that moodiness, irritations, and fears, menstrual ten-

sions in women, not darken the souls of others.
- Applications of good manners to daily living. For instance don't monopolize the conversation.
- Charity is trustful of others. It never judges another person's motives. It is not puffed up. No one "knows it all."
- Charity is not "gooey" or sentimental.
- Charity takes cognizance of little things. Don't linger in the bathroom when you know others are waiting to get in. Do you begin to see what I mean?
- Charity serves and denies itself constantly, and makes the road smooth for others, while shouldering the hardships as much as possible oneself.
- Charity also knows when to say no.

18 | The Mass Is Our Strength

Lay people in the world—in schools, shops, factories, hospitals, offices—are called to restore the world to Christ *where they are.* This is their vocation, their work. They are called by Christ not to "leave the world" for the cloister, but to remain in it, to turn its face to Christ. This task, from a human point of view, appears practically impossible in a world seemingly so far away from God. So we need the Mass.

Without full participation in the Mass, we would soon die. It is "the Mass lived" that is our very soul. The Mass is the center, the heart, the essence of our faith. It is the fire into which we must plunge to become a flame. It is our rendezvous with God. It is the only place where we and Christ become one in the reality of faith and life. The Mass is the food that will keep us on the treadmill of those gray days, chained without chains to the duty of the moment, for love is not a chain.

Infinite is the grace and strength of participation in the Mass. Daily at the dismissal—"Go, the Mass is ended"—we are reminded that the mandate of the Lord is *to live his Mass, and ours, in the marketplaces of the world!* How could we implement this mandate unless he himself was our strength? Has Christ not said, "Without me you can do nothing"? How lavishly he gives us this strength in the Mass—giving us himself—the bread of the saints.

19 | The Mass: Our School of Love

Your life as a lay person in the world is hard; and the life around you will be grim, even sordid. But God will give you strength. Everything can be borne between two Masses. Every morning you will eat the bread of the saints, and you will be able to face any kind of day. Your mind and heart will be nourished by the Word of God. The voice of the psalmist and the warm tones of the voice of Christ will give you courage and new hope. Your faith will be renewed. You plunge into the sea of fire that is the Mass and come out burning, ready to go forth and light fires of Love, even in the most wretched slums of the city.

The Mass, above all, is the school of love... of God for us, and of us for God. Our faith centers around the Mass—and the immense and infinite thought I never tire of repeating—*That God loved us first,* and that all we have to do to be fiery Catholics, is *to love him back.*

Slowly, imperceptibly, daily Mass will bring us closer and closer to God and to Our Lady. Slowly too, it will teach us silence, so that through the day, as time goes by, we will realize that there is within us a garden enclosed and that we have the key to its hidden gate. We can go into it, and there meet our tremendous lover, and like Mary Magdalene in Bethany, sit at his feet in the silence of love, while Martha, in us, goes about her manifold duties of the day.

20 | Silence within Ourselves

Deserts, silence, and solitudes are not necessarily places but states of mind and heart. These deserts can be found in the midst of the city, and in every day of our lives. We need only to look for them and realize our tremendous need for them.

They will be small solitudes, little deserts, tiny pools of silence, but the experience they will bring, if we are disposed to enter them, may be as exultant and as holy as all the deserts of the world, even the one God himself entered. For it is God who makes solitudes, deserts, and silences holy.

There is no solitude without silence. True, silence is sometimes the absence of speech, but it is always the act of listening. The mere absence of noise (which is empty of our listening to the voice of God) is not silence. A day filled with noise and voices can be a day of silence if the noises become for us the echo of the presence of God, if the voices are, for us, messages and solicitations of God.

When we speak of ourselves and are filled with ourselves, we leave silence behind. When we repeat the intimate words of God that he has left within us, our silence remains intact.

21 | More on Listening to God

Try to think of listening as an essential part of prayer. You pray, and you hear the voice of God speaking to you very gently, not aloud, but deep in your heart. If you listen carefully, you will indeed begin to know his will for you. God wants us to do his will, and he gives himself to us continually, that we might follow in his footsteps.

Because you are in love with God, you can relate to him as you would relate to a friend. You can talk to him in order to find out what he thinks. You *want* to do as he suggests. Listen to him, then, that you may know. God speaks quietly, very quietly, but he does speak, and he will make known to you what he wants you to do.

You will do his will, and it will be beautiful. To do what God wants is to be truly happy. Sometimes his will may appear to bring pain, but it will also bring you joy. To give ourselves wholly to God, in prayer and in action, is the life of a Christian, and in it we discover joy so immense that our ordinary, everyday life is completely transformed. We find ourselves living in a new reality.

Listen that you might hear and understand what it is that God wishes of you. Listen to him quietly and follow him. You will be filled with joy. You will also be filled with pain, but that makes no difference, for "your mourning will be turned to joy." This is what God wishes to share with us.

22 | Nursing and Healing

I have been a nurse, and my nursing was always directed to Christ. I always said, "This patient is Christ. Let me treat him accordingly." And I tried to the best of my ability to do so. I used to come at night to visit the patients. I really loved my patients very much. Anybody who is sick has a great appeal for my heart. What an appeal sick people must have to God's heart. He cured so many because he loved so many. He loved the world and so he cured all those who came.

Sometimes it is our lack of faith, among other things, that makes us sick. If we really had the faith of the centurion, we would be whole. Sickness manifests itself in strange ways. One can be very whole physically but very sick spiritually. Do we have recourse to God when this happens to us? What kind of sacrament do we use? There is the Sacrament of the Sick. There is the Sacrament of Reconciliation, in which two arms are open to embrace us; two lips are ready to kiss our lips, for the Russians believe confession is the kiss of Christ. There is the Sacrament of the Eucharist—the reception of the Body and Blood of Christ. But in order to enter into the mystery of the sacraments one has to be converted, one has to be changed, turned around to face God—instead of turning one's back to God.

23 | Young Flowers of the Spring

We must not forget the almost forgotten virtue of hope, which rises like a crocus in the spring. It comes forth full of joy, youth, laughter, and humor, with a yes to being. It consents to accept life as it comes from the hands of God. It has faith, not blind faith but intelligent faith, realistic faith, a faith that understands. It is a faith based on the grace of baptism, and it has its being and its joy in the immense mystery of love.

Little by little, we see young men entering seminaries. Young women are seeking religious life. They are a new breed, with few sentimental illusions. Theirs is no weak pietism. They are young men and women who know where they are going and why.

A young woman said, "Yes, I know that this order only has twenty nuns left. Well, I will be number twenty-one, with God's help. I am going in with my eyes open and my heart full of love for those nuns who must have suffered much. I enter with the faith and hope that I will make a good religious."

This trickle may be small, unimportant, hardly even worth writing about. But then, few people write about wild flowers when they are just popping their white, blue, and pink heads out of the snow. But these young people are the proof that hope is with us. Where hope is, where faith and love are, there God is. Alleluia!

24 Priests: A Sign of Hope

When I was in Toronto I had a spiritual director, Father Keating, a Jesuit, who lived not far from Friendship House. I heard one day that his doctor ordered him to walk every day. So I said, "Father, since you have to walk, why not walk in the slums—right here?" He said, "I should go out to the park or someplace away from here." I said, "There is Cameron Street here, filled with Communists." He looked at me and said, "So what do you want me to do?" I said, "Why not walk on Cameron Street? You will bring hope to them, because a priest brings hope—just your walking down these streets, especially Cameron Street." He said, "Okay, I'll walk, but I don't quite believe I am a sign of hope." I said, "The Lord will show you." Every day after that I saw him walk the slums, especially Cameron Street. He was pelted with a few rocks and bad remarks, but he was fifty, six-foot-one, and strong—he had presence. One day a woman ran out, looked around to see if anybody was watching, then whispered, "Pray for my son. He is very sick." About a week later, she came, standing straight and not running, not afraid of anybody. She took Father's hand and kissed it according to the beautiful Slavonic custom, and said, "My son is well, thanks to your prayers."

When priests are around, they are a sign of hope. They may not feel they are, or even know that they are, but they are.

25 *St. Mark, the Evangelist*
About Your "Free Time"

In a family, a mother doesn't have free time that she can call her own. It belongs to her husband, to her family, to her children. True, when all is well she can arrange some free time for herself. But if you have ever dealt with families, or remember your own, you know that a mother's free time always depends upon the needs of her family. She relinquishes it without a moment's hesitation. A mother who nurses a sick child doesn't do it as a hired nurse at night, on an eight-hour basis. She is like the Good Shepherd that the Gospel speaks about—the one who never abandons his sheep, because he is not a hireling.

When I was a waitress, a laundress, a salesclerk, I understood (by the grace of God) what it meant to be a committed Christian. I was just trying to "keep body and soul together" for myself, my sick husband, and my little son. Nevertheless, I knew intuitively if my fellow waitress was in misery, I had to help her, even though I was as physically tired as she was. Perhaps it meant going into another restaurant and buying a cup of coffee and listening to the tales of her misery until eleven o'clock at night. Perhaps it meant spending the lunch hour that I had intended to use to buy something, or to just take a walk. Instead, I would sit in a stuffy cafeteria and just listen. Love compelled me to do so. A loving, mature, adult Christianity compels millions of Christians today to do likewise.

26 | "Soul Gardening" for God

It is important to pray that the Holy Spirit give you particular insights about individuals, for no two people are alike. To think about each person, to pray about each, to plan for each who is your responsibility (short-range and long-range), all this may be part of your job at home or at work.

For instance, intuition and prayer, coupled with love and intelligence, told me that one of my staff needed academic studies to unlock a barrier within her. Another has good intelligence, but a passion for details that keeps him from seeing the whole picture. That passion of his must be slowly cooled down, lovingly and kindly. Still another person has an abrupt tone of voice, yet is gentle and loving inwardly. And so on, down the line with the rest of my staff.

The Lord desires you to grow a beautiful garden of souls for him. But you must learn to be a good gardener—to know that each flower needs a different kind of fertilizer, another type of treatment, perhaps a transplanting into new soil. But to make each flower bloom at its best, and to produce the fruits that the Lord wants it to bear, you have to tend that garden according to his rules of "diversity in unity." Like all gardening, this is best done "on your knees." Use all your spiritual and intellectual faculties, and then more prayer. Ask the Holy Spirit and Our Lady for ever deeper personalized insights for each of the people who are your responsibility.

27 | Tearing the Seamless Robe of Peter

These next two days I want to discuss with you what is known as the *mysterium romanum*, or the mystery of Rome. It may be illustrated by a story a bishop once told me. He knew a very intellectual man who was interested in coming into the church. However, this man had one tremendous stumbling block—the human frailty of the hierarchy.

The bishop answered him this way: "Dear friend, don't you see why the Vatican library made its historical files so available? It was not afraid of the truth, sad as some of it is. Such frailty has been additional proof of the divine call of the church. Bishops, priests, and popes by their human sinfulness and weakness have hurt the church for two thousand years, but it still stands!"

God did not build his church on angels, but on human, sinful, weak, frightened men who loved him, and, slowly cooperating with his grace, they became what they should have been. Therefore we who are still directed by weak men must understand that we need to look beyond the person to the *office* each holds. That office is Christ. Because Christ is in the church, he is in every office, from the pope down to the local parish priest. Otherwise, there would be no church.

28 | The Mysterium Romanum

No matter how much the men and women in office seem to wreck their part of the church's fabric by their humanness—hence sinfulness and unpleasant personality traits—it does not happen. Christ in their office does not allow the church to be wrecked because of the weakness of the persons who represent him.

Many people expect every religious superior, from the pope on down, to be a saint. Let us say that your religious superior, your pastor, or whoever is in charge has the worst personality conceivable, and that everyone has enormous difficulties dealing with him or her. Let us say that person's mannerisms irritate you. If you are a man, you dislike being ordered by a woman; if a woman, you dislike being ordered by men. I'll let you fill in the rest of the picture.

Remember, though, we are dealing with the *mysterium romanum* and—what is more to the point—dealing with the passion of Christ and the behavior of the apostles, who were not such hot potatoes. One denied him, one betrayed him, all but one ran away when he died.

There are only two possible conclusions: either the Catholic church *is* divinely founded, and Christ is *in* all the people who rule his church, or there *is* no Catholic church and the whole thing isn't worth belonging to. Take your choice.

29 | *St. Catherine of Siena, Doctor of the Church*
Defending the Church

I asked my mother once why she named me after St. Catherine of Siena, because then I have two saint's days—St. Catherine of Alexandria and St. Catherine of Siena. "Well," she said, "St. Catherine of Alexandria you just naturally have, because that's the Russian feast." But she read the life of Catherine of Siena when she was carrying me and she said, "I wanted my daughter to be more like Catherine of Siena." I said to her, "Mother, you couldn't have done anything worse! She is one of those dames who really gets you to the popes and everybody. And if you don't want to go there, she gets you there."

St. Catherine of Siena was made a Doctor of the Church when I was in Rome—can you imagine that! She couldn't even spell, not Latin but plain Italian. She wanted to say the breviary, so she told God she'd like to learn Latin. And do you know what happened? She learned Latin in a half hour. She opened the breviary and proceeded!

When I faced the death-of-God movement in the 1960s, I felt both weak and strong at the same time. The strength was not mine. I prayed to St. Catherine of Siena often during those years because she fought for the church. I have a statue and a relic of St. Catherine. I carried the relic on my person as the death-of-God issue was thrown at me. I knew that I was on guard for the church. To defend the church you have to be crucified, always crucified.

30 | Loving Our Family

It is more difficult to serve one's fellow human beings than to "serve the poor." It is easier to embrace the stranger than to love one's own family, with whom one is so deeply involved by a thousand ties, to whom one comes as a servant-giver of so many things. I want you to meditate on that.

A family is a community. A parish is a community. The world is a community too. And community living polishes our sharp edges; it is God's way to sanctity.

It is up to us to form a community of love, a family. We do so by silently preaching the Gospel with our lives, without compromise. We do so through the childlikeness of Bethlehem; through the hidden life of Nazareth in "small things done well" for love of God—and through the kenosis, or self-emptying, that leads us to Golgotha. We do all this so that Christ may live in us—and in our neighbors.

We bring Christ's love to our neighbors *one by one*, as individuals, never en masse. It would be foolish to try to restore the world to Christ en masse. We must begin to restore it person by person by person, beginning with *ourselves!* The Gospel of Love, the witness of faith that liberates mankind, is preached and given to one human being by another human being. It is not something that can be given in any other way. It is a person-to-person relationship.

May

1 St. Joseph, the Worker
Go to Joseph

Go to Joseph, of course, the young, strong, silent man. His silence, once entered into, heals all it touches. His silence is a school of courage, faith, and love. It makes a beautiful bridge between humanity and God, a bridge we need to find, oh, so terribly much today, when most lives are so empty of God that men and women have even forgotten the way back to him.

To Joseph, of course, the poor man whose foster Son was born in a stable and whose family lived most frugally in a little forgotten village of Palestine but who held in his arms the wealth of the nations and the Light of the world and who can teach us all how to empty our hands of tinsel and fill them with love, faith, and happiness.

To Joseph, of course, the mender of broken toys, furniture, houses, as well as broken hearts, souls, bodies, minds, and families. Yes, let us go to Joseph, whom Jesus and Mary love so much.

2 | The Month of Mary

This is the month of Mary, Mother of God and men and women. Why not take this month off from worry and fears—from shallow amusements and useless recreations?

Why not begin a journey inward to the Immaculate Heart of Mary, to learn from her the secret of the King, her Son—the secret that would change our lives, and with them that of the world—the secret of infinite charity, of God's peace, and Mary's joy—the secret and art of *being before God and doing for God?*

This is not easy for restless, modern men and women, who have wandered far from the truths and ways of God. Fortunately, we can start by turning to a creature like us, a woman who will lead us along the royal road to God, her Son. Yes, we can start easily enough, by turning to Mary, the Mother of God, who has made this century her own. Mediatrix of All Graces! Queen of all hearts! A human being who clothed God with our flesh! She knows all the answers. And she stands ready—nay, she is *eager*—to give them to all who turn to her.

The woman who spent her time on earth cloaked in silence is speaking to us today from Lourdes, Fatima, and many other places. If only we took time to listen and to ponder her words, ours would be a century of peace, ours would be lives of joy.

3 | *Sts. Philip and James, Apostles*
Meditation for a Typist

Typist or computer operator or data entry person, whoever you are, typing on one of many kinds of machines, be reverent before this machine. Bless it if possible with holy water and never allow it to dominate you. You are greater than the machine! You are master of it. It can neither frighten you, stop you, anger you, nor frustrate you, because of itself it is neutral.

It is simply meant to remind you of God as it is. Never take out on the machine that which you should take out of your heart. For then you would reverse the order of things established by God.

Typist, whoever you are, praise the Lord for the skill of your fingers, and use the keys before you lovingly to transmit their symbols into words. Remember that all words, unless they are sinful, come from the Word, who is God.

Typist, whoever you are, know that your fingers are praying as you work. You are part of the Mystical Body of Christ so you are praying as you type those words. Work well!

Typist, whoever you are, remember you are part of the great tranquility of God's order, so your margins must be perfect and your ribbon changed and your touch even.

Typist, whoever you are, never cease perfecting your typing, for it is a stairway to your union with God. Love is never satisfied—it always wants to love more. If you listen well, you may hear his voice in the rhythmical song of the keys!

4	*Anniversary of Fr. Eddie Doherty's Death* # A War of Words

Words are cheap. They flow into our minds from everywhere: from the radio, the television set, the lecture platform. They greet us from walls many feet high, and from the pages of tabloid magazines. The world and its inhabitants are tired of mere words. But people are looking desperately, searching hungrily, for words that have taken flesh through being *lived* by those who utter them.

We are arrayed between two battle lines. On the one side are the words of the Prince of Darkness, which, one must admit, are lived up to by his followers. On the other side are the words of the Word incarnate, which must come alive in us, in our daily lives, in our flesh and bones, in our spirit and actions.

Have we so lost our way that all we know how to do is to denounce, denounce, denounce, again and again, with strident and sterile vehemence? Let us be done with being anti-anybody. Let us become pro-Christ and pro-love! Let us stop talking against this person and that, this nation and that. Let us begin to live Christianity!

Then Christ will come and dwell among men and women again, through us, in the simple dealings of daily, ordinary life. Then men and women shall know him again, in and through us, which is the way he meant it to be. The kingdom of God will begin in this world, also as it was meant to be. Darkness will vanish before his light shining through our souls.

5 Flower Gardening

Flower gardeners spend their time growing beauty, which the Lord can then use to heal people and bring them closer to him. Each flower is a love poem of God to us! Each reflects a small part of God's beauty. Look at each one and you will lose yourself in the infinite perfection of that one flower—its colors, its form, the shape of the petals.

Flowers give hope, returning each spring as they do. Flowers give courage. Flowers heal. Flowers are harbingers of joy.

Flowers speak the silent language of lovers, from Hawaiian leis to Catholic children's May-crowning ceremonies for Our Lady. In the old country, processions of the Blessed Sacrament were always accompanied by flower girls who strewed petals of fresh flowers before the Eucharist, just as palm branches were strewn under the feet of a donkey when children cried "Hosanna" to their King.

Many hermits and saints have spent some of their love life for God planting and tending flowers—making their desert bloom. A hermitage without flowers is not the dwelling of God. Wherever the Benedictines and Franciscans walked, they left hermitages of flowers behind them. A house without flowers is a dead house. To state it simply: where there is a loving heart in a home, there is someone who devotes himself or herself to flower gardens.

6 Mary and the Rosary

I was thinking the other day about the rosary. What is the rosary? The story of the incarnation. It began in the womb of a woman who simply said yes to God. The rosary follows the main events of the life of the Man-Child to whom she gave birth, and who for us Christians is God, the Second Person of the Most Holy Trinity.

Step by step, in awesome simplicity, anyone can follow the life of Christ in the mysteries of the decades. As the drama of his life unfolds, the tempo increases. Finally, humanity is killing God, and God is willingly dying for love of humanity. The tragedy pierces heart and mind with almost intolerable gratitude. Then, slowly, the pain is assuaged by the resurrection and the realization that the Lord is in our midst.

The rosary cannot be hurried or mumbled carelessly in rapid recitation. No. One decade a day might be better, or even one a week. Entering deeply into the mysteries of the beads is entering into the whole immense mystery of the life and death of our Lord Jesus Christ. And who better to guide us than Mary? She was there at the beginning, during his public life, death, resurrection, and afterward in the upper room when the Spirit descended. She "started it all" in a manner of speaking with her yes. So we ask her to lead us through the mysteries of her Son with devotion and faith.

7 On Selecting Good Music

Today I want to discuss music and its immense power to affect our emotions, minds, and souls. Music can lift our spirits. On the other hand, music has been vulgarly prostituted to appeal to the lower emotions. Like all the arts, music can lead us ultimately to heaven or to hell. Music affects people differently, depending on their educational, cultural, and social back-grounds. Memory also plays a part in the effect music has on people, reminding them of sad or joyful events. One can often guess people's ages by the music they select.

Men and women dedicated to God should be very careful of the music they choose. They are custodians of one of the most beautiful gifts in this world for molding people's emotions, minds, and souls. Music also can help them restore the world around them.

In selecting music, ask yourselves these questions: does the music arouse in you thoughts and emotions that lead you away from God? Does it lead you into an escape from solving your problems? Into a web of forgetfulness of the cross in your daily life? Does it lead you to a dreamy life that cannot be yours? If the answer to any of these questions is yes, it is the wrong music for you. But if it arouses in you a greater understanding of the beauty of God and his creation, and brings you closer to God in any form, then it is good music.

8 | Mother Was a Revolutionary

My mother had revolutionary ideas, in the Christian sense. She believed that all Christians must love one another! She translated this love into direct action, especially by involvement with the poor. She was a talented concert pianist, and during her undergraduate years at the conservatory of St. Petersburg, she "went to the people" every summer. This means that she hired herself out for a few rubles as a maid, to just the type of people that Joseph and Mary were—worker-peasants.

Her days were strenuous. She got up early, helped with the cleaning, prepared the breakfast, did the washing all by hand, went on with the chores of the day, prepared lunch and dinner, cleaned—whatever this peasant family needed. By fall she had succeeded in teaching the whole family how to read and write.

I have always attributed my vocation, at least in part, to my parents, especially my mother. She went to the poor people, because, like other Russians, she felt herself a member of the Mystical Body of Christ. Every Russian keenly felt this oneness with all Christians.

I thought all parents were like mine, but now I know better. Not for a moment did they ever neglect to instill Gospel attitudes in me. In my organization of Friendship House and Madonna House, I used the ideas and patterns I learned from them.

9 Helping Serve the Poor

My mother often served the poor as a nurse and midwife. As soon as I was old enough, she involved me in her works of mercy. I would carry medicine and supplies and we would walk ten or twenty miles. When we reached our destination, I would scrub the floor, clean the utensils she would need, fix the beds and generally make myself useful. Then I prepared food for the family because often the woman was in labor. Mother attended to this, and I attended to all the rest. It was quite something, believe me. I learned a great deal.

In those days, ladies and gentlemen didn't exactly do those things: at least, none of our neighbors did. They all thought mother was slightly crazy. The memory of these trips is deeply embedded in my mind. I learned identification with Christ in the poor and I grew up knowing this truth with my heart.

Also, in the Russia of my childhood, social services were almost non-existent. People felt the words of Christ, "Whatsoever you do to one of these..." applied to orphans and old people. So families took in the children and also the elderly, who were revered and catered to, as age was considered a symbol of wisdom.

This was my spiritual formation regarding the poor. Eventually it resulted in Russian spirituality at work in the slums of Toronto, then in Harlem, and now here in Combermere.

10 | Our Lady as a Little Girl

I love to meditate on Our Lady. The first image of her that comes to mind is that of a very young girl. She comes from a small town or village, and her parents are bringing her to the Temple where she can learn to read and to do many things. I see her little hands as they become accustomed to labor. She learns to weave, cook, sweep, spin. She does so many things that fourteen-year-old girls of today cannot do. I see her as being very simple and unobstrusive, melting into the group to which she belongs, unobserved—she who was to become the Mother of God, to hold Jesus in her motherly arms, to hold my own heart in her delicate hands.

Then I think of how she must have played, as all children played: jumping, dancing, running through the fields; and I feel as if I could celebrate with her. She was attentive to all the feasts of the synagogue, to the Psalms, to all the things of God. I ask myself, "How attentive?" And it comes to me that her attentiveness was probably fantastic, because it was an all-absorbing activity. She drank deeply of the Psalms. She was enraptured by the Scriptures, reading the ones that we now know refer to her. She did not know that they were going to be applied to her; yet in some way she must have absorbed them deeply, and "kept them all in her heart." I like to meditate on all of this.

11 | Mary and the Devil

I just received a letter from a woman who had gotten herself deeply into the occult. She asked for my help; but what can I do?

I can only pray for her. But I also sent her a picture of Our Lady.

In Genesis, there is the prediction that a woman will arise who will crush the head of the serpent. Mary will do this. Her heel is ready to do so, provided we pray at her feet.

She will crush the serpent that is slithering around in our hearts. We hear that serpent voice whispering to us: "Don't be a sap. All that religious stuff is for nothing. There is no God." It whispers so many things, half-truths and quarter-truths and downright lies. If we pray to Mary, *she becomes powerful and immense.* And the devil is exceedingly afraid of her, for he knows when he has met the one who can crush his head.

To go to Mary is to be near Jesus! He chose to come to earth and to us through her. The Holy Spirit overshadowed her. It should be very easy for us to go to her when we are full of tears, full of loneliness, full of slithering serpents, because she has the answers.

* See Appendix Two for more explanation of this intrepretation of the woman crushing the head of the serpent in Genesis 3:15.

12 | Holding the Hand of God

When I think of prayer, the sentence that comes to me is this: *Hold the hand of the Lord, and talk to him any time you wish.* Sometimes you talk to him and sometimes you don't, but you are with him all the time. That is what our basic approach to prayer must be.

People think you need to set aside lots of time to pray: "I need at least two or three hours a day," they tell me. I do not think so. We don't need to spend all our time at our "prayer"; we need to serve each other! When a mother is busy with her children, an employee with his job, a missionary with the poor, they may think they have no time to pray. That isn't true. You give your time to everyone and everything, but in your heart, you pray continuously. You know that the Lord is very near, and that he holds your hand, as it were, while you go about your business. That's the way you should pray.

Obviously, there are times specifically allotted for prayer. The Mass is the outstanding prayer, for instance, but the prayer I'm talking about now is simply the communication that constantly passes between you and the Lord. Prayer is conversation with him. You don't need to understand how to talk to God. You just do it. He loves to listen to you and he especially delights in your silence when you listen to him.

13 | Prayer Should Be Simple

God likes our prayer to be simple. All we really have to do is to say to him, "So-and-so is sick. Please do something for him." I think God would probably be relieved to hear such a prayer; how tired he must get of all our long windedness! Suppose you are traveling. From the window of your car you spot someone in a wheelchair. Put your heart in his hand, so to speak, and say, "Lord, help that person." In this way, you can pray for many people and many needs.

Prayer should be primarily for others. God will see to it that your own needs are met. We shouldn't always be pleading, "God, do this for *me*, do that for *me*." When we say, "God, look after this person," He takes care of us as well.

With so many people to pray for, long prayers are not necessary. That is why I simply say, "Lord, take care of so-and-so." If you say that every day, and keep close to God, you will find that he remains close to you. I wish I could take you by the hand and say, "Come with me. Let's all hold the hand of our Lord and pray in this simple way." Few people think of prayer in this fashion, however. Most of us are not used to praying as life flows along. We are used to "taking time" for prayer, when we should be praying all the time. Prayer never stops. It is such a beautiful thing to hold God's hand and to pray always.

14 | The Holiness of Farming

Farming today may be business, even big business, but the people who forget that farming is a way of life will someday weep over their forgetfulness. For there is no better place to live the Gospel than on a farm. Nowhere do men and women come closer to God than in the country, in rural areas; and nowhere are they closer to him than when they till the earth and look after the flock. Jesus was born in the countryside and he lived in the countryside most of his lifetime. He wasn't a farmer, but his Gospel is filled with examples from farming. He talked about vineyards, crops, plowing, grains, and seeds. And he loved to use parables of sheep and all kinds of flocks! Tenderness to animals was in his voice in a sense; tenderness to the earth and all growing things was there too. Have we got that tenderness? Have we got that love? Have we got that understanding?

When I was a little girl in Russia, we had shepherds and shepherdesses for our cows, horses, and sheep. They knew the serenity and peace that comes from living a life of silence and being one with nature and nature's God. All were deeply religious and the villagers considered even the young ones wise. They were respected, and they loved their work.

In Russia, the farmer is called *Krestianin,* which simply means "Christian," and the Russians have the right idea—a farmer should be the epitome of a Christian.

15 | *St. Isidore, Patron of Farmers*
Apostolic Farming

At Madonna House we have a farm called St. Benedict's Acres. There, we do what I call "apostolic" farming. Our farmers seek to make the farm rich by using the simplest means possible and the least amount of money to feed our brothers and sisters so that the money might go to others who cry out for it. We talk to God and our Blessed Mother and to St. Isidore, the patron of farmers, who were able to do so much with so little.

Just as in everything else, in apostolic farming, every action has an eternal value. A farmer hasn't "chores" to do. "Chores" implies heaviness, unpleasantness. No, a farmer has a whole world to save by feeding the pigs! And there is nothing "dirty" about farming. Spreading manure around has the same value as writing a thesis or working at any other occupation that appears to be cleaner. Everything the farmer deals with is clean and everything has a purpose. The manure is going to give us food for next year. The hog will be eaten. The cow will produce calves and give milk and meat. Everything on the farm leads to the feeding of humanity. How can it be dirty when it feeds our bodies that are temples of God where Christ comes to dwell?

There are in the world two people who really touch God. The priest touches God in his very essence. And the farmer touches God in his creation as it came from his hands.

16 | Farming, Time, and Health

Apostolic farming demands the whole of a person. It is the best way to die to self because the demands of nature and animals are there to remind one, like no bell in any monastery can remind one, of the duty of the moment. That duty leads to the goal—feeding one's brothers and sisters—and is always before the apostolic farmer.

Therefore the farmer doesn't waste one ounce of time, for it is precious. It is God's time, and of all the men and women on earth, a farmer can't waste time. If the farmer misses a day, there will be no hay. If the farmer plows a little too late, there will be no harvest. If the farmer seeds one hour too late and a storm comes, then all the work will be undone. The apostolic farmer knows the value of time and reveres it. Farmers know that time is their part of eternity that God has given them to grow in love and to become saints, which is the lot of all Christians.

Apostolic farming is a very slow process and it teaches farmers many lessons not learned in apostolic books. It strips them naked of many preconceived notions and makes them whole again. Farmers who work with the earth, from which they came and to which they will return, are healed of their wounds. In a strange way, a farmer is somehow deeply reconciled with God again and walks at eventide with him while they both look over the creation of their hands.

17 | *Foundation Day for Madonna House* New Beginnings

May 17, 1947 was sunny and very warm. My husband Eddie and I arrived in Combermere about three o'clock in the afternoon and our first sight of the little, unfinished six-room house was exhilarating. Though it had no siding and was unpainted, it still looked cozy. The statue of Our Lady of Guadalupe, which had been enshrined the year before, stood over the window of an upstairs bedroom. We could see it from the road and it welcomed us. Hungry and tired, we ate in the living room. In a state of great content, Eddie stared out at the Madawaska River and said, "Katie, welcome to your new home."

Three dozen young apple trees had been delivered a few days before. The field for the orchard had been ploughed and manured. All we needed now was a hole in the ground for each tree—and our neighbors Desiré Mayhew and Wilfred Bouchard helped us plant them. Thus, the orchard, in a sense, is a memorial. It was planted on the foundation day of Madonna House, the day we arrived. The trees are still there today.

In those early days we had a wood stove, an outdoor toilet, and a well in the cellar with a hand pump that took a thousand strokes to fill the water tank. We filled the tank three times a day to cook and do laundry! We didn't have much money and not many clothes. I planted a garden, did some sewing, and baked bread. Such were our early days in Combermere.

** See Appendices Three and Four for more explanation of Catherine Doherty's spirituality and life at Madonna House.

18 Mealtime Conversation

Conversations at the table reflect the state of everyone's mind, heart, and soul. They are an important part of our family spirit of love that spills over to our guests as well.

Love will be watchful over table conversations. Argumentativeness has no place in our conversation, and a sullen silence of withdrawal has no place either. These are breaks in charity and therefore in the family spirit. Love will direct much conversation toward God and spiritual matters. Generally discussions will be about something worthwhile instead of a silly, wasteful spouting of words that really make no sense.

This does not mean we cannot discuss daily affairs, or laugh over little incidents that were funny. For surely during a day something funny happens to everyone. The ability to laugh at oneself instead of others is a great step forward toward emotional health and sanctity.

Laughter has been given to us by God to relax us, to sing him a song of joy. The devil hates laughter, and he wants to snatch it away from God. So he tries to use it as a harmful thing by provoking some uncharitable joke. For example, he urges us to tell an unpleasant truth in jest.

Let us remember that a meal should be an *agape*—the breaking of bread in love, reminding us always of the Eucharist and the Last Supper. If we remember this, then we will act accordingly.

19 | Vain Ambitions and Envy

Are we completely free from any vain ambitions? Do we get upset when we do not have our own way? Do we have the ambition, even deeply hidden in our hearts, to do *our* will instead of God's? Do we have the desire to be *promoted?*

Do we want to be "in" on confidential matters that do not concern us, to be specially close to persons in authority so we are a little "higher" than the next person? Do we measure our jobs by worldly standards instead of divine standards? Do we consider collecting garbage, cleaning rooms or toilets to be *beneath our dignity,* and think that we rate better jobs? Do we boast of the talents or special knowledge that we have? Do we seek the limelight, and are we shattered emotionally when we do not get it?

If we haven't left behind that type of ambition, we walk in pride. Need I tell you what happens to proud people? If you are in doubt, read the Gospel concerning them, but read it on your knees.

Do we jockey for positions? This is still part of ambition and begets envy. Do we always wish to be right, so others may envy us? Do we engage in arguments, so others are proven wrong or ignorant? This is an inverse form of envy. He who loves is open to another's point of view. Do we see every little concession given to another person and envy it? Envy is a deadly sin.

20 | Let the Little Children

Every year, whenever it was possible, my father, mother, and I, and later my brother Serge, used to go to Jerusalem for the Holy Week ceremonies and Easter season.

One year when I was a child my parents took me to the Rock

of the Ascension, the place near Jerusalem from which Christ rose into heaven. I loved to look at that rock because it showed the imprints of a person who was standing on his toes on one foot, while the other was flat.

I had one ambition: to put my feet into these imprints of the feet of Christ. But that was a bit difficult because they had this area cordoned off. But what's a rope to a little girl? One day I just slid underneath while everybody was praying, and put my little feet into those imprints, one up and the other down.

People began screaming, "Look what she's doing! Look what she's doing! Get that child out of there! Blasphemy, blasphemy!" A Russian priest came out and said, "'Let the little children come to me,' have you forgotten that?" He helped me put my feet in the imprints of the feet of Jesus Christ, then he escorted me out of there!

21 | Correction and Criticism

People confuse correction with criticism. Correction means to straighten out, to make strong and well, to help eliminate faults of character and soul. Criticism is an intellectual exercise that helps people arrive at better, sounder results—a better book, better behavior and so on. Literary critics prod writers to give their best, for instance. Without criticism, people would get into a rut. Criticism in the negative sense, is often done with an intent to hurt. It may take the form of nagging or uncharitable faultfinding, which tears at the fabric of charity. Constructive criticism, on the other hand, is a fruit and sign of deep love and friendship. It should be most welcome, as a means to improve a task or communication with others.

Now let us look at correction. One type is what comes from someone in authority who has special grace to do this: parents and teachers, superiors and employers, spiritual directors and parish priests. Should you come into a position of authority, it will be your duty to correct others. There is also fraternal correction, from an equal to an equal, and it too is a fruit of charity. It should be done gently and charitably, to show the person the error of his or her ways, for the betterment of the soul.

You who are growing in maturity should be open to, even glad of, correction and indulge only in constructive criticism. Unless we understand these two concepts, charity might die among us.

22 | Into the Arms of Hope

Let us be full of hope, for this is the era of the Spirit! We have passed through a confusing period. Vatican II, one of the first signs of the coming of the Spirit in our times, shook us all up, as powerful winds are wont to do! These winds left behind them a seeming havoc. Mighty trees fell, which no one knew were hollow! As they fell, they tore up a lot of underbrush that had begun to grow over the paths of the Lord.

Yes, let us be full of hope, notwithstanding the fact that the wind of the Spirit confused many and upset old, established ways and customs—customs that really should have changed a long time ago. But now we can begin to assess what has happened and realize that it was so very simple and beautiful, and that only God could have brought it about.

What happened was that the Holy Spirit, the Advocate of the Poor, who has always been with us, has made himself known again! As on the first Pentecost, he has shaken everyone up with his winds of change. He reawakened in us truths which we thought were self-evident but which obviously we had not incarnated into our daily lives. But now we are beginning to see that, though shaken up, we truly have been thrown into the arms of hope—wondrous, soul-healing, joyous hope. So let us be full of hope! This is the time of rejoicing, the time of thanking God for the gift of the Spirit, eternally renewed. Alleluia!

23 | The Little Word "But"

"But" is a strange little word. It is small but powerful, and can be used to break the family spirit of charity. This is especially true when it is used not always deliberately but at least semi-deliberately, to undermine morale. It also undermines authority.

Let's take an example. Someone begins the conversation, "That was a good meeting and so-and-so was really terrific, *but...*" And with a few sentences, the person sows in the minds of others doubts, hostilities, tensions, anxiety, and a host of questions that needn't have arisen.

That is how a little word of three letters can smash the family spirit of charity in two minutes. It can do more than that. Someone is given a task to do. Listen to the response: "But look, I have to do this..." or "But I haven't finished this..." or, "But one moment, don't you think it would be better to do it this way?" "But... but... but..." There are so many *buts* in our conversation that it almost makes one cry!

The little word *but* is the very soul of argumentativeness and rationalization. Used in this way, it is better left out of your conversation.

You can bring it in when someone praises you; then you can say, "But you don't know me... I'm not as good as all that." Then it will be in its proper place!

24 | Stop Taking and Start Giving

The time has come for us to stop taking and start giving. If we really examined our souls, we would see ourselves as little babies with mouths pining for the breast, yelling our foolish little heads off for the milk of attention, tenderness, and understanding. Like babies, we want to latch on, to be held, to be cooed over, and have lullabies sung to us. We refuse to *give, give, give.* We want to *take, take, take!* We are immersed in small problems of self-centeredness and selfishness. We think other people are inconsiderate; they don't understand us; they should pay more attention to us, care for us more. We are still greatly affected by the likes and dislikes of people and situations, still in the infantile, emotional state of children. As St. Paul says, we are still children and have yet to grow up. Did the Lord latch onto things self-centeredly? I don't think even his enemies could say that of him. Can you say it of yourself? We must stop taking and start giving *maturely,* as adult men and women should. You are part of the army of lay apostles that Christ is raising up to restore the world to him. He calls you to bring clarity to the confused, understanding to the bewildered, to feed hungry hearts, and to give drink to thirsty souls. But you continue to take. You act like children, refusing to take responsibility, afraid of the slightest pain. When will you arise and offer him to drink of the cool waters of your love—the total gift of yourself in service and in love to others?

25 | The Yardstick of Love

Often people talk to me about the difficulty they have in loving. They say, "Why doesn't love grow among us?" I answer, "Love—Christ himself—stands before the doors of our hearts twenty-four hours a day. He greatly desires to enter. But our hearts have doors with latches only on the inside."

Oh, Christ knocks with his graces, but we turn a deaf ear to his knocks because we are afraid that if we let him in, he will ask too much of us. Love and joy are the fruit of faith, sacrifice, and pain. True joy does not come to people who are self-centered and who view the world only from the way it affects *them.*

So Christ stands outside and knocks. He has given us free will, and he doesn't violate that gift by forcing himself in. Until we allow Christ to come in, we will not be able to love one another. First, we must love him and surrender to him willingly, and let him take total possession of our souls; then the rest will follow.

And you will not bring Love into your life by reading books or meditating about him. The yardstick of your love is with what enthusiasm, completeness, and thoughtfulness you do your duty of the moment. It is all very simple: *We* are the ones who make it complicated to escape what we fear: to surrender to Love in the daily, ordinary, little things and duties of the moment.

26 | *St. Philip Neri*
Moving Fast for God

We sometimes drag ourselves through the day instead of walking about *our Father's business* with buoyant, joyous steps. How different we would be if we were going on a date! Or working for big money! Socialites bustle and plan parties to meet "important people." Ambitious junior executives work with energy, enthusiasm, and speed to "get ahead." For God, however, we move slowly, like shadows across a screen. The phone might ring. We think, "It's nothing but another request for information," or "It can wait." In so many of us there is no "oomph," no joyful life in God, no understanding of the urgency of our tasks.

Throughout the Old Testament, Yahweh urged his prophets to *hasten.* Moses, Isaiah, and other prophets *hastened* to bring the words of Yahweh to the people of Israel. Habbakuk couldn't be persuaded, so an angel grabbed him by the head and *whoosh!* In a minute, he was down there with his dinner, and *whoosh*—in a minute he was back faster than an airplane!

God moves fast! Jesus Christ was even more emphatic. I suggest you study the Gospels for fun and count the times the Lord of Hosts used the word *hasten.* I think you will be extremely surprised.

We have to move fast too. Do we really hasten about our

Father's business? Does the zeal of our Father's house really eat us up?

27 Mary and Housework

Let us ask the Lord to show women today the fullness of the life at Nazareth. Pray that he might lift the veil of years and sentimental piety, and present his own mother as she really was—a housewife, a mother, a spouse, a woman busy at the sublime creative work of the "kingdom," which was his home on earth.

Instinctively we imagine their Nazareth house to be spotless. But do we today know what goes into that kind of spotlessness? Have we experienced the utter joy of scrubbing a floor? Do we know how to make it a prayer, a song of love and gladness? Have we recited the litany of dusting and sweeping whose goal is a home bedecked with cleanliness? Or are these humble tasks irritatingly monotonous to us?

Have we experienced the exhilaration of creativeness in cooking a meal or making a loaf of bread fit to eat? Do we understand the sublimity of service—humbly, daily, constantly repeated? Or do we dream about more gadgets to take all the zest and creativeness out of life so that we can be free for long hours of leisure that only serve to lead us ever further from God?

Let us ask Mary to help us restore our work in the home to Christ, and to restore all the work of our hands, all our labors, to Christ.

28 Cemeteries and Spring

In old Russia, spring brought out the villagers to clean the cemeteries and plant flowers. To clean and adorn cemeteries was considered one of the corporal works of mercy, but to me it was a human joy too. For Russian cemeteries were indeed fascinating. They sprawled unevenly in the country, surrounding the church. They were enclosed by wooden picket fences, painted red, white, or blue. Some were unpainted. Each grave had a wooden cross, surmounted with a little roof; it made a sort of shrine, under which an icon might be placed, together with an enclosed lantern that would burn on big feast days in lieu of a vigil light. The cemetery looked beautiful with its big trees and simple flowers becoming immense in the shadows thrown from those gently swaying lights.

Always there were special nooks and corners in every cemetery that attracted the passerby to stop, rest a while, and say a prayer for the good souls that slept so peacefully in these homey surroundings. I remember especially a little corner by the huge lilac bushes that I could never resist. When they were in bloom their scent could be smelled afar off, accompanied by the fragrance of a white carpet of lilies of the valley, Russia's favorite wild flower. I have never since smelled so sweet a fragrance as that of lilacs and lilies of the valley.

29 | Are You Ready for the Holy Spirit?

Are you ready for the Holy Spirit? You know that he comes to you like he came to the apostles, and you can all be filled with the Holy Spirit. To be filled with the Spirit is really something. He explains everything to you. Remember what Christ said, "What you don't know, the Advocate will explain to you."

When you want to understand something, why don't you pray to the Holy Spirit? Sometimes you get to know something better from him than from any of us. You should be praying to the Holy Spirit constantly, especially if you are in a seminary, because he is a special friend of the priests. He looks after the priests in a very special way like he did with the apostles.

The Holy Spirit gives answers to your questions. From my

own experience, when I can't solve something, I begin to pray to the Holy Spirit, and receive answers in my thoughts. I advise you to do that.

And don't be afraid to call upon him if you are in danger. He keeps you safe. I remember once I had to go out at night to nurse somebody in Harlem and I saw two guys coming toward me and I knew exactly what they were going to do. I didn't have any money, but they didn't know that. They were coming toward me and I said, "Holy Spirit, help me because they are going to attack me." And you know what? They came up to me and said, "How are you? I hope, okay." And they passed me by! Now there you are.

30 | The Holy Spirit: He's There for You

The Holy Spirit is there for you under many conditions. Sometimes you are confronted with a very vital situation and you feel that you should talk to the Holy Spirit about it because *what you think seems all right* might be all wrong. Suppose your people want you to take a job some place and you don't feel for sure that it is a good spot to go. Well, pray to the Holy Spirit and he will give you an answer. At least he always does for me. When I was deciding to give up everything and follow God directly, it was quite a struggle, you know. So I talked to the Holy Spirit and asked him what he thought about it. At that time I had a strange answer: "Do it." So I did it, and here I am. Yes, here I am. It is astonishing, absolutely astonishing.

Prayer to the Holy Spirit is indicated at least once a week, because people forget him. They pray to Jesus Christ and they pray to the Father, but they forget the Advocate who teaches us. So pray to him quite often. It is impossible to tell you how wonderful he is, and how important. The average Catholic doesn't think he is important, but he is very important.

We celebrate Pentecost yearly but I think Pentecost could be celebrated every day. Each day he is with me and holds me tight. All of me. He is like my cloak that covers me up and I am safe. So are you. Yes, he keeps you really safe. So I hope you are going to pray to him. It is so very important that you should.

31 | *The Visitation*
An Ordinary Miracle

One night I was awakened out of deep sleep by my husband and the doctor. They said I must get up to help a woman who was having a baby. So I took my nurse's equipment and we started out into the night. The Canadian countryside was full of stars, frogs were singing, spring and new life were in the air.

The doctor's car became stuck in the mud and we walked the last mile to a tiny house, where we waited.

Waiting for a new life to begin is a most peculiar waiting. There is a hushed and holy quality about it, as if one were in church. It is both hard and sweet. It is as if one were listening with one's soul to hear God's words of command, of creation.

It was going to be a hard delivery and the doctor was worried. He wanted to operate in a hospital, so the woman had to walk the mile to his car. The grit of our women! We went with painful slowness. It began to rain. She was racked with pain, but smiling. "This will be my tenth baby," she said with joy. In her face was a light, a glow like the shadow of God's face. I shivered a little from sheer awe. We made it only to a neighbor's house, where water was boiled, instruments sterilized, and we went to work—and to prayer. The silence was broken only by the doctor's whisper and the woman's groans. Then—wonder of wonders!—the cry of a newborn baby. The first cry of the baby merged with the last cry of the mother and a baby boy was born. Alleluia!

June

1 | Love and the Sacred Heart

June is the month of the Sacred Heart of Jesus. For human beings, the heart has always been a symbol of love. St. John the Apostle put his head on the Lord's breast at the Last Supper and heard the heartbeats of God! Imagine how that would transform us, if we understood, even dimly, that each beat was a love letter to us!

So let us enter the great silence of our own souls. For a split second we are John the beloved; we put our head on his breast and hear, "Thump, thump, thump." That is not an average heart. No, it is God's. And what it spells loud and clear is love for us. Let us pray there humbly, lovingly, plunging into the riches of the Sacred Heart. Then we shall know God in a way that no book can teach us. Then we will love him so passionately, so tremendously, so utterly and completely, that it will become simple for us to be the kind of Christians we must be. We will not have to *say* very much. We will only have to walk upright, crying the Gospel with our lives, reflecting our lover in our faces.

The world needs the Sacred Heart today. The world needs human hearts united to the Sacred Heart. Without love the world is very dark. Let us arise and resurrect the world by bringing love to it—and it to God.

2 | Real Love of Neighbor

Love means an interior and spiritual *identification* with one's brother or sister, so that the person is not regarded as an "object" to which good is "done." Doing good in that way is of little or no spiritual value to anyone. In fact, it is a tragedy! It destroys the one who gives, and the one who receives.

Love takes on one's neighbor as one's self, and loves the neighbor with all the immense humility and discretion and reserve and reverence without which no one can presume to enter into the sanctuary of another. From such love, all authoritarianism, brutality, all exploitation, domineering, and condescension must necessarily be absent.

The full difficulty and magnitude of the task of loving others should be recognized. Love should take on one's neighbor as *one's very self*, and love that person with immense humility and never minimize it. That it is hard to really love others in this way should be recognized, if love is taken in the full sense of the word.

I have often spoken of identification with the poor. It is an identification that only love can achieve by complete forgetfulness of self and total concern for the other person. It is an identification so deep, so complete, that it becomes part of oneself, like breathing. It is a way of loving.

3 | Servers of the Altar

God loves us. He loves us so much that he seems to constantly want us close to himself. He selects ordinary men as priests and brings them close to himself during the awesome hours of his Sacrifice of the Mass. This same closeness he pours out on all those lay people who also serve at the altar.

A server at the altar of God—that is what a boy or man becomes when he walks up those steps. Does the server realize where he is? In whose company he serves? The Trinity, the saints, and Our Lady dwell on that altar of God, the Holy of Holies. Has the server prepared himself to stand in this holy place? Has he washed his soul so that it might be clean before the Lord? Is his heart open to love? Is his mind fully concentrated on what he is doing? When he offers the cruets, does he understand that he is offering the very essence of the fruits of the earth—grapes, which in a few minutes will become the Blood of God, shed for him personally and for all the people?

Is it conceivable he could be sloppy in his clothes and attire? Slouchy in attitude and posture? Hunchbacked, half asleep? How does a soldier speak to his superior? He stands straight, erect, listening to the will and wishes of his captain. He answers clearly, distinctly. He who serves at the altar should also have this proper bearing as he moves to and fro in the Holy of Holies, showing his love by the way he stands and walks and moves. Nothing is too good for Almighty God.

 # 4 | A Practical Question about Order

Today I have for you a practical question about order. People are not always aware that proper record-keeping or file-keeping requires an intelligent approach and a periodic rethinking, redoing, rearranging. I propose that you meditate for this month on these questions:

In what state of affairs have I left my files and other records?

Are they so arranged that my successor will have no difficulty in taking over? Or is my office an "unholy mess"? If it is, will that set the person who takes over my job, at least six months behind—or more?

In charity to others, we should remember that we are all mortal, and might die within the next twenty-four hours and also that we might be moved or transferred suddenly.

These are serious questions, and not to be lightly dismissed. Do not say to yourself that you are very busy (so am I!)... or "too busy." That is not an excuse; it is more likely a rationalization. If you really want to, you can *make* time.

5 | The Green Feast

The great feast of the Most Holy Trinity was also called the Green Feast in my youth in Russia. Then the Church and many of the homes were decorated with freshly cut green boughs—the color of spring and hope, and of love, and of God, which to us were synonymous.

It was also the day of the birch. The village youth would gather at eventide and, with special songs and much laughter, go in search of the nearest and prettiest birch tree. The girls then, with the help of the boys, would decorate it with multicolored ribbons and flowers. The task accomplished, they would dance around it, special dances, to special old songs that had been taught from generation to generation. The boys at certain intervals were allowed to take a ribbon off the tree and pair off with the girl it belonged to. Many a true romance started there and then. No wonder the birch tree is the national Russian tree.

Old and new were intimately interwoven in Russia. Many pagan customs survived and were "baptized" by the church.

May Our Blessed Lady, whose shrines form so beautiful a rosary around the land of my forefathers, bring Russia back to her Father's house, and give back to her people the right to enjoy the old, holy, and joyous ways of their ancestors that made every year a new adventure in living and being.

6 Fire, Flame, and Movement

To me the Trinity is fire, flame, and movement. It is like an immense disk from the ends of which shoot out huge flames, the whole of which cover the cosmos. But this is not all.

I feel myself being drawn into the center of this fire, flame, and movement as if into the eye of a hurricane. I am enveloped in it and I envelop it! Because, incredible as it might seem, *the Trinity dwells within me.* I am its temple even while I am, in a manner of speaking, in its centre.

To use human words to explain an unexplainable mystery, I would say that the tips of the wings of the Spirit—for there seemingly are wings—in this movement, in this fire, touch the tip of my heart.

Within this movement and this fire, the Father bends over me, as fathers do, with an infinite gentleness, tenderness, and love; and Jesus Christ is at my side, strangely reflecting the face of the Father, whom no person can see and live—unless it is reflected by his Son.

7 Meditation for Repairmen

The repairman often has to handle the result of somebody's mishandling of a machine, perhaps because of that person's emotional problems. In most cases, he will be repairing the result of a fragmented person, a thoughtless person. The workshop, therefore, must be a place of prayer, atonement, mortification, silence, and recollection. It is not enough to simply repair something of God with the knowledge of one's mind and the skill of one's hands. One has to repair also the harm done to the creation of God and the slight done through it to God himself.

Repairmen have the opportunity to atone for their sins and the sins of others through their work, which is a great grace. They can easily associate with Gethsemane. On hot days, greasy sweat will run down their face and bodies. It won't be bloody, but if they accept it lovingly, it will mingle with the bloody sweat of Christ. The eternal dirt and grease on their hands, so hard to get off, will remind them of the dust and dirt that must have added much agony to Christ's body when he was carrying his cross. His wounds were filled with spittle and the dirt of the road. Mechanics and other repairmen often have to assume strange and difficult positions to work, and these postures will tire their back muscles. Then they will know how tired God's muscles were when he was crucified. They will know in some small way of God's sufferings for them, and God will accept that, lovingly, passionately.

8   *Our Lady of Combermere*
 A Place of Devotion and of Pilgrimage

In the early days of Madonna House, we called on Our Lady for her help, using the local name of our tiny village, Combermere. We later learned the word Combermere derives from old French, meaning "mother of a plateau in the mountains." Combermere is a thousand feet above sea level and lies on a plateau in the Laurentian Shield mountains, with higher peaks all around us. Later, little by little, our love of the Mother of God using the title Our Lady of Combermere grew to include a song to her and a picture and prayer. A visitor who received a favor through Our Lady of Combermere offered to help with a statue, which eventually was sculpted and erected, then blessed by our bishop on June 8, 1960.

Eddie Doherty called our new shrine "the humblest and least pretentious in Christendom," adding, "It was no miracle that produced this shrine. No apparition. Only the coming of a beautiful statue, and the love of people in and around Madonna House, that caused it to become a place of devotion and of pilgrimage."

This is the way of the Mother of God through the church of her Son. How quietly she worked it all out. No startling apparitions. No great flaming miracles. Just little favors here and there. Souls moved to pray to her under this title. Graces flowing through her gentle hands. Noiselessly, as she walked this earth.

9 | Social Amenities

Now I want to speak a little of ordinary social manners. They include posture, ways of sitting, ways of eating, and certain niceties, such as men opening doors for women.

Remember that politeness and good social manners really stem from love. Your concern should be for the other person. So note this—it is very important—being concerned for others should be for you like *breathing*.

Posture is important. Saints teach by the way they sit, the way they stand, the way they walk. Let that be a lesson for you. Consider how a saint would sit, stand, or walk; then, do likewise. And of course charity demands that you assume a posture that doesn't offend others.

You may not know which fork to use for salad, but charity makes it very simple. Without false shame, you simply acknowledge that you don't know, and ask someone for help.

Can you imagine Our Lady, like a lump, sitting with her two elbows on the table and taking no part in the conversation? Can you? I can't. Doesn't the Gospel give you a tremendous picture of the graciousness, gentleness, and good manners of Christ? And I am sure that Mary was like him. In spirit, go to Nazareth! Then act as if you were in the presence of Jesus, Mary, and Joseph, and you will automatically be a gentleman or a lady.

10 | Who Is the Greatest?

In Matthew 18:1-4, the disciples ask Jesus who is the greatest in the kingdom of heaven. Read through it now. It's a revealing story.

Those disciples were just like us. We always ask metaphysical questions. "Who is the greatest in the kingdom of God?" Now isn't that a stupid question? Each one wanted him to say, "You." They were only thinking about themselves. And God knocked them for a loop. He brought a child and said, "I tell you solemnly, unless you change and become like little children, you will never enter the kingdom of heaven. And so, the one who makes himself as little as this little child is the greatest in the kingdom of heaven."

Now *that* I have always understood. When people are like children, they have to accept handouts. A child accepts handouts for a long time—in school, at home, everywhere.

Then, later, in chapter 20, verses 20-23, Mrs. Zebedee goes to Jesus. Read through that! Now Jesus says, "Can you drink from the cup I am going to drink?" To drink his cup is to be a martyr. Now there is bloody martyrdom, when you must drink the cup in one swallow, while the blood is flowing from a wound inflicted. And there is another cup that's slowly poured out—drop by drop. Sometimes you find martyrdom right next to you, in daily, ordinary life.

11 | The Greatest Is Servant of All

In Matthew 20:24-28, Jesus deals with the other apostles, who were pretty indignant after the episode with Mrs. Zebedee. From this, we see we should strive to be the servant of all. But we want to dominate. Leadership through service really goes against our grain. We don't like that. We don't mind *being* served. We don't even mind serving the poor officially, on a committee. We certainly like giving a couple of bucks for the poor, and serving on a committee for the elderly, the retarded, the disabled children. It doesn't interfere with what we want to do, with our way of life. Definitely and positively we do not wish to do the will of God.

Now it's clear what Jesus did, and we must do the same. But we don't want to, because it's hard, and takes away from us the feeling that we are in charge. If you think you are in charge of yourself, well, there is only one character who can put that into your head. It's the devil. He mixes everything up, making a mishmash of your life. He says, "You are in charge of everything." In other words, making an idol of yourself.

We make idols out of power, money, prestige, and even ourselves! But to adore yourself is the greatest idolatry. Once you begin to adore yourself, you're finished. You're nobody, because once you're in the power of Satan you become a blob, just a blob!

12 | Christian Recreation: Re-creating

With more leisure time and shorter hours of work, spending one's leisure time intelligently for the glory of God has become more and more important. High standards of living, the mobility of cars, and the changing pattern of family life have made deep inroads into the whole concept of recreation. Our young people say, "There is no place to go," and "There is nothing to do." It takes a little time to bring them to the Christian idea of recreation.

Christian recreation is truly *re-creation*, a renewal, a re-gathering, a re-collecting. Recreation is, above all, a change from the everyday routine. And it doesn't mean *doing nothing*, which is very boring. Recreation is to re-create, to make new.

It is done with God, for God, for his honor and glory. Re-creation includes self-expression, imagination, creativeness, and leadership. Let me be explicit. You might be swimming and having a lot of fun, then afterward, lying in the sun, you take a little snooze. Or you might be reading a book quietly, re-creating your mind with new understanding. Or your recreation might consist of a square or folk dance, or take the form of learning a new handicraft, or engaging in a work of art, for in creating beauty, one re-creates oneself. Nature study, sports, gardening, reading aloud, and the art of story telling are all possibilities for re-creating oneself.

13 | Recreation, Togetherness, and Family Spirit

The best recreation is spent together with others. A family, parish, or group that recreates together stays together lovingly on the natural level. Doing things together makes us know and love each other more. Joy binds us, and laughter cements our relations. Knowledge gathered and shared with one another creates a deeper union. Creating things together, such as a skit or planning games, helps make us one in spirit and truth. Family spirit comes into being that cannot happen through work alone. One has to pray, work, and recreate together to make the family spirit come alive. You are children of a society that divorced fun from God—that is part of secularism, which is a heresy. You may have to get used to doing things together, and by doing them learn how much you grow in knowledge and love of one another. Then, in a perfectly natural order you will see how much fun it is.

Organized recreation and spontaneous recreation are both good. Perhaps you will visit a museum and decide what to do afterward. You might plan picnics or a night of reading together, or you might just have free recreation, depending on your circumstances. Be simple about these things. Try to recreate this way and that way, and eventually you'll find the best way. Let the intellectuals have their say, the sports fans their say. It is give and take. That is what teamwork is and that is what love is.

14 Recreation and Teamwork

Recreation can also become teamwork and team play. These are a must for democracy and for good social intercourse. Good team play is a weapon of Christian lay people. If your recreation includes members of minority groups or the poor, or any people you work with, a new spirit will develop.

People who play together can never hate each other. On this, incidentally, the British Empire was built. British fair play and teamwork fostered the virtues of justice, charity, and in ordinary language, fair play and sportsmanship. All of these natural virtues are really the reflection of the Ten Commandments applied to recreation.

Remember, the key word is *togetherness*. Don't go on a picnic and separate yourselves for the whole day, then come together only for a hasty picnic meal. Do things together. If you read a book, share what you have read with others. If you take a snooze in a shady corner after swimming, join the others after the snooze. Togetherness is the foundation of recreation!

Slowly recreation will become what it is meant to be—fun, a builder of unity, a refresher of the mind, spirit, and body—all of which will help to mold your group or family into a whole which knows and loves each other better. May the Lord of all creation be with you and inspire you to recreate in tune with him and his Blessed Mother.

15 The Duty of the Moment

When I was a nurse during the Russian Revolution, I was called out late one night to help with wounded soldiers between the Russian and German lines. It was about ten miles on horseback, with bullets buzzing all around. I miraculously escaped unharmed. It was doubly miraculous because my horse stumbled, I fell off, and he kicked me. He was so sorry afterwards that he licked my face and helped to revive me. When I came to, I remembered what I had to do.

Getting back on the horse took some courage because I coughed up blood every time I tried to climb into the stirrup. Finally I made it. "The duty of the moment is the duty of God," I said to myself. Only God knows how I made the last two miles because every time I moved I spat blood.

I arrived and found no doctors or nurses, forgot about my injury, and proceeded to nurse the wounded as best I could. In the middle of it all the doctor arrived. He took one look at the wounded, and one look at me and said, "You've got to go to the hospital!" I really was spitting blood badly.

This was one of the reasons I received a decoration for bravery. There were others, but this was one of them. I never thought much about it, for I was only doing my duty.

16 What Is a Christian Community?

A Christian community, first and foremost, must be a community of Christian love, founded on love of God and neighbor. Its members communicate with one another in the way Christ told us in the Gospel. This kind of communication requires an openness that transcends human understanding, especially in our present day when people feel so alienated from one another.

Members of a Christian community should be open to one another, know how to listen to one another, know when and how to speak. And each knows these things because each knows how to pray. This is how communication reaches the dimension of love that God desires. By this openness, by each member living the Gospel without compromise, each can slowly shed "human respect" as men and women shed garments, each one can slowly learn to accept injuries, persecution, gossip, etc. Peacefully, then joyously, each will learn a constant listening to the needs of the brethren within the community. Unless this law of Christ is applied, the community will never grow into true Christian maturity.

Christian communities are called by the Lord to leaven the community of the world which Jesus bought for his Father. The words "I have built a dwelling place for you to live in forever" (2 Chronicles 6:2) apply to the whole world. The ultimate reason for forming Christian communities is to make humanity realize that the world is God's dwelling place which he built for men and women—that life in this world is an entry into the kingdom of the eternal God!

17 How to Build Christian Communities

How is anyone to achieve this miracle of grace? How can any Christian community—religious, lay, married, or single—achieve this life of pilgrimage, of prophecy, of openness, of listening to the hearts of men and women and to the Spirit, of making one's life into an icon of the life of Christ? The same answer comes again and again, unmistakably: *through prayer*. What is impossible to us is possible to God *and* us. Prayer brings together, in a mysterious way, the mystery of our humanity and the mystery of God. Above all, to be filled with the strength of the Lord and replenish ourself, we must go to the house of the Lord, which is the church. There we will center our life on the Eucharistic Sacrifice.

A community is a group of persons who have joined together because they are in love with God and in love with men and women. They want to bring God to men and men to God. They can do it better together than alone. Together we have each other, can console each other, pray for each other, encourage each other.

But to persevere in such a community, one must pray, really pray, without ceasing. While making the Mass the center of one's life, communication with God must continue constantly; otherwise, communication with men and women will cease. The ways and means of prayer of the members of such communities must be determined by each community. But prayer there must be. Otherwise there will be no communication and consequently no community.

18 | The Two Holiest of Hearts

I wonder if we understand what the Sacred Heart and the Immaculate Heart are all about? Quite a few people say, "Oh yes, that used to be the nine First Fridays, and so on." They are a little hazy about it.

Just let your mind drift; let it enter the mystery of his heart. You will find a strange, incredible heart that God accepted when he became human, a heart that beats forever, in a manner of speaking. When Christ's heart was pierced, the church was born. The church, reviled by so many. Yet where the church is, he is. And with her, Christ stands; and his heart comforts and cures the church.

He stands there like a beggar, begging the pennies of our love. How many pennies have we put in today? Yesterday? He is a beggar for our love and solace. His beating heart spells love for us! That is why on certain days we bow low and thank God for his faithfulness toward us. And the humble little girl who became the Mother of God—Mary—we know that she is the mother of humility, simple and still. As he lay in her womb, and his heart began to beat, she was the first to hear it. And her heart answered his.

So we have before us a mystery—the heart of Mary and the heart of Christ—both immaculate, both of beauty unsurpassed. What more could you desire, except to give yourself totally to these two hearts, especially the one of God!

19 | God the Forgotten Father

Our utter, complete forgetfulness of God the Father is a tragedy. Who remembers that it is he who clothes the lilies, feeds the birds of the air, leads the lamb to pasture and the hart to water? Why have we so utterly forgotten him from whom all paternity, all fatherhood descends? Why do we not turn to him at all times? Why don't we pray to him? Run to him? Love and adore him constantly and greatly?

Where is our devotion to God the Father? Today more than ever in history we need him. We are affrighted beyond the ordinary fears of humanity, living as we do under the shadow of strange bombs that in the twinkling of an eye can destroy us and the very earth we tread. But we do not even think of him when we say "Our Father."

If only we turned our faces toward him, who loves us as only a Father can! If only we prayed to him, reminding him that he so loved us that he gave us his only Son for a brother! For where is the father who will refuse the plea of a loving son, even if that son be now a prodigal?

Let us fall on our knees and, embracing his feet, implore our Father to forgive us for our forgetfulness, our neglect, begging him to take us once more into his arms, and make us safe.

20 Run to Your Father

I get irritated and miserable when I don't run to my Father, when I don't remember that I am little, when I don't say, "Abba." Instead I say, "Now, Katie, you are a pretty brilliant dame. You've known this apostolate for thirty-nine years. Okay, I'll solve the problem."

But if I run to my Father, and take his hand, and cry "Abba," and become very small—realizing that I can solve nothing—then the big, bad dog, which seemed the size of a mountain in Switzerland, suddenly becomes the size of a Pekingese. My Father solves the problem, because I was childlike; and I approached the problem in a childlike fashion, instead of in the pride of my intellect.

Being little, always little, being small, being poor, being childlike—this will solve every problem.

You have a terrible problem in your house? Remember, you're poor; so do not be ashamed to be a failure. What do you expect? If the Son of God saved us through a failure, then why can't you save the world by failure too? At least your little world. I thank God for showing me that I am poor, which is what our Little Mandate at Madonna House tells us.

21 First Day of Summer A Meditation on Frogs and Snakes

This summer, as I cross my bridge here in Combermere every day, I meet frogs! They remind me of the many bullies I know, and of little people who try to be important. These frogs of mine can really blow themselves up to strange and immense sizes. They do not realize that the more they blow themselves up, the uglier they look. I watch them bully the little frogs as some people bully others. Having bullied them a long time, they then push them around. They (the frogs!) often end up by eating the little guys. Doesn't this often happen among people? There are a thousand ways of eating and swallowing a human being.

There are water snakes in my marsh here too. I watch them swim silently out of nowhere, blending with the water lilies and vegetation. It's fascinating to watch them approach their prey, swimming in ever-decreasing circles, hypnotizing their victims, who watch, immobilized, fascinated, unaware that death is closing in. The eternally repeated story—the tree and the apple, the serpent, the man and woman—comes vividly to me. I find myself with tears in my eyes as I watch the snakes finally get their prey. I think of the millions of men and women who, like this prey, could have escaped, jumped away, if only they had not been fascinated by danger and knew the truth which is God.

22 | We Are the Dispossessed and Forgotten

I am, as most of my friends know, a fool for Christ's sake, and also one of the *humiliati. Humiliati* means the dispossessed, the forgotten, the unrecognized, the rejected.

Would you like to meet the *humiliati?* Go to an old people's home, where thousands of mothers and fathers are forgotten, unvisited, uncared for. It is not difficult to do that. And it is not difficult to be a fool for Christ's sake and try to penetrate the seemingly impenetrable greed and selfishness of such places.

Do you have the courage to go into racially mixed neighborhoods or the neighborhoods of the poor? Yes, it takes courage to go there. Not because you are going to "see" the poverty that perhaps you have read about in the papers or in a book. It takes courage to enter. It takes courage to knock at the door. Who am I, who are you, that we dare to enter the "Holy of Holies" that Christ loved so much? He was always with the poor.

Yes, it takes courage to go there. But a fool for Christ's sake can go anywhere, because people will laugh at him and will let him in. That is the joy of being a fool for Christ's sake, and one of the *humiliati*, one of the despised, forgotten, neglected.

23 | The Ones Who Most Need Our Help

I am tormented. I am tormented with the situation of the old, the helpless, the hopeless, the ones who "die" from loneliness! My torment is not only for those in hospitals and in nursing homes. (There are people who are already doing good work in that area.) It is the others—the even more forgotten and rejected ones, the other *humiliati*—who need our help. How we are going to do this, I do not know. We have to pray, and we have to search. God will show us the way.

It is a very simple thing I am asking. We are already doing much of this already, but we have the capacity to do more! Go out... be free... do it! They are on the streets, in rooming houses, in offices, in condominiums. They are the hidden ones, the overlooked ones, the neglected ones.

The "real" rejects of society already knock on our door, seeking our help. But these others we have to look for! They may be very poor in the economic sense. Or they may be very rich. They may be politicians, or civil servants, or wards of the state. It is up to us to seek them out. It is up to us to make friends with them, to help them in a very special manner—the only manner by which they can be helped: *love!*

24 | *Birth of St. John the Baptist* A Holy and Joyous Russian Feast

In old Russia when I was a girl, St. John the Baptist's Day was celebrated with huge bonfires. They seemed to reach the very skies, and they always brought out daring young men who jumped through the dancing flames! Strangely enough, they all came out unscathed and untouched by those fiery and dangerous fingers! Probably each whispered a quick prayer to the fearless saint.

On the same day the girls would weave beautiful wreaths from the many field flowers that bloomed about that time of year. Laden with them, they would go to the nearest river or lake and, taking careful aim, throw them into the water to the accompaniment of age-old verses whose origin was lost in the dimness of centuries gone by. These rhymes expressed their hopes and desires. This rite performed, the girls would run along the banks, a colorful and beautiful crowd, dressed in their native costumes. Each would watch her own wreath breathlessly, for the wreath that kept afloat longest promised its owner marriage within the year. And where is the young heart that does not yearn for love and romance?

This is one of the old customs of my homeland; it marks the occasion forever in my heart as both holy and happy, a joy forever! I am glad of it, for this and other old Russian customs make my life fuller and richer, and somehow bring home to me the fellowship of men and women under the Fatherhood of God.

25 Practical Tips for Supervisors

I would like to help you in training your staff. First, *take nothing for granted.* Check and recheck; and be explicit in giving directions for a given job. Then check to see if the person has understood the directives given. A good technique is to have them repeat the instructions back to you. Many people today have emotional problems, and though a person *seems* to be listening, he or she is *not* absorbing! We must take this into account. Be sure the person is familiar with the equipment needed: hammer, rake, typewriter, ironing board, or whatever. Be ready to teach and correct, *as needed*, not at some future time.

During the first few days of a given job, check the quality and timing of their work. Encourage a slow but steady speed-up in the work to a normal rate. Where you can, try to work with them on new jobs. This will often be of great help in instructing them by your example and bringing about better use of time. This means you will examine *your own* use of time and become more efficient. And you must always be ready to connect each job with the spiritual. A nice way is to explain that Christ often used the words "arise" and "hasten," as well as the Old Testament prophets such as Moses and Jeremiah. This constant "taking nothing for granted," this checking and rechecking, this explaining and re-explaining, this timing and encouraging, will subject you to a certain crucifixion, but it will pay dividends and will be worth the pain.

26 | Supervisors, Plan Your Day!

The proper use of time is something many of us have not mastered. The key, of course, is planning. We must *plan our day*, knowing that a phone call, a visitor, or need of an individual person or several, will shatter those plans as a sharp blow shatters glass. Nevertheless, we must still plan daily, or preferably the night before, for the next day. It is good at the end of the day to jot down whatever was not accomplished and try to fit it into the next day.

Into this daily planning must come a firm understanding of a simple fact: that a supervisor is not one who does everything him or herself, but one who knows *how to delegate both jobs and authority*. That, plus planning, are the two keys to using to good advantage God's precious commodity of time. Appraise your staff and assign jobs according to their ability. Some tasks require no decision-making, for instance. You must consider the emotional and physical state of each person on any given day and plan accordingly. Monotonous or onerous jobs should be rotated occasionally. Then you roll with the punches, and accept that some jobs are never "done" and try to squeeze them in when there is time.

Another key, of course, is *your own* use of time. You also have your duties. You are the schedule maker, planner, counselor, the busy person who finds some time to finish that which was left unfinished.

27 | Prayer and Peace for the Supervisor

There are a thousand rationalizations (and a million other excuses) ready at hand to remind you why you can't take time out to read or pray. The pressure of work is the most common one. But the cornerstone of your life is meditation and prayer. It is vital that you remember this. For a life of action, and action only, of allowing yourself to be dominated by action, will result in your *worshiping* action—the good *works* of God—instead of God himself.

Immerse yourself in the essence of your vocation. Do not engage in the "heresy" of good works. Some of you go overboard without noticing it, and the next thing is that you are all tense, exhausted, nervous. And the essence is lost somewhere along the line. What is this essence? To give love and peace—person to person.

Even in your actions, let the atmosphere be loving, peaceful and unhurried. Your own tension can be transmitted to those you wish to train and they will become confused. Show them that you are kindly disposed toward them, and want to help them. Take a deep breath, untense yourself, and begin to speak in a clear, peaceful voice, remembering to smile with your eyes as well as your lips. Be peaceful and take your time. Even though you are hurried and may have to dash somewhere, don't show it.

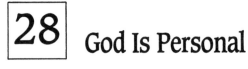

28 God Is Personal

If we operate without spiritual motivation, but just on the natural level of "getting the work done" or of inculcating good training habits (order, cleanliness, punctuality, efficiency)... important as these might be... we will be wasting our time and achieving nothing. Our goal is a spiritual one, that of answering the call of God to a specific work that has a specific accent and spirit. To have this spiritual motivation, Christ must become a *personal* God... and God the Father really a *Father*... and the Holy Spirit likewise... as in the reality of faith, deep faith.

But for the majority of people, God is *an abstraction!* He is someone with a big stick, a frightening judge who sends one to hell if his commandments and precepts of his church are not obeyed. So people respond by living more in the letter of the law than in the spirit, and emotional crises keep recurring. Without a personal God, without the supernatural motivation of loving and glorifying God, and serving him and (for him) loving our neighbor as ourselves—and loving ourselves well!—the vocation you have been called to cannot be implemented. Without a personal God, we will put more emphasis on counseling techniques than on spiritual verities. Not that we should cease to clarify emotional problems; however, we must help an individual solve them. But emotional problems are a part of life, the average "cross" we all bear.

29 | Sts. Peter and Paul, Apostles
Toward Unity between East and West

I have been asking myself why I, a refugee from Russia and from communism, should be chosen by God to found a lay apostolate. God might have chosen a Russian in order to bring to this land in North America a little bit of our simplicity, a little of our contemplative spirit, and of our passivity. Perhaps he just wanted a humble bridge between the Latin and Eastern rites, for in Russia I was brought up in both rites. I am Polish and Russian, with an Orthodox mother and a Catholic father. From early babyhood I had been steeped in both and have absorbed them both, as it were.

Now at Madonna House we have icons of the Lord Christ of Russia and of the *Bogoroditza*, which in Russian means Mother of God. These icons were gifts from Archbishop Joseph Raya while he was a priest, pastoring a Melkite rite parish in Alabama. They were given to us on the occasion of the ordination jubilee of one of our priests, Father Emile Briere. When they were installed in our chapel, they blessed our Western world in an Eastern way, bringing by their very presence a unity based on love, on prayer, and on understanding of one another's traditions. In a way, they represent my work and prayer for many years for the unity of the Eastern and Western churches.

30 | The Virtue of Simplicity

Simplicity is vitally important nowadays, because people are so complex, so filled with fears and inhibitions, so fragmented.

The dictionary tells us that simplicity means *consisting of one thing; single; uncombined; not complex or complicated; without embellishment; sincere, artless, and free from affectation,* which correlates with innocence rather than sophistication. Apply this to the spiritual life and we see a person who is single-minded, whose mind goes to the essence of things without embellishment and complicatedness. It conjures up a person innocent of guile, truthful and direct, who—psychologically speaking—*lives directly,* which is a sign of maturity.

Now "holy" simplicity is the state of mind and soul that is totally occupied by God. The colloquial word for holy simplicity would be childlikeness and would bring us immediately to the Gospel verse, "Unless you become like children (single-minded, uncomplicated, humble, trusting) you shall not enter the kingdom of heaven!" To be simple also means being emotionally or psychologically simple, in the right sense of the word. It does *not* mean being naive or foolishly ignorant. Intellectual simplicity should blend with this psychological simplicity, and be practiced in a way that will help us to become spiritually simple—or childlike—as Christ wants us to be.

July

1 | Blood Shed Recklessly

July is the month of the Precious Blood, Love recklessly shedding his Blood so that you and I might have life everlasting. If Christ had not shed this Precious Blood of his in the Garden of Olives, at the flagellation post, in the crowning with thorns, on the dry, dusty road to Calvary, and on the cross, we would still be walking in utter darkness, devoid of grace.

What price Love dying for the love of us? It seems as if we still do not know the price, or do not want to pay it. For the price is love in return! We are afraid to love gloriously, joyously, in complete surrender, perhaps because we dimly realize that love is synonymous with sacrifice. And we do not want to have anything to do with sacrifice, which means self-denial, discipline, and submission to authority.

But the Lord's cross is light. And if we assume it *willingly*, for love of him, he will carry most of its weight for us. The key to carry it is in our hands, the key of love, ready to open the lock of sacrifice. They fit, one into the other. And they give us life—not only for our earthly span, but for eternity.

The formula is simple: "Not my will, Lord, but thine." A little sentence that, if lived up to, will give us sanctity. And all because, two thousand years ago, Love, who is God, spilled—lovingly, recklessly, joyously—his blood for us!

2 | Taking Christian Vacations

I would like to discuss with you the topic of vacations. A vacation gives you a change, a chance to re-create yourself, to "re-collect" yourself in Christ, with his help. Therefore, you do not really take a vacation from Christ or Christian behavior and attitudes.

You might want to "recreate" yourself by taking a summer short course, in crafts or arts, for instance. Or you might take walks, go to museums, look at art. Do things with your family. If you are interested in some hobby, learn more about it. Locate books about your hobby or craft. Try to visit the sick or shut-ins you know.

A Christian vacation isn't lolling around, doing nothing, and indulging all of your whims. And don't spend your vacation watching TV all day! That's not a vacation, but sliding backward in your spiritual life. On the other hand, don't overindulge in too many good activities either. It is a pitiful state when you come back from vacation more tired from the social rounds and activities than when you left! Surely, that is not re-creation, rest in the Lord, and recollecting yourself!

Finally, a retreat for a week in some quiet spot may be good for those especially "on the go" and in the public eye. There, people can catch up on spiritual reading and have time for meditation and contemplation, while giving the body a much needed rest.

3 | *St. Thomas, the Apostle*
Showing the Wounds of Love

Today, across a confused world, men and women seek the *real Christ* of the Gospels, the one they have read about but cannot seem to find. In this seeking, men and women ask one another,

"How do you find Christ? Where is he? Where can I find him?" It seems to me the answer is exceedingly simple: We meet Christ in a real Christian. Human beings have to be *shown.* The time of mere talking is over.

After his resurrection, Christ showed his disciples his wounds and they believed. These wounds were visible signs of Christ's love for them—and for all of us. They saw his wounds of love and they believed. None of them needed to say anything. It was only Thomas the doubter who later spoke on seeing those wounds, "My Lord and my God!"

Today, it seems to me, we must likewise show the wounds of Christ to men and women, for only then will they believe. This is what men and women are seeking today: someone who will show them the wounds of Christ so that they may touch him and be reassured!

But we must go further. Christ prepared breakfast on the beach for his friends. We too, by our service, must *show* how much we love our brethren, all those who are seeking the Lord. We also must accept all human beings *as they are,* without wanting to change or manipulate them. It is a benediction and a joy in itself that they come to us.

4 | Loving God in Others

Men and women will not know God unless we show Christ to them. We must open the doors of our hearts and homes, accept people as they are, serve them, and show them the wounds of love.

Love is always wounded because love and pain are inseparable. Even a young girl barely falling in love worries about her boyfriend traveling on hazardous roads. There is no love without pain.

But where do we acquire these wounds that we must show? Where do we get the strength to cook a supper for someone when we ourselves are already exhausted by the day's toil? How do we get the strength to open our hearts that we want to close against the noise of our incredibly noisy world? How? The answer is always the same: prayer.

The Lord said we must love our enemies. Until we do, we cannot show Christ to other men and women. We must empty ourselves, according to his commandment of love; and with his grace, we can allow God to love in us.

No, words are not enough. A loving glance, a meal cooked for a friend, a welcome through an open door into an open heart, these will do it. It is only then, when my brother or sister has been filled with my supper, when the person has beheld my wounds of love for him or her, when that person has experienced a totality of acceptance, only then will he or she be open to the glad news!

5 Are We Christians?

We should ask ourselves, are we Christians? To be a Christian means to live in such a faith and commitment to Christ, that it will revolutionize—turn upside down—not only our lives but the lives of others. To be a Christian means to incarnate, actualize, literally implement the teachings of the Gospel. It means preaching the Gospel with one's life. This alone would be a revolution, a spiritual, intellectual, political revolution!

True, certain signs of an awakening are visible: the charismatic movement, more concern for the poor and so-called useless, and a new flourishing of prayer. Praised be the Lord!

Yet, something is still missing. A vibrant, passionate totality of commitment seems to be missing, and faith that would transcend all limits of time and space. What is missing is a discernment which can distinguish between a security that depends on human resources and the security of faith that is the heritage of every Christian.

The law of love demands that we become people of the towel and the water, that like Christ we wash the feet of our neighbor. This simply means that we wash the feet of one another when we implement the Gospel. That and that alone is the true revolution that will change the face of the earth. What does it mean to be Christian? It means to revolutionize the world the way Christ wanted it to be revolutionized. When shall we begin?

6 Meditation for Maintenance Workers

To "maintain" means to keep whole and intact, to prolong life and usefulness. It also means to repair what is broken, damaged, dented, or misused. Sometimes it means changing ugliness into beauty, as with restoring antiques. Maintenance means to restore something that seems useless, to put to use again by loving care.

The tools of this may be stains, sanders, wax, nuts and bolts, power tools. And maintenance men must have a hunger for knowledge about every tool and the best way to use each. They must be men of ingenuity and order, great order. For it behooves them to enter into the tranquility of God's order. By ordering all things, the Lord restores broken souls and hearts and minds. Maintenance men must realize that God has given them a very special grace, the grace of healing and "restoring" his creatures. Houses, furniture, tools—all these are creatures of God. What a grace—to be a restorer, a renewer, a healer of God's creatures! Our vocation is the *restoration of the world to Christ!*

Maintenance men must be men of prayer. Then the creature of God upon which they work with loving care will easily yield itself to them, and their job will be as perfect as it can be under the circumstances. And that job, that repair, that restoration will continue to praise God as long as it exists. And the whole Church will be enriched by the graces God gives maintenance men for their work.

7 Fundamental Community

You seek community? The greatest and most fundamental community is the Trinity who dwells in your heart from the day of your baptism. I touch the Trinity within me. I extend one hand toward God and the other toward my brother and sister. This is community. If I don't reach out toward them, the hand outstretched toward the Trinity will fall limp, because God will not grasp it. God and humanity, humanity and God. I am now cruciform.

In his inimitable way, God continues to bring forth this prayer from our hearts. In this prayer of love and service, all arrogance, enmity, and desire to manipulate must disappear. Unless we love each other as Christ loved us, we can pray and read Scripture all we want, but nothing will happen. At the core of our prayer, there must be love.

We must strive for hospitality of the heart. Without it, hospitality of the house is nothing. We must accept those who come to us just as they are, without judging them, and with deep respect. The traditional Russian greeting to the neighbor says, "My brother is my life, and my sister is my joy." When you meet your brother or sister, do not probe and do not ask questions. If you stand there like Christ, accepting the person—as is—into your heart, God will reveal what he wants you to know about that person.

8 Opening Your Heart

This attitude of always and everywhere opening one's heart to the other requires spiritual warfare. We must fight against all that is not God within us. This is the *kenosis* I have talked about, the emptying of oneself in order to be filled with God.

This is true poverty. People are always asking questions about poverty, but it is very simple. When you touch God, you serve others, and you are crucified. What can you hold on to? Nothing. Not even your will. *That* is poverty! The things of God are so simple—*we* are complex.

When I am cruciform, I am free. I am holding on to nothing. Now I can be a carrier of the towel and water, wiping the feet of my brother and my sister. This, my friends, is the answer to all our social and political problems. This answer is based on my forgiveness and love of you, and your forgiveness and love of me. Until this takes place, we can expect nothing to happen.

We have sinned in not fulfilling the second commandment of Christ, which tells us to love our neighbor as ourselves. We haven't loved ourselves and, thus, we haven't been capable of loving our neighbor. We present-day Christians have sinned by not showing the face of Christ to the world at large. The early Christians showed his face to such an extent that the pagans said of them, "See how they love one another." We must do likewise.

9 | Hell in a City

In my Harlem days, from our window, we saw a land of loneliness, despair, and hell. Thomas Merton came and looked from our window and wrote a poem about it all. Then he put his face upon the window sill and cried, and said, "I have to spend my lifetime to atone for this."

And I agreed, because I already was spending my lifetime in atonement. I cried too, and my tears spilled onto the floor, and strangely, they seemed to reverberate. They seemed to fall as if on a tin roof.

There was a little Black boy in the midst of this desolation, this hellish trap permitted in the city that is New York, and I saw the Christ Child holding a bat, wondering if there was a tiny place where perhaps he and his friends could play a game of baseball. But my mind reeled before this picture, for I lived in the midst of it. I cried, because the Christ Child was holding a bat looking for a field to play in. He was a Black child. And I cried out: "Lord, have mercy! What have we done to you? What have we done for you?"

And at that moment it seemed to me as if my heart got bigger, bigger, bigger. Until it embraced all the Harlems in America and all the Black children who held a bat but could not find a field to play in.

10 We Are Weak Little Vessels—So What?

You, like Christ, must incarnate yourself in utter simplicity, humility, and seeming weakness—into the stream of the day-by-day life of people who live in the world, in its marketplaces, its pleasure places, its slums and its palaces, its studying places, its holy places, and its sinful places.

There you must begin to witness to the incarnation. To Christ. There you must begin to enact in your own person, or should I say re-enact, Bethlehem and Nazareth.

What does it matter if you are inadequate in your own estimation? What does it matter that you think you are not contributing too much to the church?

What does it matter if you think you are a sinner? Take it for granted. You are. So am I. So are we all. But don't bother about it. Do not impede his grace in your soul by dwelling on your poverty. We are all paupers of this kind... all sinners.

Dwell instead on the *incomprehensible mystery of his choice of you.*

11 Praying the Jesus Prayer

When you are in love, only one person matters to you, and that is your beloved. When your beloved is God, you must surrender to him. The self has to disappear. Prayer is this self-emptying. It means that we stand still and wait.

The Jesus Prayer might be enough for you. "Lord Jesus Christ, Son of the Living God, have mercy on me, a sinner." Why would it be enough? Because it brings Jesus into your life. The repetition of the holy name brings the presence of the person, for in the Hebrew tradition, the name of a person *is* the person. Thus it says in the New Testament, "At the name of Jesus, every knee must bend." When you invoke the name of Jesus, you are drawn into his name, immersed in his name, immersed in him.

Don't try too hard to concentrate. You might be reciting the Jesus Prayer even though your mind is on a hat you saw a few days ago. You can continue saying the Jesus Prayer with a hat on your mind. You don't have to get all upset, saying, "That damned hat! I wish it would go away! It's been interrupting my thinking and my prayer for days!" You needn't worry about things like that.

Russian Christians don't know anything about yoga, mantras, special breathing, and all the prayers of the non-Christian East. Nor did the Greek monks—they prayed the Jesus Prayer naturally, and the Russians learned it from them. "Lord Jesus Christ, Son of the Living God, have mercy on me, a sinner." In and out. You don't do it consciously; it just happens. This is the Jesus Prayer.

12 | The Name of Jesus

Even in our secular society, a name is something very powerful. Some names suggest tremendous beauty; others evoke fear. Say the name Adolph Hitler and everyone shrinks, even the younger generation that barely knows about him. But when you say the name of Jesus, "It is accompanied by its immediate manifestation, for the name is a form of his presence," says

Russian theologian Paul Evdokimov. Just say "Jesus," and *whoosh*, God is here! You brought him. You made him present. When you say "Jesus," many things begin to happen.

When you say "Jesus," the word is already a prayer. You remind yourself, "If two or three are gathered in my name, I am in the midst of them." How much truer this is when we say, "Come, Lord Jesus," as we do in Advent. "Come, Lord Jesus." And he comes! This is reality, one of those strange mysteries that exist between God and humanity. We call and God abases himself and takes again the form of a servant.

Once you really understand what you are doing and begin to pray the name of Jesus, it will continue even without your consciously willing it. Once you've called on the name of Jesus, his name will remain with you because you desire it to be there. He desires it to be there too, and the two desires merge into one.

13 | Prayer and Doing the Will of God

It terrifies me to hear young people say, "God told me to do this or that." It is easy to say, "I received all this in prayer," but unless it is checked by someone with a real knowledge of the spiritual life, such a statement will ring false.

I firmly believe that God inspires and draws people, but when he does, it invariably makes some kind of sense in terms of the circumstances surrounding that person's life. A woman once wrote to see if she could come join us. She was absolutely convinced she had a vocation to the lay apostolate. When she arrived, it turned out that she also had a husband and five children. It didn't take much to figure out God's will in that situation!

Today young people want to make pilgrimages. I'm all for pilgrimages. My mother made pilgrimages. She loved them and would readily walk two hundred miles or more to visit a shrine or holy place. But first the children had to be cared for. Then it had to be a time when my father was away and didn't need her. The household had to be in good order. Only then did my mother go. If any one of those conditions were lacking, she would not go.

This is how God normally works. He speaks to us, but what we hear must be checked out in relation to our responsibilities and our particular way of life.

14 | Love, Truth, and Prayer

Truth is love. In order for our prayer to be rooted in love, we must be willing to face conflicts openly. When people are angry with each other, they have to come together and talk it out. They must be willing to say, "Look, I am angry. This is why, and this is what is really in my heart." They also have to be willing to take the consequences of such openness. It may be the other person shouting the truth back to them: "You're angry because you want attention and no one could possibly fill the need you have!" Or the consequences might be much more drastic, and then we are called to say what we have to say without fear. Being human, we may well be afraid. But we will speak the truth, regardless. If we do, people will not only believe us, but believe in us.

Throughout our lives, we will have to face things squarely. We will have to do it with our husbands or wives, with our friends, our co-workers. We will achieve nothing by trying to hide our anger. As long as we fail to confront situations as they are, acknowledging our fault when the fault is ours, or asking the other if he or she is in the wrong, there will be confusion and a lack of truth between us and God. We are called to truth and forgiveness, but we are also called to become the cross on which the other is crucified. We have to be honest about this. When we live in truth, our hearts will be at peace, and our prayers, purified by truth, will rise before the face of God.

15 Accepting Rejection in Christ

A psychiatrist named Jung concluded that all human beings feel rejected by God. He found there is a deep rift at the bottom of their souls, between themselves and that someone greater than themselves.

Let us consider mortal sin, which today is hardly spoken of at all. Mortal sin is an offense toward God, and the guilt of it, if it is not verbalized (confessed), is like a cancer eating up one's heart and soul. It upsets the equilibrium of the entire person. The answer to this terrible state of affairs is to share what is in the soul and heart with someone else. And to have the cancer of guilt removed, the individual must go to a "surgeon," who is a priest. When the guilt is removed, the person can proceed and be receptive to rejection.

When one receives rejection in its pure form, it means accepting the rejection Christ accepted. *Rejection accepted in faith is acceptance by Christ.* Did you ever think about that? If you accept rejection because you love God, a strange thing happens. God comes down to you—into you—and you begin to feel as if you are walking on air. Why? Because you chose something much more powerful: your rejection is Christ's rejection. You share it. And in the fusing of the two, you walk directly into the resurrected Christ. In him, rejection becomes joy, not sorrow.

16 *Our Lady of Mount Carmel* Mary and Rejection

Mary was truly a marvelous person, sensitive beyond all normal human sensitivity. How did she make it through the way of the cross with Christ? She watched him fall; she watched his body being beaten; she saw that face that had been so dear to her covered with mud and dust. Just as Simeon had predicted, she felt the sword going through her heart. As Jesus fell down amid the jeers and rejection of the people, she was there. She united herself with him. They were always united. What he felt, she felt, for was she not his mother and did she not, beyond all others, understand who he really was?

When the ordeal was over, they laid him in her arms; she held him fast. I looked hard and long at the Pieta in Rome. How profound was her feeling. Both he and she were rejected by the mob, by those he had cured and helped. As she held him in her arms she must have foreseen, with the wisdom that was hers, the bitter rejection that would come to her Son and to herself down through the centuries.

But she remembered the words he had said to St. John and her. He had asked her to be the mother of men and women. But was she accepted? How many of us accept her? How many of us accept her Son?

17 Keys to Tranquility, Order, and Happiness

In the great tranquility of God's order, all things come to rest —all things except men and women, who, with their stupendous gift of free will, can refuse to accept either the order or its tranquility, or even God himself. Thus, men and women can choose to live without hope, without rest, without love.

Because so many of us refuse to accept God's order, there is a darkness, a fear, an unhappiness, and a disorder that rule the world. We are besieged on all sides by forebodings of annihilation and destruction. How could it be otherwise? No one can challenge God with impunity.

Men and women seek vainly to escape darkness, fear, and unhappiness, or to find some natural solution for these things. But it is vain because their "escape" is directed *away from God*, and their solutions are not rooted in *God's laws*.

Yet what they must *do*, and what they must *avoid*, if they desire peace, happiness, order, and a life without fear, is blue-printed for humanity in the Ten Commandments.

Let us turn our attention to those commandments, repeating with the psalmist, "Your testimonies are my meditation, and your justifications my counsel.... Open my eyes that I may consider the wondrous things in your law.... Strengthen me by your words" (Psalm 119:24, 18, 25).

18 | The First Commandment

I Am the Lord thy God, thou shalt not have strange gods before me.

How few of us remember the first commandment! How small the handful who still examine their conscience by it! We have outgrown and deserted the crude idols of bygone days. Statues with calves' heads would bring but a smile. But we do worse. We have given free rein to our passions. And we have made them into gods. While rendering lip service to God, we have burned the incense of our devotion to these new idols—we make gods of success, wealth, power, and sex.

Sex, a great and divine gift, given us for the procreation of children and the raising up of God's saints, we have made into a monstrous and hideous idol. And we adore it ardently, in utter defiance of God's first law.

If we disregard the first commandment, the rest cease to have any meaning. Let us all go down on our knees while there is still time. And, with tears of sorrow and compunction, let us ask God's forgiveness for our sinful ways, offering ourselves and our lives in atonement for them. Let us ask for light and courage to obey more strictly God's first and most important commandment, and teach others to do likewise, by our example. Thus, together, we and the world we seek to restore to God, may love and worship him daily more and more, and come to rest in the great and holy tranquility of his order, here and hereafter.

19 | The Second Commandment

Thou shalt not take the name of the Lord thy God in vain.

This commandment is a continuation of the first, in which God makes it known that he desires our worship and our adoration. In this second one he commands us to be filled with veneration and respect for his divine name. He commands us to honor it, and to refrain from using it in vain.

It is not fear alone that should keep us from profaning the name of God. It is Love that should seal our lips, and Love, again, that should open them to use his holy name as a blessing, a joy, a word spoken with all the reverence and respect our minds, hearts, and souls are capable of.

Let us stop for a moment... stop and *really* think about what is asked of us! Incredible as it may seem, God asks us, his creatures, to love him. That he should demand from us adoration is understandable. But love? The very thought should make one happy, with happiness that is beyond all understanding!

If we begin to love him, others will too. Where love is, there is respect. When love enters, sins against the second commandment—blasphemy, perjury, and the misuse of God's most holy name—will vanish. Could there be a greater goal than to spend our lives in making his most holy name loved and adored—so that every knee, indeed, will bend at its sound?

20 | The Third Commandment

Remember, keep holy the Sabbath Day.

As more days are added to our lives, more of us fear their passing. But how joyous our fleeting days would be, if we framed them between two Masses! How holy they would become, rooted in God! Our faith, our hope, and our love would change them into the golden steps of a stairway leading straight to God. But, perverse creatures that we are, we keep on fearing, wondering, bemoaning their passage. Yet God gives us the secret of days, the secret of life itself in his third commandment.

One out of seven must belong to him. One out of seven! How gentle, how good, how kind God is! Giving this chance to us to pause and remember that we were created to love, worship, and serve him. So little to give—one day out of seven. So much to gain by giving it! Let us give it fully, completely, utterly.

The least we can do on God's day is to refrain from sin. And let us refrain from work for gain! We have six other days to buy and sell in. Why profane the seventh, the one the Lord asks for himself? Unless our "buying and selling" is of such a nature that it belongs to God and our neighbor, let us be done with it for the love of him who gave his life for love of us.

If we do this, we shall lose the fear of the passing days of time.

21 | The Fourth Commandment

Honor thy father and thy mother.

The first three commandments deal with God. This commandment is the first of the remainder that deals with the love we should have for our fellow men and women.

We must honor our fathers and mothers in our youth by implicit obedience in all things but sin, and in complete respect, and a filial fear that has its roots in a love that aims not to hurt the object of its love. We must honor our fathers and mothers in adult age, even unto death. We must care for them in need at the expense of our vocations, plans, desires, and dreams, and even at the expense of our lives if that is required. For they come first after God, being our most beloved and closest "neighbors."

If only modern youth were given this training—if only it accepted its lessons—how changed our world would be! They would bring its fruits into their daily lives, and transfer them into obedience to all lawful authority, understanding that it too comes from God. Yet, in the modern vocabulary, the word obedience is obsolete. Perhaps it is because obedience requires self-discipline, and the sacrifice of one's own will for a common good. But obedience also means, ultimately, freedom! For only the obedient person is free, as all children of God should be free, in him.

22 | The Fifth Commandment

Thou shalt not kill.

Modern society rationalizes away, quite easily, the fifth commandment. We go on killing, not only in wars, but out of them—skillfully, sadistically, professionally, eagerly—as in the Nazi concentration camps, where killing reached diabolical perfection, or in the Communist prisons and labor camps. Human life has become cheap the world over. Murders, the most sensational, have almost ceased to interest us. We take them languidly, matter-of-factly. Yet the evil goes deeper. There is murder by abortion. This is the most common kind of killing. Few care. Birth control has clothed itself in the garments of respectability and "science"—the science of making God's noblest creation vanish from the world.

We are children of God's love, peace, and light—what are we doing about all this? Are our voices heard above the conspiracy of silence and indifference that surrounds this incredible breaking of the commandment of our Lord and God? Or are we silent? Silent with the dastardly silence of torpidity, fear, or complacency? It appears that we are silent!

Lord, have mercy on us, Your lost children! Holy Spirit, give us the gift of fortitude, so we may cease to remain accessories after the fact, by our criminal silence, by our sinful indifference. Let us become witnesses to your law, witnesses in the love that casts out all fears, witnesses unto death, if need be.

23 | The Sixth Commandment

Thou shalt not commit adultery.

Love is the most misunderstood word of our loveless age. Perhaps it has never before been used so much and meant so little. We are confronted with it from morning until night, with the media suggesting a thousand ways of arousing "love." Yet real Love was born in a manger and died on a cross. Real Love is synonymous with sacrifice and service. Marital love was begotten by God himself, and raised to the tremendous status of a sacrament by his Son. A man and woman united in holy wedlock are a miracle of love—two distinct persons, yet one in a fusing creative beauty. They are lifted by God to become co-creators with him of another human being, another immortal soul—a child.

No wonder then the sixth commandment sounds thunderous and formidable to our human ears. And well it should. Adultery is a sin that wounds love, a sin of injustice against an innocent person or persons, a sin against marriage, a social sin that undermines the very fabric of society.

If we want to restore the world to Christ, we must first clarify what marriage really is to a world that has forgotten the very meaning of the word love, let alone the sanctity of marital love. Then we must restore the home.

Lord, have mercy on us! Open our eyes. Give us the grace to understand the virtue of purity. Restore marital love to the heights it used to occupy—the heights of your cross—which is the key to joy, happiness, and life eternal.

24 | The Seventh Commandment

Thou shalt not steal.

Although everyone seems to agree we should not steal, stealing goes on, day in and day out, on a large scale. We take our neighbor's goods—not violently, of course—but without his full knowledge and consent, under false pretenses. Sometimes it is done through wholesale political graft; or else by white-collar crimes; or by taking in "suckers." The poor, when caught, are always prosecuted to the limit of the law. The rich, who steal on a grand scale, seldom are brought into court. And when they are, people shake their heads with pity that such big-time operators have been so careless as to be found out! To "get away with it" is considered a sign of intelligence and bravery!

Honesty, truthfulness, uprightness of mind and soul—these old-fashioned virtues are seldom practiced. Perhaps because of this, our international situation is what it is. When men and women become lenient toward theft, when the foundations of God's design are lost sight of, when honesty becomes synonymous with being a sucker or not being "in the know," or not taking advantage of others, then it follows that nations, composed of individuals who have lost all sense of proportion, become thieves on a grand scale. And they steal whole peoples, and their countries too, while the rest of the world stands helplessly by!

We live in such times. Yet let us take courage and be honest with ourselves and our fellow mortals. Let us teach ourselves and others that we are damned by what we steal; for whatever we steal from men and women, we veritably steal from God himself.

25 | The Eighth Commandment

Thou shalt not bear false witness against thy neighbor.

This commandment forbids lies of any kind, slander, detraction, calumny, vicious gossip, and perjury. Yet so many of us think nothing of these. Across the nation, reputations are ruined, souls are wounded, hearts are filled with sorrow, and minds are distracted with grief by those who use their tongues maliciously regarding their brothers and sisters in Christ.

People trying to serve God, each in their own fashion, and each according to their vocation, are subjected to the tortures of unjust accusations that attack their morals, their lives, their motives and intentions, and discourage and handicap the work of God they are trying to do.

Thousands of upright citizens are brought close to ruin by those who have forgotten that God gave us this commandment. Isn't there enough sorrow on our tragic earth, without letting loose this tidal wave of treachery and falsehood?

We cannot restore the earth to Christ, its Lord, on the shifting sands of gossip and lies. How can we dream of bringing the fullness of truth to men and women, if we are traffickers in lies? We must cleanse our hearts from the evil desire to speak carelessly, wrongly, about our neighbor, so that when we appear before Christ, the Lord, on judgment day, we may not be too frightened.

26 | The Ninth Commandment

Thou shalt not covet thy neighbor's wife.

This commandment and the next one forbid us in thoughts and desires. Only God could make these laws, for to do so it is necessary to know the individual human heart with all its inner workings. Human justice cannot know the hearts of men and women. Hence it cannot, and does not, forbid internal thoughts or desires. Nor does it punish them. Only external actions opposed to justice are within the power of human law. But God's law regulates not only our external actions, but even our internal desires—how holy and pure is God's law!

How far our generation has wandered from both the spirit and the letter of God's law! Consider our media, our whole manner of life and thought and action. Were we suddenly to remember the Decalogue in its fullness of the spiritual and natural order, life would abruptly become different.

All around us, by every means imaginable, people try to awaken in the soul of their fellow men and women thoughts and desires contrary to God's laws. They smooth the paths of evil to make easy the fulfillment of those thoughts and desires. How the devil must rejoice!

Lord, have mercy on us! Give us ears to hear your voice, eyes to see your ways! And give us courage to reform, lest we spend eternity in hell.

27 | The Tenth Commandment

Thou shalt not covet thy neighbor's goods.

This commandment, like the others, is a commandment of love—love of God and of our neighbor. Can a person who loves bring him or herself to envy or desire the possessions of the one who is loved? Yet look at our crazy world. Some nations desire goods, lands, people, even the minds and souls of their neighbors. Men and women everywhere look with fear and envy on the goods of others. And they keep striving, ever more desperately, to devise ways to get them.

Consider the common idea of "keeping up with the Joneses"

—trying to match what they have. It is a race of envy, of strange and dark desires, of restlessness and greed. Any means to achieve "parity," we seem to believe, is good enough for individuals, for business concerns, for nations.

We are in a mad pursuit of acquiring possessions that possess us more than we possess them. In the process, our hearts become attached to things. Because of this we are perishing. For whoever makes a god of goods, makes idols. Whoever desires what belongs to another, and uses unjust and dishonest means to acquire it, is damned.

We should remember that we came into this world with nothing; and with nothing we shall leave it. *Our dead hands can offer God only that which we have given away.* What we have taken, we must pay for, somehow, some day. Shall we pay for trash with undying fire?

28 | We Are Pebbles in God's Slingshot

In everyday life, what does God expect of us? A great simplicity, absolute naturalness, and humility as ordinary as the air. For we are little. Very small. Remember David and Goliath. David saw little pebbles in the brook and he bent down and put them into his childish slingshot—and slew the mighty Goliath!

The Lord does likewise with us. David is a prefiguration of Christ. The Lord looks at the world's Goliaths of darkness, waxing strong and fat, plucking away from him souls for which his Son died. Christ his Son, with the sling of his grace, bends down and picks up little pebbles—you and me—to fix in his sling. So what must we do? Just be there like little pebbles. It's up to God to shoot.

Here is the hand of the Lord, and here are the pebbles. They are worked over by the water. They are shiny and ready. They lie still on the palm of God's hand. It's for him to pick them up, put them into his divine sling, and shoot wherever he desires. That's all!

But oh! What goes into those tiny pebbles! Chastity, poverty, obedience, humility, simplicity, naturalness, death to self, and love! The pebbles lie still in the palm of God's hand, content just to rest there.

29 | *St. Martha*
Four Dirty Pennies

Theologians have their own ways of discussing weighty matters of doctrine and dogma, but to the ordinary person, it is the little ways that matter—and the little people. Many of God's little people—the *anawim*—came through our doors of Friendship House, doors painted blue in honor of Our Lady.

I remember only the first name of the person whose story I am now going to relate. I remember her very well. Every Saturday, rain or shine, this woman would come through the Blue Door. She would enter, oh so softly, and close the door gently behind her. Slowly, with tired step, she would walk up to my desk, and, after a few words of greeting, lay on top of it a tidy row of four dirty pennies. Then she would explain, almost in a whisper, that this was all she had left of her pay to give to Christ in the poor. Then, with a little smile and bow, she would ask for our prayers, say a soft goodby and walk out through the Blue Door, again closing it very gently.

She was a Black, a widow. She earned her living scrubbing a few office floors at night. Her name was Martha. She brought her four pennies every week for four years. Then, one Saturday, she did not come. I never saw her again. Months later someone on the street told me about a poor woman buried in an unmarked grave. I asked the woman's name. All they could remember was that her first name was Martha.

30 Do You Realize God Loves You

The greatest tragedy of our world is that men and women do not know, really *know*, that God loves them. Some believe it in a shadowy sort of way, but their belief in God's love for them is very remote and abstract.

Because of this, they do not know how to *love God back*. Often they don't even try, because it all seems so very difficult and remote. But Christians must realize that the Christian faith, in its essence, is a love affair between God and each human being. Not just a *simple* love affair: it is a *passionate* love affair. God so loved each of us that he created us in his image. God so loved each of us that he became human himself, died on a cross, was raised from the dead by the Father, ascended into heaven— and all this in order to bring each of us back to himself, to that heaven which we had lost through our own fault.

Yes, of course the Christian has dogmas and rules, but they all concern love, which is the essence. Dogmas and tenets without love are dead letters, not even worth spelling out. God is love. And where love is, God is.

It is time we awoke from our long sleep, we Christians. It is time we shed our fears of God, or what is worse, our indifference toward him. Then we shall know true peace, true joy. The answers to our international and national problems will become clear in proportion to the amount that we love.

31 *St. Ignatius of Loyola* A Blessing to Pray for Priests

When I was about twelve, in Egypt, a Jesuit priest gave us little ones a talk. He was holy and simple. He touched my young heart deeply. I didn't like it, however, when he asked us to pray for priests when we became "a little more grown up." I asked myself, "Why should I wait an eternity—until I reach eighteen or nineteen—to pray for priests?" I spoke privately with the Jesuit and explained my longing to pray for priests at once. He looked intently and earnestly at me and asked if I truly desired to pray for priests. When I responded affirmatively, he placed his hand upon my head, prayed to the Trinity, patted my cheek, and said, "Now, I have blessed you so that, as young as you are, you can pray for priests. Don't forget to do so, child!"

I have never forgotten that special blessing. Even as a child, I loved priests with my whole heart. In my youthful mind, I firmly believed that Christ left us priests because he didn't want to leave us orphans or to part from us. I didn't understand a great deal about the Mystical Body and the many ways Christ remains in our midst. I sensed, however, the very special role that priests played in Christ's plan and I found it terribly important to pray for them. Since the age of twelve, therefore, I have prayed for priests, acting on the blessing given to me so many years ago.

August

1 Our Teacher in Loving

This is the month of Our Lady's assumption. It is the month of Our Lady's love, the Mother of Fair Love, the Mother of God. Let us turn to her, and beg her with all our hearts, all our souls, all our strength to teach us how to love. Unless we do, we shall perish in the hate begotten by our fears and our lack of love.

Gentle Mother of God, virgin most powerful, terrible as an army in battle array, resplendent Spouse of the Spirit, humble daughter of God the Father Almighty, bend down your beautiful face and gather us up into your loving arms. Do not give us up; do not forsake us, even though so many of us hear not your voice that speaks so constantly to our generation.

Speak now in accents of love, in a whisper as gentle as a distant breeze singing in your trees, or in a mighty roll of thunder that can be heard to the ends of the earth.

Behold our deaf generation! Behold our blind millions! Look pityingly on us who neither hear the voice nor see the face of perfect Love! Behold and pity us.

Teach us how to love, Mother of Fair Love, so that we may lift up our hearts and walk upright once more, like men and women created in the image of Love, your Son.

2 Superficial Communications and Loneliness

Many people are the "Hi, how are you?" type of person. They realize, though, that this doesn't communicate anything to anybody. They can go through life with shallow greetings and senseless questions, but when they try to love others, the "Hi" interferes. These people do not want to shed their loneliness or reveal themselves. They do not desire to communicate even with the persons they love. Are we like this?

It is most difficult to always communicate superficially, to have no friend with whom we can talk or share. Feelingless greetings run shallow and communication is really nonexistent. It may be better than nothing, but loneliness laughs at us when we do this. The reason we speak so superficially is because we are hiding ourselves from people. We do not wish them to have a part in us. We want to be alone, and yet we desperately desire friendship and understanding.

Yet there are moments when Christ calls us to become human, to cease to be alone, to begin to love and to get involved with others. We must do this to get out of the morass of our loneliness. We need to speak and really communicate with others, perhaps with others who are lonely. Did you ever go into nursing homes for senior citizens? There are whole floors of lonely people there. Do something about it. Do something for others. Break the loneliness of others, and you will never be lonely again.

3 Start Reaching Out

I recall one time I was in a subway in Montreal. I was reading a book when an elderly lady, who sat across from me, looked at me and said: "You have a kind face. Would you mind talking to me a little? I have had the flu for the last three weeks and only a nurse visited me for half an hour. The landlady would bring me a tray, but neither of them spoke very much. It seems I am hungry for human speech; I am hungry to share with someone. That is the way I feel."

We made two trips on the subway from one end to the other. Then I invited her to a coffee shop and we became good friends. I did not live in Montreal, but we corresponded until she died. I hope—in fact, I know—that her loneliness disappeared because there was someone on the other end. There was an ear that listened lovingly. That is all we have to do.

Loneliness has many levels, and we can slip deep down into it, become depressed and emotionally ill, or we can ascend and overcome the superficiality of communication. We can stop and really look our neighbor (whoever it might be) straight in the eye, and say, "Friend, how are you? Tell me about yourself."

This is partly why Madonna House began "listening houses." You would be surprised to learn how many people come to them just to talk.

| 4 | *St. John Vianney, Patron of Parish Priests*
What Is a Priest? |

A priest is a lover of God. A priest is a lover of human beings. A priest is a holy man because he walks before the face of the Almighty! The Russians say that the face of God is reflected in the face of the people, so the priest who offers the Eucharist must reflect the Eucharist.

A priest understands all things. A priest forgives all things. A priest encompasses all things. Perhaps he doesn't intellectually understand many things better than you or I do, but he understands much more than we think he does, because Christ is his teacher. Look at St. John Vianney, who is now the patron of parish priests. He was almost thrown out of the seminary because he couldn't do well in his studies, yet he became a saint, and a great confessor. That is what I mean by understanding.

A priest is a man whose goal is to be another Christ. A priest is a man who lives to serve. A priest is a man who has crucified himself so that he, too, can be lifted up and draw all things to Christ. A priest is a man in love with God. A priest is a gift of God to humanity, and of humanity to God.

A priest is a symbol of the Word made flesh. A priest is the naked sword of God's justice. A priest is the hand of God's mercy, and a priest is the reflection of God's love. Nothing in this world can be greater than a priest—nothing but God himself!

5 | The Kitchen—A Holy Place

The kitchen is the heart of a home and is a holy place. From time immemorial, eating was a tremendous act of great importance. Sharing one's food with a stranger was considered a sign of friendship, as was all hospitality. Preparation of food, and its acquisition, is an expression of love. There is always love in the transformation of raw material into edible food for the family.

Our Lady sanctified the kitchen in a special manner by transforming the fruits of the earth for the nourishment of Christ's human body which he assumed for our sake. Then it became holy because Christ used ordinary bread and wine to feed us by transforming them into his Body and Blood.

Whether a kitchen is modern or humble, those who work there lovingly and joyfully transform—*transubstantiate!*—the raw products of God's earth into food to feed their brothers and sisters. This is a service and privilege almost beyond compare. Our Lord said, "Whatsoever you do to the least of my brethren, you do to me." He was very explicit about it all. We are to feed the hungry and those who work in the kitchen assuredly do. If we do it in the right spirit, we are assured of God's gratitude—and heaven too.

May the Lord who used bread and wine to feed us so lovingly with himself bless all cooks and show them his face in those who partake of the meals they lovingly prepare.

6 | *The Transfiguration*
Food, Nourishment, and Strength

Matthew 17:1-8 describes the transfiguration of Jesus. Take a minute to read it now.

That's a fantastic Gospel. It always cheered me up in my poverty, in my loneliness. The Gospel is my companion. Without it I don't think I would have survived. In this scene of the transfiguration, one line stands out for me: "Jesus then came up to them, touched them, and said, 'Stand up, do not be afraid.' And when they raised their eyes *they saw no one but Jesus.*"

That, to me, is the only thing that matters. In the terrible, horrendous, awful, lonely days of my life, it seemed as if he touched me and I opened my eyes filled with tears and despair. Suddenly, I saw Jesus, and I got up and washed my face and went on about the duty of the moment. That's what the Gospel means to me: the duty of the moment. It gives me courage. It gives me food, nourishment, strength, and the ability to keep plugging along against every opposition.

Then, in the next verses, Christ went down the mountain and found his disciples had not cured the epileptic. He got quite angry, let me tell you! "Faithless and perverse generation," he called them. Then Jesus delivered the epileptic from the devil. He told those little pipsqueaks called apostles that they had very little faith. Neither do we. Let us pray "Lord, I believe; help my unbelief."

7 | Blue Door Stories

Someone once asked why the doors of Friendship House, and later Madonna House, are always painted blue. I answered, smilingly, "Because of a very old, old saying of my people in

Russia: 'Every front door painted blue in honor of Our Lady brings her blessings on all who pass through it.'"

In the next few days, I want to share with you some of the many wondrous stories of God's grace and mercy and of Our Lady's tender love which have occurred in my life, and that continue to occur. Telling these little stories—adventures in grace, as Raissa Maritain called them—are my way of thanking the Lord for his many gifts.

Many people have passed through our blue doors, each receiving, I know, Mary's blessing and her divine Son's grace and mercy. The blessings were not always visible, but when they were, they were beautiful to behold and joyful to witness. They also encouraged us and helped us to persevere in our vocation: to love God and to prove it to him by loving one's neighbor and spending one's life in serving him. This is the "witnessing to Christ" that changes the world, the extraordinary ordinariness of our daily life that passes through Our Lady's Blue Door.

 # 8   God Knows

One day I was alone in my dark Harlem apartment. The loneliness of Christ encompassed me so utterly that I literally cried out. I could not take another minute of it. I thought I would pack and leave that hell on earth where man's inhumanity to man could be seen in every face along the treeless, crowded, dirty, segregated streets.

Then, suddenly, there she was—Miss Russell, soft-spoken, shy. Yet shining from her lovely light brown face was a charity whose other name is love. She told me haltingly that she wanted to assist me in helping the Blacks in some way. What could she do?

There was a deep repose in her and I felt refreshed. There was peace in her gentle speech, which was punctuated by a warm, friendly silence. I was healed of my pain and my fears.

I led her across the way into the rectory basement, into our first "clothing center," to which many "naked" came to be clothed. It was depression time in Harlem. The door of the clothing center was painted blue.

Fifteen years later Miss Russell was still there, after walking quietly into my heart that first murky afternoon. Few people noticed her working, fewer still will ever know about her. But God knows. Through her being there, I was blessed, and all of us in Friendship House were blessed. Just a simple, quiet person who wanted to help. Not famous. God knows.

9 The Gunman

I received a call one day at Friendship House, asking if I had room for a man just out of prison (he'd been serving a sentence for manslaughter) and his girl friend. We had room, they were destitute, and they belonged to Christ, so I said we would be glad to have them. In a few hours the Blue Door opened and in walked a tired, haunted man and a girl with fearful blue eyes, all paint and paste, nails dripping red. I welcomed them warmly and went back to my business at hand: counting pennies, nickels, and dimes from selling our little paper in churches. The man surveyed the piles of cash, produced a gun, and announced that, in return for food and shelter, he would guard the money!

The next day I wondered what we would find. We found the gun out of sight, the money intact, and the girl washed clean and looking very young and demure. They stayed a week, making themselves useful. She loved to sew; he liked to cook. No one spoke to them of religion, the past, or the future.

Years passed. Then one day, a limousine stopped in front of the Blue Door and a kind, middle-aged man, his wife, and child approached with a check for a thousand dollars. He smiled and we recognized the gunman! He said, "This is a little token of my gratitude for all the hospitality, love, and trust that I found at your place many years ago. This is only the first payment to Lady Mary who has blessed us ever since we passed through her Blue Door."

10 St. Lawrence, Deacon
A Man of the Towel and Water

Dr. Karl Stern passed many times through the Blue Door of Madonna House in Combermere. He played our old piano, and under his fingers it sang. It made us weep and laugh and brought us peace. He told us about the books he had written and about his patients, stories that gave us courage.

We talked about the terrible mental sickness of anxiety, and ventured to say that Christ must have been very anxious facing the sins of all humanity in Gethsemane, so anxious that he sweated blood. Dr Stern agreed and said he had a patient once who also was anxious to the point of sweating blood.

I thought of Christ washing the feet of his apostles and wiping them with a towel, and suddenly it all became clear. God had given Karl Stern the towel of profound intelligence and the water of discernment to know when and how to wipe the faces of people who sweat blood in their anxiety. In a flash I understood the role of the psychiatrist—to wipe from the hearts of men and women the pain inflicted on them by others, by the inhumanity of society.

When I think of Karl Stern, I think of him as a consolation. I think of him as a Christian with a towel over his arm and holding a basin of fresh, cool water. He is wiping the heart of Christ in the hearts of men and women.

11 A Vision of the Whole

On a blustery March day in the early 1930s a priest walked into Friendship House. Zeal, understanding, and a love of souls shone through every word he spoke. This fiery priest, a bearer of light, warmth, and truth, was in love with the Holy Spirit. He was Dom Virgil Michel, a Benedictine monk from the Abbey of Collegeville, Minnesota, later the heart of the liturgical movement in North America.

That day he gave us the vision of the whole. He showed us the whole Christ who was not crippled by compromise or touched by the fear of human respect. Lavishly he fed us with the Bread of Truth and the Wine of Love that were his own food. The vision of the whole Christ, he said, begins with the Mass, where we are filled with Christ like empty chalices with wine. The Mass is sacrifice and sacrament, food and drink, the bridal chamber where the bride (the human soul) enters to become one with the bridegroom, Christ!

To go forth and live the Mass is to restore the social order and world to Christ—beginning with oneself! That is our vocation and we must persevere in it. He said this to us in a shabby storefront of a big-city slum.

Later, in 1951, kneeling at the feet of the Pope, I heard the same words repeated: "This is the hour of the laity. Persevere. Be steadfast and you shall renew the face of the earth. God needs you. The church needs you. We need you."

12 The Pity of God

The priest who walked through the Blue Door of Friendship House asked me to help a family in his parish. The father was a

Communist, the mother a practicing Catholic. The father would not allow their seven children to attend parochial school or any of them to set foot in church. Would I go see if, with God's help, I could do something with him? I followed the priest through the slum streets to a little shack, where he pointed out a man chopping wood, then left me with a whispered blessing. I approached and we began to talk amiably. But as the content of my message began to penetrate, he became furious, raised his ax, and shouted he would brain me if I mentioned God again. Gathering courage, I continued. He lifted his ax and started for me. I ran! Past garbage cans and down alleys; then suddenly I stopped. He *had* to be made to see God loved him! I turned and saw him, panting, ax held high. We stood looking at each other. Fear left me, an immense pity overtook me and I wept. He asked why I was crying. I told him from sorrow and pity for what he was doing to Christ. Suddenly he fell face down in the alley and sobbed the deep-heaved tears of a strong man. Then he arose, dropped his ax, and shook my hand. Weeks later, the priest came to see how I persuaded him to send the children to parochial school and the whole family—including him—to go to church! I simply said it was the pity of God, which for an instant took hold of my heart.

13 | The Man with the Deep-Seeing Eyes

One day a young man with a very interesting face came through the Blue Door of Friendship House. He had eyes that took in everything they saw. He was a poet, writer, and teacher and had left his university job to come to Harlem and offer his services. Poets, writers, and teachers are great people, but all of them seem to have, at least at the beginning, a complete inability to concentrate on practical things. But it wasn't long before our friend could mop a floor with the best of them. He fit in very well. One day, a few months later, he came to me and said,

"Catherine, I am going to enter the Trappists in Kentucky." I was very happy that he finally had found his real vocation.

Before he left, he gave me a manuscript and said, "If you can sell it, the royalties are yours." I tried, but no one would accept it, so I put it away in a filing cabinet. The manuscript proved to be a rough outline of what later became "The Seven Storey Mountain." Many years later, I came across the manuscript that the now-famous Thomas Merton had given me those many years ago in Harlem. It was later published under the name "The Secular Journal of Thomas Merton." If you read the foreword of that book, you will learn more about the relationship between me and this young poet, writer, and teacher who one day came through the Blue Door.

14 | Student and Worker

We were expecting Peter Maurin of the Catholic Worker to come for a lecture at Madonna House in Combermere. He had left New York for Canada a week earlier! With Peter, anything could happen—he would start for a city in the north and perhaps wander through the south to get there. Peter Maurin, co-founder of the Catholic Worker movement, inspiration of thousands, was, to my mind, a veritable saint!

When he finally arrived, he was at his best. He spoke in blank verse of God and Mary, of Jews and Gentiles, of justice and injustice. In sharp, concise and precise phrases, as only his wisdom and knowledge could mold them, he spoke of heaven and hell, of workers and management, the whole social scene and the church. He spoke of what he really knew. He was that perfect combination of student and worker.

To all, he made it clear that we were all *responsible for the state of the whole world,* for each person individually and for all collectively. We all in fact *were* our brothers' and sisters' keepers. Under his clear exposition, the doctrine of the Mystical Body became luminous. Peter could take sublime verities and, unwrapping them from the heavy garment of words with which centuries had clothed them, bring them forth into the light of day. Peter is dead now, but he lives on in his "Easy Essays," still available at the Catholic Worker. Peter Maurin, pray for us!

15 | *The Assumption of Mary into Heaven* Mother of God and All Peoples

She sits upon a throne, the assumed Mother of God and all peoples. Though no one saw her go to sleep, nor saw her being taken up into heaven, still she is there, in the flesh, touchable to the fingers of faith.

The glorified body of Our Lady is a sign and symbol of what we hope for. Her assumption is the prefiguration of what will happen to me if I gain heaven.

Mother of God—what awesome words! How could it be that femininity enfolds Divinity? And yet it did.

Mother of God, yet child of earth. Miracle of the love and grace and mercy of the Lord. Mind folds its wings, faith opens its arms, all understanding ceases to be, and the soul is plunged into the heart of a mystery that is timeless.

Mother of God, flesh hiding Light Eternal which has entered time. A seed lying in your holy womb, clothing itself with your flesh. God incarnated through your *fiat.*

Mother of God, through his birth and death you became Mother of all men and women. Pray for us then, that we in truth may all become brothers and sisters of your own divine Son.

16 | Our Complex World Needs God's Truths

Life has become most complex. Gone are the days of simplicity; gone too, the times when the world was stable. Today, between two wars—the one just fought, and the next one yet to come—there is neither peace nor security, neither simplicity nor stability. Simple decisions are hard to make.

Natural life has become unbearably complicated; and supernatural life, for which we were created, makes *heroic* demands on the followers of Christ. Indeed this is the time of heroism. Ordinary virtue, practiced well, has become heroic in the utter confusion of today's world. It is hard to think, let alone pray, in the modern din. It is harder still to hold to the royal road, what with all the distractions surrounding us.

Yet human hearts have never been hungrier for the Lord than they are today—the Lord and his truths. Nor have Catholics, ordinary average Catholics, ever had a greater role to play than in this century. Yes, this is the acceptable time to bring the Living Waters of Truth to the thirsty, and the Bread of Life to the hungry. But to do so, we must be clear, sure, and ready. Are we? The verities of our faith are simple, as are all the things of God. He gave them to us himself. We need much love, and a clear understanding of God's truth.

17 The Beatitudes

It must have been a soft spring day, the grass a tender green, the light breeze from the lake playing caressingly, lovingly, with the hair of the Lord. Sitting on a knoll, he spoke to the "little ones" of this world: the housemaid, the gardener, the bookkeeper, and you and me—to those whose births and deaths go unrecorded and who never make the headlines.

It is to *us* he gave the beatitudes, those bylaws of heaven. Not to a few chosen ones. No. To all. And yet look at us! How few of us can even remember how many beatitudes there are, let alone realize that they are to be considered daily. And that, unless we live up to them, our entrance into heaven is very dubious.

We persist in excusing ourselves, saying the beatitudes were meant for the few, the called ones, the priests and monks and nuns. Why do we try to fool ourselves? Even if we succeed, we cannot fool God. All this seems to be part of the modern Christian apostasy: abandoning our faith, of which so many of us are guilty. Still more tragic, we lack the honesty, the courage to *examine* this cancer that eats out our very souls—if indeed we even dare to acknowledge it is there.

Still—piercing the centuries—the gentle voice of Christ pursues us with the beatitudes.

The First Beatitude

"Blessed are the poor in spirit, for theirs is the kingdom of heaven." To be poor in spirit does not mean to give up all things and embrace holy poverty with one swoop. Nor is this meant for priests and religious only. No. It is a beatitude for *all of us*, for it detaches our hearts from earthly possessions and places them into Christ's Sacred Heart.

To be poor in spirit simply means that we understand well that we are but *stewards* of our earthly goods, and the Lord is the owner thereof. It means that all the goods that are over and above our necessities (food, clothing, shelter, education, provisions against sickness and old age) belong to our brothers and sisters in need—belong to them *in justice*, not in charity.

Such worldly goods as we have help us to fulfill the obligations of our state in life, and should be enjoyed fully and used for the glory of God. But should he take these away, we will neither miss them, nor pine for them, for our lives are rooted in the most holy will of God, and it alone. Joyously we fulfill it—with a free and detached heart.

To be poor in spirit, to be detached, to live according to God's will, means simply to be happy, at peace, and full of love and hope.

19 The Second Beatitude

An old priest died. Among his papers was found an ordinary card on which was written, "Every time I look at me, I seem to see only me. Please, Lord, kick me out of me, so that you may find some room for you in me." The people sorting his papers remarked that these few sentences summed up the whole life of this gentle man. He had permitted the Lord to take full possession of him. He had become selfless.

Selflessness! That is the key word for the restoration of the world to Christ. It is part of that new kingdom which he gives us himself in a few simple words: "Blessed are the meek, for they shall possess the land."

This second beatitude is closely related to the first, for while to be poor in spirit is a passive state, it also means to be full of Christ. And to be full of Christ means also to be active—working with him, by him, for him. Therefore this second beatitude opens a large field to us. Nothing less than the *whole world* to win for Christ! And it is the meek, the gentle, the kind who are going to do it. But we cannot be any of these things until we are selfless—for how can we be kind to others until we have put selfishness away? Let us, then, begin today on this eviction of self so as to make room for Christ.

20 The Third Beatitude

"Blessed are they that mourn, for they shall be comforted." Never before have we needed to meditate on this beatitude as much as we do now, for this is the time to mourn over our sins.

Yes, this is the acceptable time to mourn over our sins. To do penance and to pray. To fast. To wear sackcloth and ashes—if not factually at least spiritually. For if we Catholics, who are supposed to be "the salt of the earth," are to restore the world to Christ, then we must do so with clean souls, clean minds, clean hands.

This is the time for all of us to make this third beatitude our own. We must realize what a tragedy mortal sin is. By it, we lose God. A mortal sin cuts us off from his friendship, with a sharp cut. We stand alone. And how insignificant, how small are we without God. So let us meditate and ask the Lord for tears of repentance to wash the stain of all sin from our souls.

To sin mortally is to move from light into darkness, and lose one's way. That is what has happened to our generation. We must mourn—really mourn—before the Lord for the sins of our brothers and sisters the world over. If we do this, offering ourselves as holocausts for them, then (as he promised) we shall be comforted. Not only in heaven but even here on earth.

21 | The Fourth Beatitude

"Blessed are they who hunger and thirst for justice, for they shall be satisfied." Here is the answer to our search for peace, the fruit of justice. And for happiness. And for all the things our hungry human hearts cry out for in the night of our atomic age.

To be hungry and thirsty for justice—true justice—means to be hungry and thirsty for God himself. It means to see him in our fellow men and women, and to try to assuage that burning hunger, that all-consuming thirst, in being *just* to all.

True justice walks in charity, whose other name is love; walks firmly but softly, remembering always that—though theologically, charity precedes justice—sociologically, justice precedes charity. As the Holy Father says, "Charity cannot take over until justice has had her fill."

Can you imagine the social revolution this beatitude would bring, if Christians practiced it? Like the fire of the love of God, from which it came, justice would sweep the world. It would change the social order, bring peace and happiness, convert our enemies, make others whole again, and restore Christ's inheritance to him. It would also make our salvation sure, for we will be satisfied, says the Lord. And only God can satisfy a human heart. Imagine eternity with him. Isn't that what we were created for?

22 | The Fifth Beatitude

"Blessed are the merciful, for they shall obtain mercy." What an awesome and consoling sentence! Awesome because of the implication of what will happen if we are *not* merciful: we shall face the full justice of God, untempered by his mercy.

This beatitude is ours, or it should be, in this crazy atomic twentieth century, when people calmly discuss the utter destruction of their fellow creatures. There seems to be no rhyme nor reason to it all. Yet... the signposts of Christ are clearly marked on the road of life.

Blessed are the merciful, for they shall obtain mercy. What is clearer, simpler than that?

Let us stop for a moment—forget the mad pursuit of a security that is not to be found on earth—forget the driving urge for perishable goods—forget, above all, *ourselves*. Let us begin to think of God, and of the quality of mercy that will bring us face to face with him tomorrow and give peace to our hectic todays.

Having meditated prayerfully on this beatitude, let us make it our own in daily living. Remembering that mercy extends far and wide into the social fabric of our lives and that of our brothers and sisters in Christ, let us start now, being merciful, and then rest in peace, his peace that no one can take away. If we do, we shall obtain mercy.

23 The Sixth Beatitude

"Blessed are the pure of heart, for they shall see God." Many think this beatitude refers only to chastity or virginity. But it takes in all who walk the earth in holy simplicity, who shun sin because they love God and realize the price the Lord paid to ransom us from its dark embrace, and so keep their hearts pure for him to rest in.

Think of it. *Holy simplicity.* Two words that would solve so many big problems. To walk in holy simplicity through life means to trust implicitly in God. To trust in God is to be free from worries, to be mentally healthy, joyous, and happy in all circumstances and conditions.

To be free from sin—because one is in love with Love, because one really and truly shudders at the sign of a crucifix, the emblem of Love dying for our sins—is to look at life with the eyes of God. It is to choose always the "better part"... his part. And that means, in everyday terms, to be well-balanced, to have real security, that of today on this earth, and that of tomorrow in eternity.

To have a pure conscience is to walk unafraid, free from the fears that beset humanity. A Catholic in the state of grace walks in the glory of the Lord; he or she is a temple of the Holy Trinity, a companion to the mother of Christ and all the saints. Such a one is surrounded by choirs of angels and archangels. How can fear dwell anywhere near such glory?

24 The Seventh Beatitude

Christ's constant refrain of peace swells into a mighty song in this beatitude: "Blessed are the peacemakers, for they shall be called the children of God."

Of all the qualities of his kingdom, our Lord seemed to have liked peace the best. It was his universal and tenderest greeting: "Peace be to you!" "Have peace among you." "My peace I leave you, my peace I give unto you." The Gospels are full of this tender, warm little word that does not simply mean the absence of strife, but so much more, for its real meaning is happiness.

Peace is right *within* us. To find her, we must arise and, turning our faces *inward*, go into the very depths of our own souls, where God indwells. It is a long journey, and dark, so we must take with us the lamp of love to light our path, for where love is, God is, and where God is, peace is, and the fruit of peace is happiness.

He who has real happiness, real peace, is indeed a child of God. But before any one of us can attain this peace, he or she must make peace with God, thus being also at peace with oneself. And such an individual must share this, the fruit of grace, with the whole world, becoming that synonym for a Christian, a peacemaker.

Lord, have mercy on us! Give us the grace to be at peace with you, with ourselves, and with our neighbors.

25 | The Eighth Beatitude

Listen! The Man of Sorrows speaks, he in whom all the beatitudes had their complete fulfillment, he who died on a cross to redeem us from our sins: "Blessed are they who suffer persecution for justice' sake, for theirs is the kingdom of heaven." He makes pain the condition of union with him. "If any man will come after me, let him deny himself, take up his cross and follow me." Suffering was the measure of *his* love for us, and suffering was to be the measure of our love for *him!*

All of us who have loved know that love is pain. Perhaps the world today is in such chaos because so few really love. Fear of pain has become almost morbid. We run from it as fast as our puny, spindly spiritual legs can carry us. Husband and wife divorce at the slightest pinprick of pain, mothers leave children, children seek escape in ways that bring about vandalism and juvenile delinquency.

But Lady Pain is beautiful. Her face reflects God's for she was his constant companion. And it was at the foot of the cross that her white garments were dyed crimson in his Blood.

To love is to bear witness to someone or something. To love God is to bear witness to him. But his kingdom is at war with the kingdom of the world which belongs to Satan. Where there is war, there is pain. Especially in a war where Love fights hate. And we must all wage this war or perish.

26 | Boredom

Today I would like to discuss boredom. Do you know what boredom is? It is a kind of *death* in a human being. It means that people have let their interior resources dry up and have reached a sort of coma akin to death. Their motivation is at an absolutely low ebb. Boredom is the forerunner of many emotional problems.

But when we are in love with God, it is *impossible* to be bored! Those who are bored have ceased to love or are in danger of ceasing to be *in love*. How is it possible to be bored when we believe, as St. Paul said, we can make up what is "wanting" in the sufferings of Christ? In his infinite mercy, God calls us to become co-redeemers of the world with him! We are co-redeemers with Christ! He has given us an immense power! So our grayish routine isn't gray at all, but resplendent with light—at least it is in our power to make it so.

How does this work in our daily lives? A secretary who "offers up" the tiring task of hitting those typewriter keys is co-redeeming the world with Christ. Cooks making stew, men doing chores, driving trucks, doing repairs—all can save souls from the jaws of hell! How in the name of the All-Holy can you be bored with this typing, cooking, repairing when—in faith—you know everything helps to redeem the world and to render glory to God.

27 Just Anger

At what point in the hidden depths of human heart and soul does "just anger" begin? At what point does a Christian lift the cords of that anger to chase the moneylenders out of the temple?

I personally know the terrible storms of anguish when just anger shakes a person. I knew it in the slums of Toronto during the Depression, when the poor went hungry while a Catholic audience to whom I lectured at a swanky hotel ate rich and costly food. I knew when I used words like cords in my lectures on social justice and, upon returning to my bedbug-infested room in Harlem, was tempted to use the talents of my words to arouse the Blacks to violence. I am still filled with this just anger, because the face of poverty and injustice is still everywhere—in the rural slums, among the minorities, in the under-developed countries. How long can Christians watch the poor being ground into the dust by the rich?

I have only one answer for myself: unceasing prayer, fasting, and a *fiat* to God to remain crucified on the cross of tense, just anger. I feel safe on that strange wooden cross. For he who is nailed to it cannot succumb to the temptation of violence, for temptation it really is. A crucified person can only hang there, and slowly die for those with whom he or she identifies.

28 St. Augustine, Doctor of the Church
Peace Comes through Silence

There is unpeace in our hearts. Why? Because we are not silent. We have not lifted our hearts to God. We have not communicated with him. We have not taken that inner counsel with the other, that strange counsel that flows from the union of love.

How many of us are silent enough to be able to really listen to another? Peace is a way of listening to others. When one is really listening while another is talking, they begin to understand each other. We don't know how to listen because we have no inner peace, no inner silence of mind and heart. Silence is the way to peace and it flows from love. Only those who are capable of loving can be silent.

It is not easy to be silent. We begin our journey inward to meet God who dwells within us. Jesus said that his Father and the Holy Spirit would come and dwell within us. That's what the journey inward is all about. Once we meet the Trinity, then our silent communication with them will transform us into the icon of Christ. Icon means image. We shall bring forth out of the depth of silence—out of this silent communication—the likeness of God. Isn't this what all our hearts hunger for? It is. This is what we really crave. St. Augustine has said that our hearts are restless until they rest in God.

29 | Silence: Our Key to God's Secrets

We need to become the icons of Christ, because what does the world need most of all? It needs to touch God. I used to ask my mother, "Mommy, how can I touch Jesus?" She said, "Touch me." In my own silence and in the silence of others I will realize that I can touch Jesus. Silence is the key to many secrets of God. Why don't we ask him to give us this key?

True silence is always restful. Silence is a cradle. It was the cradle of the incarnation. There was a great and awesome silence when God was born. If we continue our inward journey, we too can become cradles for the child. We must make cradles of our hearts for any who wish to come and rest in them like children.

There is no man or woman living who deep down doesn't long to become a child. Jesus expressed this secret longing when he said, "Unless you become as little children, you shall not enter the kingdom of heaven." This is why my favorite prayer is, "Lord, give me the heart of a child and the awesome courage to live it out as an adult."

Silence is more than a cradle. It also is an inn, for the man picked up by the good Samaritan after he was besieged by robbers. Who of us is not besieged by robbers? Who of us does not need the inn of silence, rest, and peace of another's heart? That is what silence can do when we understand that it is the quickest way to peace and communication.

30 Teach Us How to Pray

If the question were asked, "What is the one thing needed for the success of the church's mission?" the answer would be contemplative prayer. This answer would not be understood in our secular society. But prayer must become an integrated part of our daily lives, the most important part! But in order to have this happen, the whole approach of "teaching" in the broadest sense must be changed. In the home, in the school, in the parish, *prayer* must be given full and first place.

Every third-grader knows that prayer is lifting up one's mind and heart to God. But there are many ways of lifting. It begins with vocal prayer, the one all of us are so familiar with. Then it goes on to mental prayer and meditation, a prayer that all too many people are *unfamiliar* with. This "lifting" also includes the prayer of silence, the prayer of the heart, and contemplative prayer, unknown to still more people.

How many of us have been taught to pray? Why this defect on the part of our teachers? Could it be that they themselves do not know how to pray? You who are appointed by God as our teachers—you fathers and mothers of families, you religion teachers in our schools, colleges, and universities, you parish priests, retreat masters—teach us how to know God better, teach us how to love, *teach us how to pray.*

31 Learning

My father said that a year in which a person learns nothing is a year wasted. Knowledge of any kind is useful and absolutely necessary, but there is something bigger, something greater— great as the horizon and so incredible that no words can encompass it. It is the study of the spiritual life, or spiritual things, which is the crown of all knowledge and of all natural learning.

One must always remember that *grace works on nature.* The diet of pietistic spirituality that we used to have disrupted this order and did not allow grace to work to the fullness of its depth.

In my estimation, there is nothing secular in the world, for the world has been created by God—touched by God—and so is sacred. Our ancestors used to divide it into the sacred and the profane. But I cannot imagine anything created by God as being profane. Therefore, I repeat, all things are sacred to me.

My passionate desire is for you to develop to the fullness of your capacity and talents. These talents may be latent and you may have to dig for them, but you must overcome every difficulty to develop them. It is worth everything to enlarge your natural horizons so as to allow the supernatural ones to have room to grow and expand. In other words, *to give Christ room*, not only to grow to his full stature in you, but to have a place within you to roam as he may wish, a place for him to breathe and stretch.

September

1 Teaching

The way to teach is by being. That is to say, you don't teach the spirit except by example. And so, to restore one to God and to oneself, a teacher has to lead students to the Lord. To do so, the one who is appointed to be teacher must him or herself become an icon of Christ. I remember my parents were.

The very essence of your vocation—which is glorious, even if it seems hidden and humble—is to love God passionately by loving others. God loved us first, and that is what our faith is all about. We must respond to that love and love him back! To love God passionately is to die to self. We allow ourselves to be crucified on the other side of his cross, and then our vision is the whole world, as seen from that cross.

We must constantly seek to expand our vision, review the means to our goal, and choose the ones that best fit our fast-changing times. We must be flexible and open to change, never set in our ways. Flexibility must be prepared for by observing, thinking, research, prayer, and by "folding the wings of our intellect" and letting *God* tell us what he wishes our work to be.

At one time God may ask us to forget we have a Ph.D. and wash dishes. At another time he may ask us to use that Ph.D. Scholars and scientists who pray as well as study can transform their "ivory towers" into "upper rooms" from which a great wind and tongues of fire can fall.

2 | Intellectual Learning and Spiritual Wisdom

I remember growing up in Europe, where no one sought learning for the sake of degrees, nor for earning high salaries. Knowledge, generally speaking, was sought for its own sake.

I remember my father blessing us for grade school and throughout the years. "May the Holy Spirit overshadow you, child, so that you may understand that all knowledge must be used for the glory of God and the service of your fellowmen."

I am not at all against intellectuals. I am, believe it or not, an intellectual myself! But in the 1930s, when I began working with the poor in the slums of Toronto, I realized that I had to "fold the wings of my intellect" indefinitely. There would be no time to satisfy the hunger of serious learning or opportunities to enjoy the company of other people with intellectual interests. Yet I was an adult, hungry for intellectual companionship, for books, and study. I did not realize how terribly hard it would be! Then, later, the Lord seemed to smile and I was catapulted into lecturing, writing, studying, and exchanging thoughts with others. It was then that I understood that I had been through the highest school of learning—God's School of Love. I began to see that if we give up our intellect to God, at his request, he will return it to us cleansed of all that is not of him. And our secular and spiritual knowledge will become new and powerful in him.

3 | The Vision of the Whole

The "vision of the whole" is really staggering. Through the motley crowd that we are, filled as we are with all sorts of emotional and other wounds, the Lord wishes to restore his church. Perhaps "restore" is too big a word. But nevertheless, it seems he is molding us, shaping us, healing us, blessing us, guiding us toward this end.

In proportion to our service and our faith, we will grow in the love of Christ until the "I" in us is blotted out and each of us, utterly penetrated by Christ, will become one with him. God wants a totality of love from each of us.

We must be careful not to evaluate ourselves and our work on activity more than on spirit. We need to take care that we are not living in a deadly routine of work. Work is prayer, true. But we should not be satisfied simply with work accomplished. Action should be the fruit of the Spirit. Our greatest contribution to all work that we undertake for God is our being united to Christ inwardly, to contemplate him in the depths of our souls.

As we love Christ in our neighbor, everywhere and always, he will draw us to himself. For our vocation is to be contemplatives, to contemplate God in the depth of our souls, even as we go about our daily routines. *It is given to us to touch him, converse with him, serve him—in others. Christ always comes to us in others.*

4 Rock Collecting

I think it was God who got me interested in rocks. It all started with my constant interest in everything pertaining to nature. Walking one day up a wooded path, I found several beautiful rocks, brought them home, and wondered what they were. I had had a smattering of mineralogy, but decided it was time to learn more. With the help of a friend who was the Minister of Mines, I received more rocks for a collection, learned their names, and then subscribed to magazines about rocks and what can be made from them. I sensed that rock collecting shows us a tremendous and interesting dimension of nature. My husband Eddie loved to collect rocks.

Today at Madonna House we have a lovely library on mineralogy and rock collecting. We even have a cabin to house our rock collection. I have always believed in emphasizing the spiritual, and I look for saints to help. St. Stephen was stoned to death with rocks, and like Christ, he forgave his enemies while they were killing him. We decided to call our cabin for the rock collection St. Stephen's.

If ever you deal with rocks, be like a rock in your faith and remember that the Lord is an eternal Rock. Christ said, "Unless the house is built on a rock, it will not stand firm." The Rock, of course, is Christ.

Thoughts on a Certain Manual Laborer

We were discussing work the other day, and I somehow became lost in the past of Palestine. I saw a hammer, a chisel, a hand-plane. Somehow I was utterly astounded—as if I had never thought of it before—a carpenter's shop! The challenge that it presented was beyond my ability to absorb. The Second Person of the Trinity—someone who could have been a rabbi, a king, an emperor, a man of tremendous renown, a philosopher, someone at whose feet the whole world would come to sit and listen—the awesome person was right there, bent over a workbench in that shop, chiseling and planing pieces of wood, doing little "unimportant" tasks: building a table for someone, making a cradle for somebody else, crafting a chair for another. I saw his calloused hands (for he did have calloused hands!) and I asked myself, why did he choose such humble, uninspiring, unchallenging tasks? On some side street in an unimportant village, he worked as an ordinary carpenter, just as his foster father did.

And what did his mother do? She washed and scrubbed, and took the laundry to the river, and milled the kernels of wheat manually between two stones. She wove cloth; it is said that she wove the cloak that the Romans threw dice for because it was so beautiful.

As I re-entered our discussion about work, I came back from watching Jesus doing carpenter work; and I thanked God that he became a manual laborer to show us the way to the Father.

6 | In Praise of Work

All work is holy. Through it we walk the royal road of Christ. There is no other way to God except work. The church uses the word *works* of mercy, both corporal and spiritual. These works encompass intellectual and physical labor, prayer and sacrifice. The summit of all work is the Cross of Calvary on which hung a carpenter who worked with his hands—God who worked with his perfect creative mind in a flame of love. Yes, all work is holy, but we seem to have forgotten this. Especially have we forgotten that manual labor is holy. Perhaps this is because so few of us read or pray the Psalms during these hectic days: "Let your work be seen by your servants and your glory by their children; And may the gracious care of the Lord our God be ours; prosper the work of our hands for us! Prosper the work of our hands!"

The hands of God and the hands of men and women both work—or at least *his* do! Do ours? The hands of men and women were made to work with wood and earth and steel, to glorify God through the ripple of every muscle.

Jesus, the Carpenter, bends down to us and takes our hands into his own. He feels in their roughness his own roughness. Thus, two sets of work-worn hands become entwined—one pierced with nails, the other wounded with service. They meet in utter love. Lord, help us to see the beauty, the creativeness, the joy, the power of manual work!

7 | Sacramentals

When I was a girl in old Russia, icons, medals, and other religious objects were deeply venerated both for those they represented and for the blessings that were upon them. They were "holy things," to be used reverently and lovingly.

And holy water—water blessed by God and the church—was the most powerful sacramental! Few Russians would be without it. Where is the Russian who does not believe in its potency against the devil and all the powers of darkness, in sickness and in health? If there be such a Russian, he is not any sort of Christian.

And I wonder if you realize the blessing of a vigil light? There is something about its flickering, soft light as it burns steadily before a favorite statue or icon. It makes any room or any house, be it ever so humble or ever so magnificent, truly "blessed." Perhaps this is because the light—so constant and faithful—reminds us of God and the things of God, or because we left it there as a more constant prayer than we who are so busy could give. The beloved vigil light that always burned in Russian homes brought God and Our Lady closer, making one feel secure and at peace. It still does in my home—and can in yours.

The power of God is infinite, and his blessing even on inanimate things is most powerful, especially when they are used with faith and the simplicity of utter trust. It can, and has, performed miracles.

| 8 | *Birth of Mary*
 # Mary, Patroness of Laypeople |

It occurred to me today that Mary should be the patroness of laypeople. Let's face it, she was a laywoman, lay in the fullest sense of that term. To all eyes she was the wife of a carpenter, the mother of a Son. She was a housewife who kept house, sewed, wove. Didn't she weave the seamless robe of Christ? She washed the laundry at the same pool as all the other village women. She lived with her Son, a carpenter, for an indefinite number of years, and was supported by him.

What better model, what better patroness, what better helper could ordinary lay folk have than Mary? Shouldn't we ask her help in times of turmoil, in a world filled with confusion, anxieties, and problems? I think that she must have had a harder time than we do. She probably heard rumors about her Son during his public life, not all of them flattering! So many accused him! Shouldn't Mary be, then, patroness of a laity that hears all kinds of rumors about Christ? Rumors like "Christ is not God," "Christ is only a prophet," and "God is dead."

She will give us courage to sort things out in the silence of our hearts. She will help us to grow in faith and love. I give Mary a very simple name: Mother of the People of God, patroness of laypeople.

9 | *St. Peter Claver*
Unconscious Superiority

What is our attitude toward other people? Do we feel a superiority? Do we always talk about them with grave humility? I wonder.

I want to talk about thoughtlessness concerning our conversations, attitudes, and expressions regarding minority groups. What is our attitude toward Hispanics, Asians, and Blacks? Are there now and then accents of unconscious superiority and pride? Especially when they are poor? Is there a division in our minds between us and them that is subtle, yet dangerous to our spirit?

I heard that someone said, "And do you know, you do all you can for them, give them the best, and they say nothing, or find fault and are not grateful." Frankly, this remark horrified me. That any one of us does anything for Christ in the poor and then expects Christ in the poor to be grateful! Spiritually speaking, we should kiss the feet of the poor and be grateful that Christ allows us to serve them. If we have any other ideas, we are way off base, and we have neither charity nor common sense.

I have said what I wanted to say. I leave the rest to the Holy Spirit, and to your examination of conscience. None of us can say, "Not guilty." Let us do away with this thoughtlessness and uncharitableness.

10 The Tragedy of Conformity

The majority of North Americans are very much bound by this tragic attitude: "What will the neighbors think?" They are conformists to the depths of their beings. This is what is responsible for so many of our emotional problems, because at the bottom of conformity lies insecurity and a sickly need of approval at all costs.

See how you are still bound by styles: there is little originality regarding hair or clothes. You really wish to be like everybody else. You are still subject to the need for conformity.

But saints (and you are supposed to be saints-in-the-making) are the most original, individualistic, adventuresome people in the world. As you get to know the lives of the saints, note how no two of them are alike. The Lord loves diversity in unity! If we can compare the saints to a garden of flowers in which he takes delight, I personally imagine that he would be very bored if the garden were all lilies, all roses, or all any one type of flower. The beauty of a garden is its diversity, its originality, its individuality. So it is with the minds, bodies, and hearts of the saints.

I've been thinking lately that we are commissioned by God to bring variety, holy individuality, originality, and a spirit of adventure into a world that is robot-like in its conformity.

11 The Beauty of Diversity

We must take the cords of love and, like Christ, chase conformity out of the temples of human souls—chase it in firmness and gentleness and love, but chase it nevertheless. Yet first we must smash conformity within our own minds, souls, and hearts. This is a task for each person.

Let us be adventuresome in eating foreign foods, especially

when we travel. Let us be adventuresome in our appearance. Let us be adventuresome, individualistic, and experimental in seeking out hobbies and creative outlets. Our soul will perish without creativity, for it is one of the basic human needs.

Let us be adventuresome and individualistic in proclaiming the truths of God. One must speak differently to kids on skid row than to undergraduates in college. Let us become all things to all men and women, without fear and trembling. Let us be original in our sanctity, our prayers, our efforts to go to God. Let us share the wealth we find with one another.

Let us plunge into the depths of God's love and come forth a new man, a new woman, with ideas and thoughts that will enrich the church by our individuality. Let us not be afraid to think, to seek answers to our questions. Let us be different, bringing forth the talents that God has given to each of us. Let us conform to one thing only: let us all love God daily more and more, together.

* For more explanation on what Catherine Doherty means about the beauty of diversity, especially in applying this wisdom to daily life, please see Appendix Four.

12 Dispossession

Dispossession—what a strange word. Today it is haunting many Christians who are looking for the face of Christ. Dispossession. The Greeks had a different word for this same idea. They called it *kenosis,* which means "self-emptying."

All over the Western world, men and women are trying to dispossess themselves of their many goods and possessions in order to follow their visions. It appears that the modern conscience cannot stand anymore the disparity between rich and poor.

So begins the strange pilgrimage of today's youth. They travel across land and sea, often with only a roll of bedding and a knapsack. Restless feet. Longing souls. Hungry hearts. They seek to dispossess themselves—not to have anything, searching for God, for mystical experiences, for some escape from their intolerable pain.

It is time that we examine this hunger for dispossession, for it is often a hunger inspired by the Holy Spirit. Yes, the wind and the fire of the Holy Spirit are abroad today. Dispossession haunts many Christians who are looking for the face of Christ. The basic thing we have to dispossess ourselves of is our self-centeredness and our selfishness—individually, collectively, nationally, internationally. The world cannot remain divided between haves and have-nots. It is time for the haves to become for a while the have-nots, so as to know what it is to be hungry, to be tired, to have no place to stay.

It is time to face ourselves, to get rid of anything in us which impedes us from becoming brothers and sisters to one another. This is the real goal of all the travail of modern youth. This is what they are seeking in all their attempts at dispossession.

13 | *St. John Chrysostom, Doctor of the Church*
The Need Not to Have

The Gospel is addressed to all—monk, nun, lay person, married or single. St. John Chrysostom reminds us that the monk and the lay person must attain the same heights of holiness. This Father of the Church goes on to say, "When Christ orders us to follow the narrow path, he addresses himself to all men."

A wealth that belongs to all Christians, then, is evangelical poverty. When we discuss poverty from the point of view of Scripture, we must plunge into the depths of the human soul and the Gospel. Russian theologian Paul Evdokimov said, "Absence of the need to have... becomes *the need not to have*." Here is the very essence of poverty—spiritual, physical, and emotional.

Are we filled with this need not to have? Are we cleansing ourselves and our houses of all the extra things we really don't need? Are we in search of simple lifestyles, or are we cluttering up our apartments with a thousand gadgets which only add to our feverish activity? Are we filled with the cleansing fire which strips us of all that is unnecessary? And I don't mean only physically. Physical poverty is only kindergarten in the school of poverty. It is but a plowed field preparing itself for that beautiful seed which is true poverty of spirit.

When the need not to have really begins to take root in the heart, then we have come to the essence of poverty.

14 | *Triumph of the Cross* | Glorying in the Cross

I cannot visualize a love story with God without a cross. To me the cross is *the thing!* I desire it. I accept it. And I ask the grace never to fear it, because at the end, I shall know its joy.

You think maybe that I am just talking through my hat. But with God as my witness, I look at the cross as the marriage bed of Christ! It is *union* with him, at the price of being crucified. Then, though my flesh flinches, my soul cries out, "Where are the nails? Where is the hammer?" You get that picture? Or is that too high-falutin'?

Of course the cross is there for you! When I talk about the cross, you see, I think that you misunderstand what I mean by the cross. For me, the cross is the key to him whom my heart loves. Without the cross there is no Easter. Unless I lie on that cross, I can't see him in heaven. And I must lie on the cross that he made for me, not the one I am making for myself.

God embraced the cross! He wanted it! For this he was born! And for this we are born—to lie on it with him.

When you see your lifetime of little things and say you can't take it, I want to weep. Because that's not understanding our faith! Never see your life as a lot of little things, monotonous and so forth. Think of it as the glory of the cross.

15 Our Lady of Sorrows
Our Mother in Anguish

We who believe in Christ, we who suffer, who are in anguish and anxiety, we should stand with Mary under the cross. We will find, through her, the courage to keep believing and to stand still while the church, the bride of Christ, bleeds from a thousand wounds. We should turn to Mary, who held her Son in her arms, in order to find the strength to bear the burdens which tear the souls of Christians apart.

We have a Mother who understands, because, before he died, Jesus handed her over to John, the well-beloved disciple, to become his mother—and ours. She not only understands, but she loves both sinners and saints, and holds them in her arms and makes saints out of sinners.

If we do turn to her, she will lead us to his resurrection and show us the essence of an unshakeable faith. She will give us the courage to sort things out in the silence of our hearts. She will help us to grow in faith and in love and to follow her Son as she did.

Yes, Mary is a profound mystery of consolation. If we turn to this woman wrapped in silence, she will speak to us. The one through whom God came to us will lead us back to him.

16 A Production Mentality

Production is the great heresy of the North American continent, of its culture and its spirituality. By production we mean that we value ourselves *exclusively* by the tangible goods that we can produce for society. We tend to estimate our self-worth by the amount of these goods works that we can achieve. Truly, this is a poor way to evaluate a living human being who is created in the image and likeness of God.

Many saints were often utterly "nonproductive" members of the Mystical Body of Christ. Gemma Galgani, a twentieth-century saint, spent much of her life confined to bed, suffering for the church and the people of God. That was her joy, her "loving service."

Insane or psychotic persons; the blind, the lame, the retarded and the Mongoloid are useless to and despised by the world in general. According to the measuring scale of "good works" these people are not only unproductive, they are considered a "burden" on the productive ones. Such thoughts are but a further extension of the heresy of production. But in the economy of Christianity, in the reality of God's love for human beings, these afflicted ones, far from being parasites, are the beloved ones of God and holocausts of love for us. If we had an ounce of sense, we would "hold onto the hem of their garments" in order to be carried by them into heaven!

17 | Productionitis—Workaholism

The pressures of work can push us into a production mentality. Unfortunately, into this picture comes another element— one I call "productionitis" or workaholism.

From childhood on, we measure our self-worth by the reflection of that worth in the eyes of those who matter, meaning that we value ourselves the way that we are valued by others. If "those who matter" did not give us our true value, our true dignity as children of God, then our self-esteem is very poor and we have to *prove to ourselves* and to the world that we have some use, some value, some shred of dignity. We seek to prove it by our production. This is the disease of "productionitis" or workaholism.

So many of us find "escape" in work and in production, escape from our own tensions and our own emotions. So many of us still have a very low opinion of ourselves, so we measure ourselves by the amount of "more strenuous" work or "longer hours" of work we do. Add to this the way the world evaluates the specific *type* of work done, and the idea of *status* develops in us. This makes the chains of misery grow, and our human dignity is destroyed further.

But, by the very essence of the Gospels that we try to preach with our lives, we must spiritually and intellectually reject this mentality as a terrible heresy. We must wage war on this heresy.

18 | War on "Productionitis"

We have to use all our insights and really start an all-out *war* against "productionitis" and the workaholism mentality that is so inbred in us by the culture of the North American continent. I have tried to combat "productionitis" for years.

Here are some areas that need to be attacked, some "battle stations" in this war:

- Face yourself honestly; see yourself through the eyes of God, your loving Father. In the light of what you know about Scripture, liturgy, theology, salvation history, re-evaluate your dignity and self-worth.
- Look at the world around you; see how and where its "production mentality" has invaded your intellectual attitudes.
- Arrive at a basic truth: that your own "personhood" and the people around you are more important than "things" and "actions."
- Learn to accept the normal frustration of putting *people before things*. This may mean that you will have quite a few unfinished or half-finished jobs "left hanging." Develop the ability to peacefully bear with this situation.

19 More "War Plans"

Here are more plans to wage war on the heresy of "productionitis" or workaholism:

So many of us rationalize the things "needed" for the common good. We tell ourselves that we must fulfill our obligations by being useful. While we are being "useful" we also are trying to be charitable and loving, of course, but the major accent of our work is still on its usefulness.

Therefore, keep a watch over your heart; continually clarify the intentions you find within it. See clearly when your production is motivated by the need of charity and when it isn't. Any form of "loving service" will have an aura of peace and joy about it. But the heresy of measuring human worth against the amount of work produced can only create in people the "joyous" frenzy of hell.

At the same time, study carefully your work methods, looking for any slackness or inefficiency. Constantly review your routines and techniques for "getting things done" each day. The use of time is God's greatest gift to each of us, and it must not be wasted.

To know when to work hard, to know when to stop working at a moment's notice, to know how to accept peacefully the frustration of a hundred unfinished jobs because people (and situations connected with people) come before things—all this takes wisdom and charity. And, I think, sanctity.

20 The Church and I

I have always loved the church. This is a very strange statement to make: all Christians should love the church. But from earliest childhood I have had a deep, deep feeling for her. As a child, the building itself attracted me. I would just walk in and sit down. Sometimes I collected flowers and strewed them in front of the iconostasis or the holy doors. In a Catholic church I used to climb the altar steps and lay flowers in front of what I called the "little house," the tabernacle.

When I was a small girl I didn't know much about the Stations of the Cross, but I loved to walk along and follow the pictures. I was always very sorry that Jesus Christ had had such a tough time! I remember once collecting all the crucifixes my mother had and taking Jesus off each one! In school I used a small ladder to reach the bloody feet of Jesus. I scrubbed the red paint off! The Sisters were terribly incensed, and wanted to know who had done it. They gathered all the children and asked "Who did it?" In front of everybody, I walked up and said "I did." They asked why. I said, "I couldn't stand to see him with all those nails and all that blood. I just wanted to make him more comfortable." I wasn't punished!

In church buildings, I sensed what people call a "presence," and it held a very deep attraction for me. Through it, God was laying in me the foundation for something else.

21 | *First Day of Autumn*
The Church: Bride of Christ

As I grew up I began to understand the Christian idea of the church. I began to realize who and what the church was. I saw that the church was the spotless bride of Christ. I saw her clad in the King's robes, beautiful and glorious. This vision stayed in my heart like a warm, consoling thought and I applied to the church that beautiful passage from the Psalms, "The king's daughter is decked in her chamber with gold-woven robes: in many-colored robes she is led to the king" (Psalm 45:13-14). The church was something holy, precious, something you should even give your life for.

In Canada I discovered that the church was the people of God. It took me a long time to understand that the people of God was the Mystical Body of Christ, and that Christ was the head of this body. Why didn't I understand? Because of sin, the terrible sins of the people of God. I was torn by a contradiction: This sinless bride of Christ was also the sinful bride of Christ! How could that be? It took me a long time to understand a very simple thing—that Jesus came to reconcile us sinners with his Father. As Dostoevsky wrote, "He loved man in his sin." God had rescued us from our sin. The whole picture of the church was now completed for me. I understood something else: The sin of one member of the church was the sin of all; that is, if I sin, I affect the whole church.

22 | The Church: A Reality of Faith

I have seen ruined churches in Russia, Spain, and Germany. Even in them, I experienced the "presence" of God, experienced in my body the awesomeness of the church's spiritual nature. It has shaken my whole being. At those moments I understood why the Lord calls himself the bridegroom. I can't explain it. But I understood one glorious day that he was *my* bridegroom, and that I was part of his people, part of his flock, part of his Mystical Body. I understood the mystery of the church. I still live with this mystery.

When a person falls in love with God, then the church becomes a reality of faith. This cannot be explained rationally. The head must enter the heart, close its eyes, and adore a reality which can only be embraced in faith. I walked into that reality, that mystery, not knowing that I was walking in faith.

To walk into the mystery of the church is also to walk into the mystery of the priesthood. The priest, whether he wishes to acknowledge it or not, is Christ. Before Jesus ascended into heaven, he said that we would not be orphans and, through his priests, he gives us the Eucharist, so we might feed on him. Yes,

Christ is the bridegroom, and every man and woman is his bride—all men and women together. He wishes to introduce each one of us to his Father. He who drinks his Blood and eats his Flesh becomes known to the Father in the most intimate fashion, as the bride becomes known to her husband.

23 Our Journey Inward

A leaf drifted lazily, golden against the blue autumnal sky. Slowly, it fell on the quiet water of a garden pool. It floated gracefully, a tiny speck of color on the mirror of the heavens. This is the first memory I have of "being." I was then four. It was autumn in Russia. The pool was in a public park to which my nurse had taken me.

Now, many years later, I often think of the first, strange moment in our human existence when we first realize that *we are*. It is an awesome moment. It is the conscious beginning of our journey of life, which, for all of us, should be a *journey inward* to meet the God who dwells within us.

For what does all else matter? All else but that search for God is as nothing. Human existence is to live in his presence, now by faith, and constantly to strengthen the arms of that faith, so that they may gradually become strong enough to part the heavy curtains that separate us earthbound humans from him, so that even in this life our souls may know union with him. To be possessed by God, to surrender to him utterly, completely, so that even before death one may say with St. Paul, "I live now, not I, but Christ lives in me"; to do this because one is passionately in love with him, because one's soul is filled with but one desire—to make him loved and known by others—that, to me, is *life*, the *journey inward* all men and women must undertake if they want to become one with the Triune God who dwells in our souls.

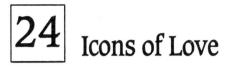

Icons of Love

The theologians spoke in learned words. Chastity, they said, was continency. It was aloof. It kept itself apart. It lived on pinnacles, snowy white, difficult of access, reached by few. They pondered further amidst austere, cold rooms of ancient cities and "comfy" ones of new metropolises. They took chastity apart and when they were done, they put it back together again. It seemed so lusterless, so cold, dead somehow, perhaps from too much handling.

A prostitute was strolling down the street, mascara'd eyes were kind and painted mouth tender, soft—the swaying body, young. A small child came up to her and said, "You smell so nice. I like you." The girl blushed and bent to kiss the little face, so pure, so innocent. The kiss was chastity itself. It shone like blinding light.

A happy, singing, pony-tailed woman-child was walking by. She sang a jazzy song. A man stopped, turned and followed her, his heart full of lust. But then she turned. He looked into her eyes and quickly walked on, for chastity had smiled at him in the fullness of its purity.

A mother of a brood came next, heavy of body and step, burdened with a lot of bags and one infant, chubby, heavy. Men smiled and women too, for chastity was passing by, fruitful and full.

The theologians did not know the face of chastity, for they had cut her up to see what made her tick.

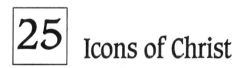

Icons of Christ

Christians are called to become icons of Christ, to reflect him. *Icon* is Greek for "image of God." We are called to incarnate him in our lives, to clothe our lives with him, so that men and women can see him in us, touch him in us, recognize him in us.

When we don't live the Gospel without compromise (or do not try to) we are skeletons. People do not care to deal with skeletons. The Gospel can be summed up by saying it is the tremendous, tender, compassionate, gentle, extraordinary, explosive, revolutionary law of Christ's love.

He calls us *directly* and there is no compromise in his call: "Whoever is not with me is against me.... If you love me, keep my commandments." We can find umpteen quotations in the Gospel that will vividly bring forth to our minds and hearts how simply and insistently he calls us to be like him, and to accept his law of love without compromise.

His call is revolutionary, one that would change the world in a few months if we implemented it. The Gospel is radical, and Christ indeed is the root from which springs all things. His commandments mean risk, great risk. They imply a lack of security, humanly speaking. Yes, God offers us risk, danger, and a strange insecurity that leads to perfect security.

26 | The Gospel Is Risky Business

The security to which most people cling is mere illusion. We are not secure walking big city streets. In planes we never know if we'll stay up or not. Wars flare up in almost every part of the world. So where is that security everybody is supposed to value so dearly? God doesn't give us this material security. Instead he offers faith... which begins, in a sense, where reason ends.

God's security begins when we start loving him with our whole heart, our whole mind, our whole soul—and our neighbor as ourselves. I speak of this so often, but it is the only message that can never be overstressed. We must clothe the skeletons of our lives with the flesh of his love, or we shall perish.

For this kind of loving we have the Holy Spirit in us. With his help, we will have the courage to risk loving our neighbor. It's a tremendous risk, because we must also love our enemies. We have the power to change them into friends and beloved neighbors. To love one's neighbor is the ultimate risk, for it may even mean death for my brother or sister's sake if need be.

All this sounds idealistic and unobtainable, but Christ assures us it *is* attainable. Through little steps day after day, one slowly accepts the other as he or she is, and begins to love totally, tenderly, compassionately. Once begun, the involvement becomes deeper and deeper and deeper.

27 Celibacy for the Kingdom

Celibacy is the absence of sexual relations between men and women. It is the relinquishing of one of the most precious things that human beings have—the power of procreating, begetting, nurturing children.

Perhaps the young priest, the night before his ordination, sees the children that will never be born from his seed, the woman who will never lie at his side. Perhaps the nun has similar thoughts; and we here at Madonna House, I'm sure we do. But then we look this gift straight in the eye, and we lift it up to the Lord like a chalice.

Of course, sex will be with us till the day we die. Sex was created by God the Father and raised to tremendous heights of dignity by God the Son. It is a difficult thing to give up.

But it was difficult to hang on a rough cross for three hours too. It was difficult to be scourged, to be pushed around. Christ did that for you and me.

No one is stopping us from getting married, just as no one stops us from loving. We give it up out of love.

28 The Sacristan

Being a sacristan is one of the most shining, glowing moments of life in the church. Though it consists of doing a thousand little things, you will find great joy and peace in being a sacristan. For the sacristan is a person truly invited to the House of Nazareth to serve the Lord. Everything you touch, everything you do, is connected with him in a deep, personal, and beautiful way.

Most of your work is also connected with Our Lady because what you are doing in the chapel is preparing the things for a meal—seeing to it that everything connected with the table is spotless, clean, and orderly. The special garments worn by the priests (who represent Christ) are also your responsibility. You must know the colors for the day and see to it they are well ironed and that the slightest rip is mended.

This is also a time when you can really talk to Christ as you go about your business. It is as if he were sitting on a bench in the house of Nazareth while you go about what has to be done. You have a special closeness to him in this exceedingly holy place—use it well! And get used to him. This is the place to meet him in the depths that we all dream about.

The word "sacristan" already pertains to the "sacred." To me a sacristan is someone who has been especially invited by Christ to dwell in his house. Pray for the whole world when you are in chapel. Here especially, each step you take, each gesture that you make, is a prayer!

29 *The Archangels*
Call on the Angels for Help

It seems that you and I come together more often these days. Perhaps it is because we have so much to talk over. Often too, I see that you need to have more clarification about the spiritual life. I love to talk to you, my spiritual children, and here I am again to discuss with you the topic of angels.

I want to share something with you that Bishop Sheil of Chicago once told me about angels. I was working in the slums of the city then, and it was dangerous there. He said to me, "Catherine, have faith in the theological truth that there are angels to answer your calls and protect you. By angels, I mean the seraphim and the cherubim, angels and archangels, powers and principalities. When you are in danger, call on them, especially Sts. Michael and Gabriel and your own angel guardian, and they will come tumbling down—a power beyond your understanding."

Do *you* call on the angels? If not, you should. Sts. Michael, Gabriel, and Raphael are very powerful. Here is a prayer to St. Michael:

> *St. Michael the Archangel, defend us in battle. Be our protection against the wickedness and snares of the devil. May God rebuke him, we humbly pray, and do thou, O prince of the heavenly host, by the power of God, cast into hell Satan and all evil spirits who prowl through the world seeking the ruin of souls. Amen.*

30 | *St. Jerome, Doctor of the Church*
Confusion and Order

The enemy of tranquility in the hearts of God's people is *confusion.* A confused person cannot think straight. Today we have a tremendous number of confused Christians.

How does one get confused? By allowing disorder to enter one's mind and heart. How does one get "unconfused"? By seeking first the order of the kingdom of God. This means taking time out from activity, from "doing good" even, and entering into the great silence of the Lord.

Alone in that silence, Bible in hand, we will discover that the terrible noise inside us slowly dies away, and the voice of God will be heard. The Bible, which in Eastern spirituality is another incarnation of Christ, will speak to us in depth, and we shall clearly see which are the first items on our agenda.

Unless we do this, it is to be feared that we shall be drowned in our own inner noise of dialogues, encounters, meetings, and discussions—in which either all speak at once, or each speaks without listening much to the other.

Let us stop for a while reading what *others* say about the Bible, and let us begin in silence and solitude to read the Bible ourselves. Then, when we return to our place in the world, we will have something to say. What is even more important, we will have learned how to listen.

October

1
St. Thérèse of the Child Jesus
Little Threads of Love

I think of you there, working day in, day out, let's say in your kitchen, peeling potatoes with great love for God, in your duty of the moment. I see you there, and suddenly the very peelings are transformed into threads of silver and gold, stretched up to heaven as hosannas to glorify God! Each thread is a prayer, a glorification of God. And the angels, reverently and gently, are winding them up, weaving out of them a beautiful carpet for Our Lady's feet. I see this with the eyes of my soul, and I understand that the beauty of the threads depends on the intentions and thoughts of your heart. You have the power to turn dross into gold; but also, alas, gold into dross.

What makes the beauty of the threads and the design is charity—charity in thought, in speech, in understanding—and patience and lack of envy. To some people God gives great graces and opportunities. But you have a hidden life, a life of small things through which you can come to God in a little way, like the Little Flower St. Thérèse did. Many others do big things, their name is on everyone's lips, yet their temptations are great and often part of their reward is already obtained on this earth. Not so with you—if you walk your way, all of it is in heaven.

and are rooted in God they never go overboard in a sentimental, gushy way. Who of us doesn't feel slightly disgusted at seeing a spinster who has twenty cats in her house, lavishing on them the affection that is due people? Who of us doesn't get angry when we hear of some rich person endowing a home for cats and dogs when there are children orphaned and going hungry? You see what I am getting at? There is a right and orderly way to love cats and dogs, and there is a disorderly way which would be abhorrent to St. Francis himself!

A disordered love of animals indicates that such persons are in need of counseling! They withhold their love from human beings and lavish it upon animals because animals do not talk back, cannot hurt them, do not cause them suffering and pain. This isn't love at all, but an unhealthy caricature of what love really is. Another perversion of love is to endow an animal with human feelings. This bespeaks a lack of knowledge of animals.

Christians are lovers of all of God's creation, which—if theologically kept within the proper order of God's plan—is fine.

4

St. Francis of Assisi
St. Francis and Pain

There is much pain in life. How could it be otherwise when we are following a crucified God, whose whole incarnation (to say nothing of his crucifixion) was not exactly without pain? Consider the prayer of St. Francis of Assisi:

> *Lord, make me an instrument of your peace. Where there is hatred, let me sow love; where there is injury, pardon; where there is doubt, faith; where there is despair, hope; where there is darkness, light; and where there is sadness, joy. O Divine Master, grant that I may not so much seek to be consoled as to console; to be loved as to love; for it is in giving that we receive, it is in pardoning that we are pardoned, and it is in dying that we are born to eternal life.*

These words are a cry of pain that conveys the hurt of a soul. He is asking God *not* to be consoled, *not* to be understood, *not* to be loved. Just these few sentences are pain—terrible pain. If you pray this prayer, and mean it, you are already allowing pain to enter your soul.

But this is a beautiful pain, my friends, because it is a pain offered for the world. It is the pain of abandonment, of surrender to God. Did you really expect to have a life without pain? That is an impossibility, my dearly beloved, because it is through this pain that you share the lot of humanity. It is through this pain that you will resurrect!

5 | Love Is a "Can Do" Attitude

There was a young, married couple who had just enough money to purchase a rather dilapidated house. They bought it and moved into it. The husband was an intellectual, white-collar worker, who had never held a hammer in his hand. Somehow, through sheer necessity, he repaired, rebuilt, and remodeled the house. They were both so proud of their achievement. Their friends were amazed, knowing his former lack of ability in this area. Smilingly, they both answered: "Love can do everything. Love does such things."

Does it? Do you see what has to be done without having to have it called to your attention again and again? Do you approach work with an attitude that is eager and willing, yet humble and truthful? When you do not know how to do a job, do you candidly acknowledge that fact, but say that you are desirous of being taught?

Love is also ingenious. Take for instance, a good cook. There is a recipe that calls for five eggs, but it is wartime and there are no eggs. A good cook will make a cake without eggs. That makes of her an ingenious cook. Love does this, and it does not waste anything. It is always ingenious.

Whatever your task, do you understand that this is a job for God—a job for Love who is a person, who is Christ? Does your love do such things? Do you feel that love can do everything?

6 | Nursing— a Privileged Vocation

Nursing is one of the most privileged of vocations. To render direct service to Christ is one of the most sublime vocations a person can have. The least of his brothers and sisters are those who are ill, and no one is so dependent on the mercy of another.

Nursing should be the profession of people who are dedicated, who love the sick with a love that never ceases. Our attitude as nurses must be total, utter dedication, with no limits on our service. This is proof of our love for God. Our patients are Christ, and few people are called to touch Christ so directly and intimately.

If a nurse hesitates to do something because it is menial, she remembers the man who washed the dirty feet of his apostles. That God should wash the feet of human beings means to the nurse there is no abasement in such actions. There is, rather, a strange elevation: we go down to go up.

And don't expect gratitude! The sick are often ungrateful. A nurse does not work for gratitude; she works because Christ is sick. All she sees is *her beloved in pain.* In her memory she sees him dying on a cross for her. She thanks him that he has given her such a simple way to his heart—through the sick.

A nurse says with Christ, "I have not come to be served, but to serve." We have to look upon our vocation of nursing with great reverence.

7 | *Our Lady of the Rosary* Slender Threads of Prayer

The apparitions of the Mother of God have lately become "news" in our newspapers. It is as if Mary, the mother of us all, just cannot rest. It is as if she must advise us while there is still time. To do this, she offers us the slender threads of a rosary—an ordinary, childish thing! But is it? The Creed is our declaration of faith and allegiance to the Holy Trinity, to the commandments of God and his spouse, the church. Recite it slowly and let each word sink in—for thousands have died for these words and what they stand for. The *Our Father* is our prayer for the fellowship of men and women under the fatherhood of God, a prayer of love, trust, hope, and faith. And the *Hail Marys* are the angelic salutation that brought the incarnation and the redemption to this earth! It still does, to those who say it with their hearts as well as their lips. The repetition, slow and reverent, of these prayers, is not monotonous. It is a companion to our retracing of the life of God, his mother, and his church, a pilgrimage of love and faith. Mary continually holds out to us, her children, the slender thread of a rosary, asking that we say it, perhaps because it is as slender as she, and as strong as the God we pray to. October is the month of the rosary. Let us pray it daily, spanning the world with its slender, unbreakable strength, lifting it, lifting it up, up to the very feet of God.

8 | God-Centered Friendships

Let us think a little about friendship. Christ said in a beautiful and heart-warming sentence, "I will not call you servants any more; I will call you friends." Christ, in many ways, calls us to a friendship with himself! So friendship is a good thing, and God wants our friends to be gentle, joyful, and quiet companions for us.

True friendship can easily be defined by analyzing its goal. If you make friends with someone for your own ends, it is a wrong kind of friendship. In fact, it isn't friendship at all. It is latching onto someone for your own selfish purposes. For instance, you are lonely and "no one understands you," so you just want to gripe about many things to a particular person.

If, on the other hand, you become friends with a person in order to help each other to God, if you become friends in a mutually give-and-take spirit, then it is a good friendship. If you have something to share mutually—a love of painting or nature, for instance—it is a wonderful friendship. But remember, be open and always ready and eager to include someone else in your activities as well. Friendships should be the natural outcome of *caritas*, of love. Consider each one. Is it "I" centered, selfish? Or is it God-centered and hence unselfish? Good friendships are unselfish and open to others, sharing common interests and all that is good.

9 Our Body Prays

I want to pick up on a matter about posture at prayer, to clarify it. I notice that many of you cross your legs or sit in a slouchy position when you are at Mass. Now a Catholic should realize the awesomeness of the Mass. This is your official act of worship before Almighty God. Your posture must express outwardly what I hope you feel inwardly—reverence, adoration, worship, wholesome fear, and the realization that you are creatures before your Creator! Therefore, because of this realization (which I am sure that you have) you must participate not only with your whole mind, heart, and soul in this act of worship and adoration, but express it with your body as well. Also, you must be an example to others. It is truly a scandal for dedicated Catholics to have sloppy manners during their worship of God.

It says in Scripture, "Worship the Lord in holy attire." We all realize that we must look decent according to the time of day, and the day of the week. We should "dress up" for church—I hope—out of reverence for God. Occasionally we might come in working clothes, but these must be clean, not torn—in a word, decent. I therefore beg everyone to see that this is done.

Bodily postures at worship and appropriate attire are simply part of the good order which I so often emphasize.

10 The Church Is Not General Motors

I see the church. I see myself and all of us Christians, the people of God who have been baptized in the Lord. Suddenly I understand that the church is so much more than the laity, the priests, and the magisterium. It is also a mystery. I consider the call of Vatican II to bring this church back to the marketplace where it started, to bring back the participation of the laity, to whom the Fathers of the Council dedicated a whole document in their pronouncements.

I'm afraid that we, the laity, are beginning to treat the church as if it were another business venture, like General Motors or Bell Telephone Company. We believe that we are going to restore it, reorganize it, put it on its feet by our own intelligence and by our own tremendous know-how!

But the church is not Bell Telephone or General Motors. Primarily the church is a mystery! She is the Body of Christ. If we treat her as if she were a business outfit, we will hack this body into small pieces and crucify it piece by piece on a grotesque, misshapen cross. If the body is crucified that way—the body which we are—then we shall again crucify the head who exists with the body, and without whom the body cannot exist.

The church is the Body of Christ through which his divine life flows into us! She is also his bride, and therein is the mystery which is not totally comprehensible to our minds.

11 Consoling the Church

It was but yesterday. I knelt in a dark corner of a Harlem slum and held with love a screaming girl, raped by marijuana-smoking boys in search of thrills.

Today, wherever I go in the world, I hold, with love that bleeds me dry, the church. The church forever young, raped again and again by sinful people.

It was but yesterday. I kissed the cancerous face of an old and lonely man dying in a hospital bed. Today, wherever I go, I kiss again and again (as if my kiss could heal) the thousand wounds of your church that look like cancer eating her from within.

It was but yesterday that I consoled a woman left alone, without food or money, with no other riches than children holding on to her tattered skirts. Today, wherever I go, I seem to be consoling the church deserted by so many.

O God, my love, my life, the agony of her who is your body and your bride is searing me. It seems, like Joan of Arc, I can smell my burning flesh and even more, my burning soul. What can I do, I, a nobody, except be emptiness in agony that will make room for you to come and rescue your bride.

Come, Lord Jesus, come! I cannot bear, it seems, another moment, the sight of your betrayed, abandoned bride.

12 | Faith for Today

We Christians today are a small handful of people in a tremendous sea of atheism, materialism, secularism, paganism, plain ignorance, and indifference. We are like the Jews of old—small, ghetto-like groups, lost in the midst of many Romans and Greeks. In this pluralistic society we suffer from a spiritual malady that prevents us from burning with zeal for our Father's house, from entering that society to bring love to it.

Our prayer should be, "Lord, I believe; help my unbelief." We have received the gift of faith in our baptism. Divine life courses in us, grace is given to us, and we feed on the Body of the Lord. Yet our faith is weak. In our technological, scientific age, we examine everything with our intellect and believe only what we can understand, examine, weigh, and analyze. This analytical approach cannot be used with God. We must enter into the darkness of faith to find him, to meet him. Unless we have this *personal* encounter with God, our faith will be weak.

Today we need a flaming faith, a faith that moves mountains, that translates the presence of Christ into every action. That kind of faith will send us forth and remove our hesitancy as we encounter our next door neighbor. That kind of faith will make ordinary, drab human lives things of splendor, a shouting of the Good News and the living of the Gospel of love again. We must beg God for this kind of faith.

13 | Love and Pain

What is it, fundamentally, that we all seek? Ultimately, it is God. He is the only one who can quench our thirst and still our restlessness.

Some people think that union with another will lead us to union with God. Of course, that's possible, if it is God's will for us to be married. But let us not fool ourselves that marriage will automatically lead us to God. No! Married people have to go through the same travail of the spirit, the same dispossession and death to self, as they would if they were single, a priest, or a religious.

Our passionate desire for union with God comes at a price. The images of courtship and marriage in the Bible warn us of this price, for love and marriage inevitably bring pain. We don't often think of it this way, but it is so.

Consider this common scenario. I fell in love with someone I didn't even know existed three months ago; and now I'm worried because he's driving to Chicago and it's raining, and I can't sleep for fear he might go too fast and skid and have an accident. Before I knew this fellow, I was peaceful; but the moment I entered a love relationship with him, the pain began. I didn't even have to wait until I married him! Where there is love, there is pain.

14 | Pain and Spiritual Growth

Say you are a young woman. Suppose you do get married. You are full of beautiful dreams. Then you become pregnant. You vomit every morning, you can't make dinner, you get disgusted with the whole situation. Of course, you're happy you are going to have a child; but today, you're downright miserable. Eventually, the child is born. For two years it screams and cries, and you wonder why you ever wished such a fate on yourself! You haven't got the money for a babysitter, so you can't go out with your husband. You're tied down and shut in and all you ever get for your efforts is "Mwah! Mwah!" You love the baby, but oh, how you wish it were in kindergarten. Then when the child gets to kindergarten, you're worried sick about it crossing the street, or getting measles from the other kids. When the child grows up, you worry about all the things that can happen to teenagers. Then you worry about your adult child marrying, and then you worry about the grandchildren. Love is like that!

Where there is love, there is pain. But whatever our walk in life, this kind of pain is God's way of teaching us how to pray. Everything that happens to us spiritually, everything that causes us to grow, will bring us closer to God—if we say yes. This is what spiritual growth means.

15 | *St. Teresa of Avila, Doctor of the Church*
The Marriage Bed of Christ

Sometimes in life, you watch what looked to you like God's work go to pieces. And you can't do anything about it but watch.

This happened to me. I knew dimly then what I see more clearly today, that this was the moment when God really picked me up and said, "Now I am offering you the union with me that you seek. The other side of my cross is empty. Come, be nailed upon it. This is our marriage bed."

All we can answer in response to that invitation is, "Help me, God! I don't have the courage to climb on that cross."

Now we begin to realize that prayer is twofold. Not only does God give us the grace to believe and to ask for help, but he also draws us to himself more surely than anything we can imagine. His own desire pulls us toward himself until the two desires meet. Our prayer and the desire of God come together in one brief moment of union, which only whets our desire for more. It is an insatiable taste of that which we seek—union with God. It will give us the courage to say yes to the next devastating situation that comes along, the next stepping stone to union on the cross which he, the Carpenter, has fashioned for each one of us individually.

16 A Dangerous Adventure

Prayer is an adventure, but it is a dangerous one. We cannot enter into it without risk. As Scripture says, "It is a fearful thing to fall into the hands of the living God" (Hebrews 10:31).

Prayer must lead us to total surrender, or it will lead us nowhere except back to ourselves. It is this surrender that we fear so much, and this is why prayer is such a fearsome and dangerous thing. This is why following Christ is indeed a risky business. He calls us to enter a revolution—like the fight for a cause, but one that is infinitely more powerful. This revolution takes place inside of us, for heaven is taken by violence *to oneself.* Prayer is part of this adventure. Do not fool yourself: once you encounter God, you will no longer be the same person you were before.

Today, almost two thousand years after the birth of Christ, Christianity still does not live in our so-called Christian hearts. Why is that? Why is the world not turning to Christ? It is not doing so because Christians are not living the Gospel. We Christians have not followed Christ. Somewhere along the road of life we have compromised, and we continue to compromise. Had we really followed Christ, there would be no communism. There would be no wars.

17 | The Essence of Our Call

The Second Vatican Council called all Christians to preach the Gospel to all peoples. To the Catholic laity, the Council enjoins the special task of *penetrating the secular world*, tenderly, lovingly, by putting this Gospel message into their political, economic, and everyday lives. This is a tremendous task! It can bring the light of Christ into the darkest corner of our fragmented, confused, searching, angry, and frightened world. But it demands of us that we put aside all nonessentials, that we stop all the word games, all the useless discussions. Yes, we must now come to the essence of things!

The essence is this: we must begin to live by *faith* and not by mere "religion." We must have an encounter with God and allow him to enter our very depths. We must remember that God loved us *first*, and that our religion is truly a love affair between God and us, us and God; it is not merely a system of morals and dogmas.

We must love God back, passionately! Through the *other*. We must love our neighbor, not only as ourselves but with the heart of God. Christ said to his disciples, "By this shall men know that you are my disciples, that you love one another *as I have loved you*." To love with the heart of God, we must empty ourselves totally of self, to allow Christ to love through us. Without him we cannot love anything or anyone, not even ourselves.

18 | *St. Luke, the Evangelist*
Getting Serious about Our Call

In order to show the face of Love to others, in order to empty ourselves so that Love will shine in our businesses, our stock exchanges, and our suburban residential areas, we must become poor ourselves. Not even poverty of spirit, which means that we realize how utterly dependent we are on God, is enough. We must be poor in the reality of daily life.

This is no time for Christians to be buying expensive homes. This is no time for worry about our "images." This is no time for religious orders to be building million-dollar plants and expensive altars. (I am not suggesting we become paupers!) It is simply a time to become poor; to give to others of our surplus, yes, but also of our necessity. Can we not live normally and curb our unruly desires for a thousand unnecessary gadgets and status symbols?

This is the time for becoming Christians in the fullness of that simple phrase, "followers of Christ." To each and every one of us, no matter what our state of life, Christ's life stands as our example. All we have to do is translate it for all to understand. Only love can do this. The father of love is faith. We must begin to *live by faith*, of which the outward signs of religion are but handmaidens, and of which the sacraments are the visible signs. When we do, the world will change.

19 | *Sts. Isaac Jogues and John de Brebeuf, Martyrs*
There Were No Priests

I remember the day when there were no priests in St. Petersburg. It was in the early days of the Russian Revolution, when things were so unsettled and priests were shot on sight, as were many other people. The Jewish rabbis, the Protestant ministers, the Orthodox priests, all were shot or "disposed of" in some way.

A little Roman Catholic parish was still surviving, and those of us who knew about it participated in the middle of the night in the Mass. It was a very short Mass, but still a Mass. One night when the priest had just consecrated the Host, the door opened, a rifle was thrust through; a shot was fired, and the priest fell dead. The consecrated Host rolled off the altar onto the floor. Two soldiers came up then, ground the Host under their heels, and turning to us said, "Where is your God? Under our heel!"

An old man answered, "Lord, forgive them, even if they know what they do." Shamed or embarrassed, the two soldiers left the church. The old man gave us Communion with the remnants of the Host. He washed the desecrated floor with holy water, and we buried the priest.

And then there were no priests! No one to hear confession. No one to give us Viaticum and the last rites (as they were called then). No one to offer Mass. Anyone who has gone through such a tragedy knows what it means to be without a priest.

20 | We Live in Fear—Needlessly

"Though I should walk in the shadow of death, I will fear no evil, for you are with me." Thus speaks the holy psalmist of the Lord. We should adopt his words for our own, we who fear so much. We fear the future. We fear illness and loss of security. We fear what people may say. We fear being different from the "herd." We walk the earth in fear! Needless fears keep us from living a full life in Christ.

Here is a young couple afraid of what people will say or think—they buy a house at a "swanky" address, instead of living simply and joyously in a poorer one.

Here are people who won't go near any poor section of their city, where there are "slums," because bodily harm might come to them. They close their doors to Christ in a beggar, for the same reasons!

Here is a young girl who feels she must conform to the dress, makeup, and hairstyle of the moment, or be "out of the swim." The swim of what? Of the world's backwash?

We who are baptized in the name of the Father, Son, and Holy Spirit, should be the most fearless persons on earth. We should forever walk in glory, for the Trinity dwells in us. Christ said so. In such glorious company, what is there to be afraid of? What does it matter what people think, if God is pleased enough with us to come and stay in our hearts?

21 | A Remedy for Fear

When I was little, my father used to say that, if you were a real Christian, you would never be afraid of anything or anyone. For were you not, if you were in the state of grace, the temple of the Holy Trinity? And wasn't the Blessed Mother there? For where the Trinity was, there Our Lady of the Trinity was sure to be. And naturally your patron saint would be within you too, as would your angel guardian. Furthermore, as a Christian, you had the right and the duty, when in danger or need, to call on all the heavenly spirits for help, to call on anyone or everyone in the Church Triumphant, which is all the people of God in heaven. So, living, walking, breathing in such a glorious company, how could you be afraid of anything but sin? Sin alone has the power to bring real death. It has to be feared with a great fear, but nothing else.

You shouldn't fear illness or even death—both are precious gifts of the Lord! Sickness can make you into his likeness, even as all pain and sorrow does, and bring deep spiritual peace and understanding that cannot be reached any other way. And death? Death is Christ calling your soul for an eternal rendezvous of Love. Oh, the joy of at long last being home, in the arms of the beloved!

22 | Overcoming Our Fears

Fear was made to be overcome. Because we are afraid of so many things, most of the time fear holds us tight. We have a fear of involvement, a fear of people, a fear of ourselves, and an endless sea of doubts about our security, our identity, and on and on. But fear is made to be overcome, because once fear is overcome, hosts of its attendants disappear.

How can we overcome fear? First and foremost, by prayer. Fear is overcome by courage too. Courage is not the *absence* of fear, it is the *overcoming* of it. We are faced with the same thing all over again under a new guise.

Let us think for a while. What are we afraid of? Above all, we are afraid of death. That is the crux of our fears. Other fears beset our life, but fear of death is the real fear. Death is the root fear and we might as well face it. It is the radical fear and the reason for all fears.

But why should I be afraid of death? Death is one of the most beautiful moments of life. If I have faith, the entry into death is a glorious one. It is not a question of seeing angels or Our Lady. It really means being greeted by Christ himself, of being *invaded* by his life, being one with him. *Momento Mori.* "Remember that you must die"—but I remember also that it will be a joyful event. God will greet God in me.

23 | Nitty Gritty Life— Transformed

Life goes on its way. Factually, it's a really nitty-gritty affair— repetitious and monotonous. Say you care for children: you change diapers, dress babies, put them to bed, feed them, entertain them as best you can. Day after day. It gets monotonous, doesn't it? Even the President finds, in peacetime, a certain monotony to his job: sign papers, meet with Congress, be here at this time, be there at that time. From manual labor to the presidency, monotony can be the path to doubts.

When we are young, we dream dreams; we're going to change the world—do this or that. But the years go by and we become bookkeepers or salesclerks. Our jobs are monotonous and we're assailed by all kinds of thoughts. Yes, the nitty-gritty daily life is the widest road to doubts.

God has given us a small path to follow him, not a wide road. But we take that wide road! Yet if we get off it and take the small path, we will know that this little path is holy. Now we will catch the smile of a child in both hands and hug it to our heart. The nitty-gritty days full of doubts will vanish and we will walk barefoot down the little path as pilgrims do. Flowers and trees will grow alongside it and we shall understand this is the path God made, and there is nothing nitty-gritty about it! Everything will be exciting, because we are in love with God. And to be in love with God is the most exciting thing in the world.

24 | Meditation on Doing Laundry

Doing laundry is a school of love. You are to be concerned about soap, water, clothing, and your iron, but never worried. *Concern* expresses love of God and men and women; *worry* is self-centered, showing a lack of love. What have you to worry about? You rest in the warm hand of your lover and spouse!

The laundry is a place where you can learn contemplation. The repetitive work of ironing and folding clothes is conducive to the freedom of the Spirit which allows you to roam at will, now beholding Christ in Nazareth, now meditating on the Eucharist, now thinking about the Scriptures.

Your work is redemptive too. Souls depend on the perfection of your work and the spirit in which you approach it. That spirit should be peaceful, prayerful, and full of charity. You are entrusted with the care of this clothing. Watch that it doesn't tear, that it's properly sorted. Handle it well before and after washing and see that the ironing is done properly. Also see to it that your laundry area is tidy. With God, everything has its place. Believe me when I say that peace of soul is achieved by tidiness and order outside the soul, just as the inner peace of the soul will reflect outwardly.

Pray to the Little Flower, St. Thérèse, who washed clothes in an old-fashioned tub with water heated elsewhere and brought in pails—only God knows what it cost a woman with tuberculosis to do this labor without saying a word of complaint to anyone.

25 | The Care and Use of Machines

You must look at all the machines you deal with, first with infinite reverence, and secondly with awe; for they are "creatures" of God in a sense, touched by the intelligence of God through the intelligence and handiwork of men and women. Everything in the world "contains God" and is touched by God. Chalice and Host are visible realities of God's presence, but to the eyes of faith, other realities are signs of his presence as well. The vehicles we drive, the electrical motor or fan, the chainsaw, and heater—these too are chalices of God's creation, transmitting his intelligence, love, and tenderness through the minds of men and women.

It follows therefore, that, in a manner of speaking, whenever we abuse a machine, we are guilty of desecration of a creation of God. This means we must think ahead and recollect ourselves before we even touch a button, or put our foot on the starter, or put into motion any machine that someone co-created with God. We have no right to mishandle a creature of God in any way.

When we take out on the creature of God our frustrations, hostilities, and emotional disturbances, we only hurt ourselves. It is nearly as bad to manhandle a machine as it is to take out our hostilities on a dog by kicking it for no reason at all. Better to have the humility and courage to say, "I am upset today. It would be better if somebody else worked with this machine today," than to challenge the Lord himself by abusing his creature.

26 Handicrafts and Creativity

Handicrafts serve as a means of communication among people who are afraid, shy, or sick, or even people who speak different languages. There is something reassuring, homey, pleasant, and relaxing to see someone embroidering or knitting in an airport or on a train. One feels a trust and confidence about such a person. If one has some similar work at hand, one becomes friends almost without words. Or one might ask what the other is doing; and a bond of friendship, gentle and warm, is established with this person who only a short time ago was a stranger. The handicraft is a bridge.

All creative effort is from God, and people who do handicrafts create. To create is to be at peace, for in creating one is joined with the Creator. Creativeness is one of the needs of our humanity and one of the gifts of God to us. Handicrafts also are one more way of restoring us to wholeness in the natural and psychological order so as to better restore us to Christ. The loneliness of modern people has almost reached a point of no return; but in a common effort of creativity, men and women may find someone else who is interested in similar crafts, and become friends through their craftsmanship. Friendship is still the most precious possession that a human being can share. So handicrafts open the door to both friendship and creativity. These aspects go together, for friendship both creates and demands creativity to grow.

27 A Meditation on Yelling

Good manners are the children of charity, and I must discuss one matter in particular. It is the terrible habit some of you have of yelling across rooms and down corridors. You have all been taught, I am sure, in your childhood and youth, that when you want to ask someone something, you go up to the person. Yelling startles everyone! In some lines of work this is necessary, but stop for a moment and consider that you are called to be saints; and saints teach by the way they stand, walk, and talk.

One whose soul and mind are peaceful does not desire to yell across large spaces. But it goes more deeply than that. Often we yell because we are too tired or lazy to go talk to the person. Did you ever think a good way of "dying to self" is to take the time and effort to go to the other person and speak in a simple, Christian way?

May I ask you a question? I think it is worth asking: do you think that Christ yelled at his apostles or at the people? I think that we would all be shocked at the thought of Christ yelling at them. Nor can we imagine the Blessed Virgin yelling at anyone. It is so self-evident that they wouldn't. Ask yourself why you yell. It is a good meditation.

28 Good Manners and Talking Too Much

I want to address another annoying situation. When several people are working together, some seem to have a need to talk constantly. It's often senseless conversation. Often these same people monopolize the conversation. Usually these good people have a compulsion to tell all that *they* have been doing. Almost unconsciously the pronoun "I" is very prominent in their conversations. Interesting as it might be to live with that sort of a person, it is not easy. They never seem to realize that they should also be concerned about other people, especially the shyer person who needs to be drawn out a little. If this type of person lives with others who are not talkative, the agony they inflict upon them is beyond imagining. It is like a sharp needle entering the brain. When this is done with much thoughtlessness, showing a tremendous lack of love and concern for the others, it has the power to lead us to hell instead of to the love of God!

You see, the care and attention to all these "little things" is the very essence of the spirit of Christianity. Good manners are the children of charity. This seems like only a scratch on the body of charity, but keep scratching the same place long enough and you will have a deep wound. Also, we will not teach anyone to love behaving like that. So you see how much harm can be done by a lack of good manners.

29 | The Art of Conversation

Good conversation is first of all a dialogue, alternating speech between two people or among several. The first requirement for this is *an interest in people.* There are many subjects, but formal education in them isn't necessary for the art of conversation. What *is* needed is interest in others, and an ability to express one's thoughts (which presumes that one has some original thoughts worth expressing!). What is also necessary is an ability to listen and a developed imagination.

Our life is rich in topics of conversation: the spiritual meaning of the events of the day; an individual's research on some spiritual topic; an appraisal of the doings in our city, state, or country; ways to improve our service; imaginative approaches to the daily routine of work; sharing interesting incidents that happened during the day.

A few elements of conversation are: an open mind, an ability to observe what is going on, listening to others as well as expressing oneself in a "give-and-take," patience and charity toward those who are learning to express themselves, helping people do the above, and a desire to learn and share, not dominating or "giving a lecture." Also helpful are spontaneity, simplicity, and joyousness in expressing oneself, without inhibitions or self-consciousness; cultivating an interest in many things, avoiding too much the pronoun "I," and the ability to sense whether those present are being drawn into the conversation.

30 | Listen to Yourself

Listen. Listen to yourself so as to find the path to God within the frail walls of your humanness.

Listen to yourself, for it is you alone who will lead yourself to him or away from him.

Listen to yourself. Listen to God, when you have led yourself to him.

Listen well, for if you hear his voice you will be wise with the wisdom of the Lord, and then be able to hear the voice of men and women—not as a surging sea or as a mob—but of each one individually. Each person's speech is a treasure given to you beyond all expectations, because you led yourself to that person and listened to his or her voice. Then the Lord will give you the powers to console and heal. Listen well to yourself and God. Listen well.

31 | On the Eve of All Saints' Day

Not to be a saint—that is the greatest tragedy that can befall a Catholic or any Christian. And yet behold our days and our times! How many of us today seek sanctity?

Why, we are almost ashamed to speak of it, let alone try to achieve it. Somehow, we have lost sight of our final goal and have become busy about "many things," none of which has to do with sanctity.

Somewhere, somehow, too, we have confused sanctity with drabness, suppressions, quirks, fixations, something unhealthy. Yet sanctity is so simple—as all things pertaining to God must be. For simplicity is the essence of love—and sanctity is love, lived fully, utterly, completely.

Nor is there anything "sissified" about sanctity—or anything gloomy either. Saints can't be sad, for saints are lovers of Love, and hence full of joy, of laughter, of gaiety. Theirs is a life of such adventure that it "out-adventures" all the greatest adventures of sinful men and women. Their lives are rooted in God —and anyone who makes his or her life a constant date with Christ lives a glorious adventure that spans earth and heaven.

We were created to be saints, to enjoy the Beatific Vision. To enter heaven, we must be saints—either now or later through much suffering and pain in purgatory. Why delay? Why not start today?

November

1 | *All Saints' Day*
We Need More Saints

What we need today is saints. Hundreds, thousands, millions more saints! All kinds of bombs, hates, and fears vanish like mist in the sun before saints, before men and women in love with God, men and women of sanctity.

Sanctity means much loving. That is what we have been created for—to love—to love our neighbor and, through him or her, to love God. Loving is fun. Loving is joy. Loving is peace. Loving means serving. Loving means forgetting self for others. Learn how to love, and all the rest will be added unto you.

We are almost beside ourselves today with fears—about bombs and wars. Our heads cannot rest anywhere, nor our hearts, nor our souls. We seek answers vainly in armaments, treaties, and laws, knowing, even while we do all this, that we are shadowboxing because there is nothing we can do to prevent annihilation from the weapons our own brains have invented.

Nothing can save us except *sanctity*. That's why we need saints today. If St. Francis of Assisi had an atomic bomb, would anyone worry about it? No. Because, being a saint, he loved much. And where love is, there cannot be fear or evil.

Ah, we do need saints today! We need understanding, too, to realize that the greatest tragedy that can befall us is *not* to be saints.

2 | *All Souls' Day*
Praying for the Dead

When I was a girl in old Russia, All Souls' Day was a major holy day, for love for their dead was deep and abiding in the hearts of the Russian people. Throughout the land, at Mass and in special prayers, the dead were remembered solemnly and with all the family present. All day the cemeteries were filled with throngs, praying, fixing graves, visiting the beloved who slept their last sleep. At eventide, there were more prayers in the church and usually a candle procession to the cemetery, with everybody chanting litanies and hymns. The candles were left to burn on the graves, in little containers or lanterns. They made beautiful patterns of light and shadow for passersby to see. They demanded that all who saw must whisper a prayer as they went by.

When a Christian dies, the church prays for the soul. Though he was baptized, he had been a sinner during his lifetime. But his faith in God still opens to him eternal life. That is why the church members sing the happiness of those who are waiting in Christ, sharing the hope of the resurrection. Though death may make us sad, the promises of eternal life to come should give us consolation.

Strange, is it not, how death can lead you to the appreciation of life? And how it can make your heart filled to overflowing with gratitude to God! It did mine. Life is not ended, just changed.

3 | *St. Martin de Porres*
Gratitude to God

I want to speak to you about gratitude to God. Consider, dearly beloved, the fact that God loved you first. You've heard this, but somehow it hasn't penetrated. If it had, you would be gratefully and passionately loving him back. Yet there are few signs of it!

Such love of God should be reflected immediately in your love of one another.

How many of us truly and constantly realize the bounty of God to us, just speaking in the natural order? Do we thank God for the medical care we receive, for our clothing, our food, and our holidays? I received a letter from a woman, the mother of many children, who had broken her arm. She wrote, "Only now do I realize what it is to have two hands, both of which I need so much." We walk; we have the use of our limbs, eyes, speech, hearing. Are we grateful to God for these? Or do we take everything for granted, and grumble and mumble and complain and feel sorry for ourselves?

I fear with great fear when I see a lack of gratitude. Think about it, meditate about it, pray about it, do something about it! Ours are frightening times and God is so good to us. Do we realize what we have? It is time we should. The time is now!

May Our Lady open your hearts to gratitude. May St. Martin de Porres, who was canonized in Rome in 1962 and whose feast day it is, fan the fires of this tremendously needed virtue of gratitude among us!

4 God's Icebreakers

It will not be very long before governments take over from cradle to grave all that we call the corporal works of mercy. This has already happened in several countries. I call it the "Ice Age" because the corporal works of mercy should be done with great love, gentleness, understanding, compassion, and delicacy. True, they rarely have been so performed, but in many instances they were. In the near future, however, all the above nouns will be encompassed by one word: *efficiency*.

Efficiency is a very cold word, as is bureaucracy. True, maybe no one will starve. But even if there is no great poverty at some time in the future, there will be coldness—terrible, icy coldness that begets a terrible loneliness in people, a loneliness and alienation which is followed by a high suicide rate.

We must get ready by prayer and fasting, by a self-emptying, to acquire pure and childlike hearts, hearts that are able to see God and thus able to enter this coming ice age. We must become harbingers and carriers of the fire of the Holy Spirit, for it is fire that melts ice. That will be our role in the near future.

We must prepare to be God's icebreakers. Each of us will become "God's Inn" for the people who are lying wounded and lonely and beaten up by countless robbers. We will be God's icebreakers for all the wounded and frozen ones, so that they might be thawed out by our love.

5 | "You Have to Have Faith!"

Both Dorothy Day and I were pioneers in the lay apostolate. She had a wonderful influence on me. I met Dorothy during my Friendship House days. She was associated at the time with Peter Maurin, and she was publishing *The Catholic Worker.* She was just starting her Houses of Hospitality. I met her in a storefront much like ours, feeding a breadline the same way we did—by prayer and begging.

She invited me to spend the night with her, sharing her double bed in a shelter filled with cots and people. As we were preparing for bed, a woman of the streets without a nose and with active syphilis walked in and asked if we had room for her. Dorothy welcomed her like a queen and said, "Of course, we do." To me, she said, "I have a mattress to put in a bathtub for you. You'll be snug as a bug in a rug. I will share the bed with this lady." Speaking as a nurse, I took Dorothy aside and warned her the woman had active syphilis, which she could contract if she had cuts on her body.

Then I received my first lesson from Dorothy. Usually so mild, gentle, and kind, Dorothy suddenly arose and in a spirited voice said: "Catherine, you have little faith. This is Christ come to us for a place to sleep. He will take care of me. You have to have faith!" This was one of many lessons she taught me by her witnessing and example. From our meeting a deep friendship was born and our two apostolates grew closer.

6 | When We Doubt There Is a God

There are few people who haven't doubted the existence of God. I must confess I did. Doubt is a strange thing. It comes unbidden, unexpectedly, suddenly. Or, it comes slowly, entering the intellect and playing havoc, so that for a moment, suddenly, truly, you don't believe in God.

Faith is given to us by God himself, in baptism. We are supposed to make it grow, and we do. Yet, quite suddenly and unexpectedly, the tree of faith—which seems to be so strong—suddenly looks spindly and weak.

All the doubts I ever had toward God are strange picture puzzles. They grow little roots and don't want to go away. We have to pull at them and throw them into the fire, for all our doubts apply to God. They turn to ashes no matter how clever we are, how brilliant we are, how fantastic we are.

Yes, doubts—new ones and old ones—come forth and touch us like soft kitten's paws. They are around all the time, but what we have to do is throw them into the fire, the fire of God's love. When we love him, we believe in him. When we believe in him and love him, we hope. Faith, love, and hope sweep away doubts. Try it some time.

7 | Doubting Is Okay

The Lord often says to us: "It is through doubts that you find me." That's a very strange thought, is it not? But at the same time, it's very true; for those who do not doubt God are not on a pilgrimage. We can, indeed, believe in God—superficially. But those who seek him, who really want to find the Absolute, as he is, go on a pilgrimage.

It should be a very simple pilgrimage because the way to find God is in *the other person*. The way to trust him and not doubt him is to trust another person. There is some strange kind of mystery in all this. Why does trust in one other person open such immense horizons of love? This trust is truly a mystery.

We should kneel before this mystery, and sometimes even prostrate ourselves before it. Only God can reveal mysteries to us; and even then, he does so in a quite mysterious way. As far as we're concerned, he decrees that whatever we do to the least of his brethren, we do to him. Now that's something to be thought over!

When we enter the desert of doubts, let us stop and pause and understand that we are on a pilgrimage. This moves our souls, our hearts, ever closer, closer, closer to God. And that strange mystery, of believing when there is nothing to believe in, is the key to a complete trust in God and the dissolution of doubt.

8   Doubts and Trusting

We really live amid doubts. They whirl around us like autumn leaves falling from the trees.

Doubts are a lack of trust. I might trust my husband or my wife. Then my imagination works overtime on his or her smallest faults. Doubts overcome trust. When doubts overcome trust, then love and hope shrivel up just like those autumn leaves that whisper under our feet. They become brown, dusty, and dead.

Doubts are stepping stones to total trust in God and love of him. But suppose we do not walk beyond those stepping stones? Suppose we allow doubts to have their way? The Old

Testament, the New Testament, annoy us. We doubt everything pertaining to God. These kinds of doubts lead to depression, to all kinds of emotional problems orchestrated by the devil.

Emotional illnesses can completely spoil a human life, and they do so because emotions have overcome faith. Once the emotions overcome faith, then a lot of things happen. Then the rustle of autumn leaves under one's feet becomes like thunder in one's ears. There is but one thing to do when this happens, and it is to plunge blindly into the waters of faith as Jesus did. There is no other answer to those kinds of doubts.

9 | Parcels of Love

"Shipping and Receiving" sounds so very commercial, so very businesslike. It seems to fit in so well with the cold, efficient spirit of our modern, technological times which are no longer interested in permeating this efficiency with a warm, human touch. Our age seeks merely to expedite business through soulless, cold, but exceedingly efficient machines. But to anyone who loves, the seemingly cold words "Shipping and Receiving" take on an entirely new meaning.

To one who loves God, the actions in the daily routine of sending out goods, or accepting them, is embedded in the heart of Christ in love. God is love, and his heart is a symbol of that love. And the gentle spirit that God has mandated to Madonna House, and also to you, touches even the cold words "Shipping and Receiving."

Let no one make the mistake of thinking that goods in shops, businesses, and commercial houses do not have to be handled with loving care. *Each parcel can carry God's love.* You who receive Love, can send Love on to others, in what is shipped. So everyone who handles what you send receives a grace. Some of this love of God "rubs off" on the clerk in the railway station, on the truck driver, on the postal workers. It rubs off on the shipping crew which handles all your packages.

What a strange and profound work—sending Love's tokens across the world! Yes, "Shipping and Receiving" is an awesome job, for it handles the love of God and the love of human hearts.

10 | The Proper Use of Time

Time is a precious commodity, like a piece of gold. What are we going to do with it? How are we going to use it? Waste it? Will we waste sixty seconds? Sixty minutes? An hour or two? Will we fritter time away in useless motion, in useless conversation, in taking a long route instead of a shorter one? Or are we going to use every second for God?

What do we have? Twenty-four hours between daily Masses. Our tomorrows are his. We have but twenty-four hours. And if you want to come down to a fine point, frankly, we don't even have that; we have just a moment at a time.

A woman left her husband and child to go to the movies and take a little drive to see a sick relative. The husband was going to make a lunch for them when she came back. Thus they had planned. Less than one hour later, less that sixty minutes later, she was on a stretcher with a concussion and a broken foot, the victim of an automobile accident.

Perhaps this example is trite. But it is still worth repeating, for it brings us back to this wealth that we have to offer God— time. Even those who take a vow of poverty have this wealth— time. How will you spend yours today?

Take a few minutes and think about it.

11 | Using Time to Grow in Holiness

There is more to time than just wasting it or using it. Time is a cord with which to flagellate our sluggish spirits. Be quiet.

Listen. Remember what you have read and meditated upon in the Gospel so many times. You can hear heavy cords, knotted with big knots, whistling through the air and hitting the back of the sinless one tied to a post. Can you see the strong, well-developed shape of the Roman soldiers? With bulging muscles and sheer brute force, they ruthlessly, methodically lift those cords and keep hitting the sinless flesh that suffers for your sins and mine. Can you see them?

We have no Roman soldiers. But we have cords made out of strands of time, a minute here, a minute there, a half-hour here, a half-hour there. We could weave them all together and make them strong and heavy. We could allow them, wielded by our own hands, to flagellate our laziness, our sluggishness, our love of comfort, the thousand things that we have to drive out of ourselves. Five minutes late for dinner. Seven minutes late for Mass. Needless wear and tear. Useless walking back and forth to our various premises. If we tried hard enough, we could do a job in fifteen minutes, but we take half an hour.

Be quiet. Listen. The Roman soldiers were strong. The cords whistled through the air, and the flesh of the sinless one was torn and hung in ribbons with each blow. What about those wasted minutes, seconds, and hours. What about them now?

12 | A Remedy for Burn-out

The only way you can acquire the strength to lie still in the palm of God's hand—to die to self in the unglamorous and monotonous duty of the moment—is prayer. Always prayer.

A trip to Europe or Brazil or Nigeria or elsewhere will be glamorous for a while. But then the broiling sun here, the humid climate there, the old monotony will take hold of you again. There will be new faces, but with the same old problems. There will always be the same treadmill—the feeding of souls, the feeding of bodies, the clothing of the naked, the nursing of tired minds and bodies. It will be the same story repeated ad nauseam and ad infinitum.

For someone experiencing these things for the first time, they will be new and exciting. But for you perhaps it will be like listening to the same old record again. So what is going to make this old record exciting and pulsating with life? The Lord! Yes, the Lord.

The vocation to love will give you the courage and the all-consuming zeal to listen again and again, to clothe the naked again and again, to nurse the sick again and again, to feed the hungry again and again—and all with the zest of a young person on his or her first date!

13 | Renewal Begins with Me

A strange weariness—a pain—has entered the minds and hearts of Catholics. It often comes from the Catholic press, from its books and publications. Its criticisms, of course, are necessary, for without them stagnation would set in. But criticisms that constantly aim at the magisterium and administrative arms of the church, criticisms that are constantly negative, that highlight the weaknesses and sinfulness of the people of God (especially those in high places)—such criticisms can create a depression of mind and heart that, by its very weight, brings discouragement, weariness, sadness, and pain. Too infrequently has the Catholic press discussed the essence of the Second Vatican Council and the conversion it calls for: that each person open the windows of his own mind and heart and begin a renewal in *him or herself!*

Let us begin with ourselves. Let us see the beam in our own eye before we look for the speck in that of our neighbor (bishops are neighbors, remember!). Only when our hearts are full of love shall we be able to speak the truth with the gentle and healing voice of Christ who is Truth. He alone is without sin.

He alone can take up the cords and chase the moneylenders out of the temple! We must not forget that to each one of us he addressed the words, "Let him who is without sin throw the first stone." Perhaps before we criticize so negatively, we should repeat these words to ourselves.

14 | Cleaning and Theology

In theology, everything is properly called a creature of God. Your dust rag is a creature of God; so is the dustpan. In the theology of manual labor as developed by St. Benedict, we read: "Treat all the tools of the monastery with the same reverence as you treat the vessels of the altar." Unfortunately, the average person of Canada and the United States considers manual labor somehow beneath him. This is far removed from the true principles of the Gospel and the dignity of manual labor. Christ was a carpenter, a manual laborer. This didn't just "happen" to him at random. He *chose* it. Nor can we forget our Mother, the Blessed Virgin Mary, a humble housewife in Palestine, who did all the household chores without our modern conveniences! So, for your soul's sake, for your health, look upon housework and all manual labor with great dignity, glorified and sanctified by the Holy Family—the Lord himself, Our Lady, and St. Joseph.

How can you restore the world to Christ if you cannot restore a room to its normal, beautiful order, and keep it that way? How can you restore the world to Christ if you cannot keep drawers and shelves and rooms tidy?

I suggest you make the sign of the cross before you begin. It's God's time, God's broom, God's floor. It's up to you how you're going about it. You can become a saint sweeping because God will see the motive in your heart. Let your cleaning be a song and a prayer of love and atonement.

15 Housework and Holiness

Begin to lay your life down today in the exacting, routine, monotonous, repetitive work of cleaning house. Do it well. Offer it up. Pray. Don't pray with words; pray with your hands. Your movement is prayer.

You see, if you give concentration and thoughtfulness to things today, then tomorrow you will give thoughtfulness to people. There is so much beauty in the action itself, in concentration, and in its results.

Face it: you are doing little things over and over again—exceedingly well for the love of God. This is going to make you a saint. That is absolutely positive. Don't seek immense mortifications or flagellations and what-have-you. Seek the daily mortification of doing a thing exceedingly well. Believe you me, you are certainly going to have mortification, I can promise you! You will get so that you will have the heebie-jeebies sometimes just at the thought of dusting the same chair once more. But you're going to take those heebie-jeebies in your hands, squeeze them, and throw them away saying, "This too, Lord, for love of you."

The desire to straighten things up, to empty an ashtray, not to leave a mess behind—these are the tokens of love. When the house is in order, it's at peace, and charity blooms in that order.

16 The Virtue of Perseverance

Lately I have been thinking a lot about perseverance. The dictionary says to persevere is to be steadfast; maintain an endeavor; to persist in following a course to a definite goal, especially a spiritual one. This is a cold definition, but gives some sort of essence of the word.

In my heart, as I prayed about it, perseverance means the flowering of the love of God. It grows and grows and grows, descending upon a soul like a cascade of flowers, like bougainvillea in the West Indies. As time goes on, both the flowering tree and the flowers hanging from it become big enough to offer shade to oneself and to many others. The perfume of those flowers draws countless thousands to the tree—or rather, to the human heart in which this "tree of perseverance" is growing.

When your heart has made a commitment, a surrender for life, you begin to sense that the words of the poet are true for you too: "Lord, I throw my life at your feet, and sing and sing that I bring you such a little thing!"

The Lord alone can give you the key to the mystery of this strange and awesome gift of perseverance. After that, *perseverance* will become clear to you. You will realize, then, that it is one more virtue you need to pray for. It must be a constant prayer, a continual prayer, because its crown of beautiful flowers will be laid on your head only when you are in a coffin. Ah, but what a crown it is! Alleluia! Alleluia!

17 | The Virtue of Trust

Trust is a beautiful but very delicate virtue. It is a gentle offshoot of faith. Trust begins when "reason" as we understand it—the intellect and what-have-you—folds its wings and allows the *wings of faith* to open up. For trust cannot exist without faith. If I have faith in a person, an institution, a community, a family, I will trust! Wherever there is faith, there is trust.

The first one we must trust is God—the Trinity. Do we really? Most of the time we either question the existence of God or, if we believe that he does exist, we question his ability to help us. We think that our everyday problems are *our own* to solve, and that we needn't have faith or trust in God to solve them. If possible, we would prefer to solve our own problems *all of the time!* It gives us a sense of power, of being our own master. We are willing to have God around and to rely on him *only* when it becomes quite evident that we cannot solve things ourselves.

Yet, without trust there can be no bonds between husband and wife, between children and parents, between members of a religious community, or between men and women in general. Because of this lack of trust, we have no peace. How can anybody have outward peace when there is no inward peace? Inner peace lies in the arms of faith and trust, and, of course, love and hope.

18 | The Strength and Gentleness of God's Pity

Yesterday I was meditating on the pity of God, and I wondered if you realize how it constantly envelops us in its gentleness, its kindness, its warmth.

God's pity is visible in people like St. Francis of Assisi, who kissed a leper. That was pity. Pity is *not* the condescension of one person toward another. "Oh, those poor Blacks in Harlem! Isn't it terrible? How I pity them!" No, that's not the kind of pity I am talking about. God's pity is strong, it is *very* strong. It lifts up a completely discouraged person, but it is not condescending. Having lifted up the bruised and crushed soul, God embraces the whole person and speaks words of tender affection—"brother," "sister," "friend."

God's pity is like a fresh wind that suddenly comes on a torrid day. His pity is like a cool evening when the sky is pink and blue and red, and beautiful to behold. That is how God's pity is.

It is something that we should desire to hold on to, something that we should want to delight in, to "wallow in," as it were. The pity of God is so gentle that it is like a cradle rocked by a loving mother. It puts us to sleep—that is to say, not us but rather our fears and negative emotions. The pity of God is like oil that make the skin soft; it makes the heart soft.

19 Let Yourself Go— into the Pity of God

The pity of God is "catching." If we "let ourselves go" and enter into this divine pity, we will be able to pity others with the same strength, with the same ability to lift the other one (if we need to carry someone on our back)... but certainly to embrace one, to hold one tight and call one brother or sister.

But first, we must allow ourselves to relax and let God's pity (which is another facet of his love) penetrate the deepest levels of our hearts. *To accept the pity of God ourselves is to start on the road to sanctity.* Sanctity, you know, is simply loving God. A saint is a lover of Christ. It is as simple as that.

Let us go without fear into that pity, which he offers us with such great tenderness and gentleness. Let us enter into that "fellowship" with himself to which he calls us. If we do this, so many of our tensions will disappear. So much depends upon our *allowing* his pity to enter the very depths of our souls. If we do so, we will no longer have a sense of inner "depression" because Christ will descend into the depths of it and will lift it up. So many painful things will vanish, if only we allow the gentle pity of Christ to take hold of us and to remember, each moment of our lives, that *God truly is with us.* The gentle, unassuming, yet infinitely strong and loving pity of God is ours for the asking. Let us ask.

20 Between Two Masses

Between your two Masses—the Mass of today and the Mass of tomorrow—you spend your time, your life. Yes, your days are spent between two Masses. That is all the time you have. Your tomorrows are God's, your yesterdays are his, and your today is rooted in the morning Mass.

Each day you should pray that the fruit of these Masses will be heaven, where your living with Christ, begun in faith, will be completed in his marvelous light.

In the Mass, you find the Lord. He comes to you joyfully and gladly. Can you feel how glad he is to come to you? He is happy to have you there at Mass. It is very important that you be there, for the Mass is your rendezvous with God.

You don't really "pray the Mass"; you sort of *experience* it. The Mass encompasses you totally and absolutely. It is such a beautiful time. In some profound sense, you become the Mass. Do you ever think about it that way?

You enter through the Mass into the splendor of the Lord. You span the bridge of two thousand years, and stand at the Last Supper with the Lord and the apostles. You are present at Gethsemane and under the Cross of Calvary. You do all that at Mass, and yet you also are present at an unbloody sacrifice, at which the Lord deigns to stoop to you and *lift you up to him.*

21 | The Parousia

The liturgical year of the church ends with an awesome and tremendous vision of the *Parousia,* which is the glorious return of our Lord. It is part of our faith to believe that there will, in time, be a day on which Christ will return. His glory will manifest itself before the eyes of all men and women, and we shall know that he is the Master of the universe. God has rescued us from the power of darkness and transferred us to the kingdom of his Son. This—our deliverance—is begun at baptism. It is completed only by entrance into heaven.

At this time of the year, we anticipate the Lord's Second Coming. It is our hope, our expectation, our longing; it is the reason for our life and our existence, our birth and our death. Because of this belief, we can exclaim, "Death, where is thy sting?" We feel hope and joy. We cease to be afraid of death, for the day of God's judgment is also the day of his *love and mercy.* Let us abide in this, in charity and peace.

We should be praying now to grow in faith, to get to know God through our efforts of loving him and our neighbor, to pray that his will be done in us. This is the type of prayer that God will never refuse. You are not sure? Why not try it out and see? Not tomorrow. Not the day after. *Now!*

22 St. Cecilia, Patroness of Music
Praising God in Song

Today I would like to discuss how we should praise God in song. We as Catholic Christians should encompass all ways of singing, while emphasizing our own Roman Catholic heritage. Let us open our musical horizons as we open our spiritual ones, for the two are connected. Music, after all, is the echo of God's voice. We should have the freedom of the children of God, yet such a freedom is always disciplined. We must not abandon the old for the new just because it is new, nor discard the old just because it is old. We must blend the new music with the old, which is part of our heritage and tradition.

There should be harmony among the priests and laypeople in this—blending the music. We should blend our voices in joyous praise to the Lord without too much discussion about when, whether, and how to sing this or that. If we have clashes, if each wants to have his or her own idea about music, if we forget to blend into a joyous and harmonious whole when we sing to the Lord, then our songs will fall flat and will never reach him! For it is important to sing with our whole minds, our whole hearts, and our whole souls, lest our songs be rejected by the Lord. Even if we cannot carry a tune, we can still sing from the heart, with great love. What matters is not how we sound, but what goes into our singing—passionate love for the Lord and Our Lady must fill our hearts.

23 | Footprints of Destruction

The day is gray. We are traveling over a gray road. I look and I see farms. Not so long ago, the Indians held this land. They cherished it, caught fish and killed bison and deer and other animals to eat; but they always left some intact, for these people did not kill for the sake of killing. But, somewhere along the road, we decided that we were "god." From that day on, we have polluted and destroyed, annihilating what God had given us to be steward of.

I travel though many lands, in many ways; and I see the footprints of destruction. I see how human beings have chosen to destroy themselves. Behold this "god of the universe" called "humanity"! We have polluted the earth with alien additives, things that do not belong in it; the earth is angry and vomits the stuff back into the crops. So people are unhealthy.

Cities are vulnerable. How long would it take an atomic bomb to destroy New York, Chicago, Toronto, Berlin, Paris? A few seconds, perhaps? And yet there are people who defend atomic warfare. My heart weeps. It has wept for a long time. Lord of Hosts, my prayers have turned into tears; and they are all I can offer you. You have use for tears. They can wash some things away from the hearts of men and women, and from my own heart... the gift of tears on a gray day, on a gray highway, amid pollution wrought by humanity.

24 | "Turn Up the Thermostat, My Dear"

"Oh, it is so cold! Only sixty-five! Turn up the thermostat, my dear. It doesn't matter. Nobody will know."

Do you mean to say you hesitate? Why? Oh, I see. You cut out a picture of a woman—bent in two. On her back she carries all the energy that she can get to cook her food and heat her home. Do you still want to turn the thermostat up? Oh, you do! This woman doesn't mean a thing to you, does she? You say you don't belong to the Third World. Would you mind telling me to which world you *do* belong? Stop! Stop fiddling with that thermostat. You cannot do this any more. There is no Third World, no First, nor Second World. There is either the world of fellowship or of the stones of the devil's field.

Stop it right now! It is *you* who make that woman carry that heavy load. It is you and I. Her life is on your soul. Unless you want your soul to be like a stone, stop it—and stop it now! It's not a matter of thermostats. It's a matter of completely changing your style of life.

Start putting the Gospel into your life. Preach it without compromise. And if you put your hand to the thermostat, you compromise. Look at her! She is your sister and mine. What have we done to her? We forget the Lord said, "Whatsoever you do to the least of my brethren, you do to Me." My friend, your hand at the thermostat makes me afraid of our hearts being turned to stones by greed and pride. Stop! Let the thermostat be. It's but a symbol of a whole way of life that must be changed.

25 | The Virtue of Gratitude

We have forgotten the virtue of gratitude. Gratitude to God for our very existence—for the breath we draw this moment and the next, for all we have, for all we are, and all we hope to be.

Gratitude presupposes that we know our utter poverty—that without God we are nothing. Knowing this, in a wholesome fear of him, we should prostrate ourselves in worship of him, and in thanks to him from whom we draw life. Knowledge of our utter destitution, and the wholesome fear of God, would bring to our barren hearts a rich flow of grace and love. This would make us whole again, and fruitful in his sight.

Gratitude would come to dwell in us. Then life would be full of zest. The grayness would go out of it, to be replaced with such *a glorious sense of adventure* that our days would be like a song. Our daily work would glow with life's sheen, and our daily lives would reflect God's beauty. All things would come together in us to praise the Lord. The earth would be renewed and restored to Christ, to whom it belongs. Rich would be the fruits of gratitude. Yes, all these things would happen if the virtue of gratitude would once more blossom in us. But before it can take root, we must turn our hearts away from all created things and lift them up to God. It is so simple a solution. Why don't we do it?

26 | Joy in Daily Life

Joy is very quiet and full of wonder. It is like a light that shines in the darkness and is connected with hope and with love. To give you an idea of my joyous moments, the first occurs when I wake up every morning with the incredible thought that here God has granted me another day to love him and to serve him.

Simultaneously, other thoughts come to me from the devil and from my own humanity and emotions. They creep in like shadows over the shining light of my joy. They whisper: "Look, you are going to have a whole day of problems. You are going to have to be in four places at once," and so on. Through those whispers, the whole weight of the day and of my duties creeps in. But joy smiles. I know that I don't have to face all of those things at once, that these too are works of love for Christ's sake, that all I have to worry about is doing the duty of the moment as it comes to me, with love and enthusiasm for Love's sake—for Christ's sake.

My joy is complete when at Mass I receive Communion and become one with God. Nothing equals the unity, love, and oneness that a human being can have with God at Mass and Communion.

My other moments of joy come from the *enthusiasm* with

which I greet every new task. To me, each one is a challenge; each will eventually lead souls to Christ if I do it joyfully and lovingly. Already God accepts that for other souls. Frankly, I cannot imagine why people look at things negatively instead of positively.

27 Preparing for Christ's Coming

My mother used to say that the days of Advent were the days of building a golden stairway that would bring us to a star, the star of Bethlehem, that in turn would bring us straight to the Christ Child!

So now place yourself in Nazareth in Mary's time of waiting when nobody paid any attention to her. *You* pay attention to her. *You* sweep for those who don't sweep the cobwebs and the dirt from their souls. Sweep in the Nazareth of human minds and hearts. Prepare that inn eternally, every day, for the child to be born in, the child who was denied the inn in reality, and still is denied the inns of our hearts. Smaller and smaller is the group of people who believe, and still smaller those who believe and will lay their life down for him. Begin to lay your life down now in the exacting, disciplining, routine, monotonous, repetitious work of your day, cleaning or whatever.

Remember that your humble tasks, done well with great love for Christ, can lift the world! This is your strength. You can lift the communists, the ones who hate, the ones who are indifferent. Do your work well. Offer it up. Pray. Don't pray with words—pray with the work of your hands.

28 Turning Your Face to Christ

Once again we are in or near Advent, reminding us vividly, beautifully, of Christ's first Advent in time. Even while he is coming, he is also with us now, in many ways. He is with us in the tabernacle. Incredible Love that he is, he could not separate himself from us. He also walks among us in all his priests. Through their hands, he multiplies himself in consecrated Hosts so that they can feed us with the Bread of Life—himself. How immense must be his love for us!

Meditate for a moment. Allow a few moments of silence to interrupt reading this page, then resume reading. Try to comprehend the lavishness of God's love for you. Daily, millions of Hosts are given in Holy Communion to the faithful throughout the world! Yet each Host is Christ, coming in tremendous love to be united to one and all!

Let *every day be the day of beginning again*, of loving him a little more, of hungering for him a little more, of turning your face to him. All you have to do is to look at the person next to you. Never forget that *you shall be judged on love alone*. There is only one way to love God and to prove it to him, and that is by loving your neighbor—the person next to you at any given moment. I repeat, turning your face and heart to Christ simply means turning your face to the one who is next to you *at this moment in your life*. If you do that, dearly beloved, you shall become a saint.

29 | A Short Season, A Long Journey

Advent is a short season, but it is the long road of a soul from Nazareth to Bethlehem. It is such a short distance as we in North America are accustomed to thinking of distances. Yet it is a road into infinity, into eternity; it has a beginning, but no end. In truth, Advent is the road of the spiritual life, the pathway all of us must take if we wish to get to heaven. It is the place from which we must start if we do not want to miss our destination. We must start with a *fiat* that re-echoes Mary's *fiat*. A *fiat* that each of us should say in the quiet of our chapels, and preferably at eventide when all creation is still.

Let us then arise and shake the sleep from our eyes, the sleep of our emotions run amuck, the sleep of indifference, of tepidity, of self-pity, of fighting God. Let us arise from that sleep with its dark nightmares, and journey to Bethlehem. But let us understand that Bethlehem is *our own* souls, hearts, minds.

Advent is a time of standing still, and yet making a pilgrimage. A pilgrimage in which we don't use our feet. A pilgrimage in which we stand still and walk a thousand miles across the world... just because we stand still. So let's enter, you and I, into the pilgrimage that doesn't take us from home. Ours is a journey of the spirit, which is a thousand times harder than a journey of the feet. Let us go.

30 | Little Things— Precious Gems

This Advent, let us go deeply into the significance of this liturgical season. The word "advent" means "coming." Whose coming do we expect? The answer is simple: Christ's. This very simplicity is awesome.

If he comes, then we who call ourselves Christians should make ourselves ready to greet him. Are we ready? Have our hearts really touched his heart in the sense that we are forgetting *ourselves* more and more? Are we remembering to love and obey, no matter what the emotional cost? Are we finally succeeding in making a cross of our emotional problems? Are we putting it on our shoulders, ready to go to Bethlehem? Are we walking the path he has laid out for us—the strange path of the monotonous, little duties of everyday life that could become our gifts for him, more precious than those of the three Wise Men?

What are these little things? They might be dishwashing, filing, running from one meeting to another, answering doors and telephones, dealing with uncouth or difficult people, facing hopeless situations in schools or catechetical centers.

Yet, all these daily duties can become precious gems, gold too heavy to bear, grains of incense to cover the earth, *if only our hearts touched his Heart,* and generously opened themselves to *being loved by him and loving him in return.*

December

1 The Reality of Christ's Poverty

This is the month of Christ's birthday. The Son of God and the Son of Man was born in a cave. Over the centuries men and women have sentimentalized it. It is time for us Christians of the twentieth century to take another look at this cave and him who was born in it. People who live in caves or give birth to children in caves are not the wealthy of this world. They are the poor. He, the Son of God, chose to be born in poverty. What does it mean to us moderns—this strange lesson of God's birth?

Are our hearts filled with longing for him who loved us so much that he was born in a cave, died on a cross, and took upon himself the burden and slavery of our humanity and our sin? Do we desire to follow him and to detach our hearts from all things that are not him, in order to be poor, in spirit and in reality? Are we going to share with the hungry ones of the world, the replicas of the child who had nowhere to lay his head, from our immense surplus? Or are we going to give of our necessity? Which is it going to be? Will we spend millions on gifts for the man or woman "who has everything"? Or will we give to those who have nothing, in memory of the child who was also God and who was born in a cave for love of us? Which is it going to be?

Are we going to the cave like the shepherds, who were also poor? Or are we going to render once more lip service to a

Christ of our own making, whose cave we have embellished with clean straw? His probably stunk as old straw stinks in stables.

2 | The Spirit of Nazareth

The spirit of Nazareth is humble and hidden. It is the spirit of the Holy Family, a community of perfect charity and love. A facet of Nazareth that I often meditate upon is the pregnancy of Mary. She was already carrying God within her when the Holy Family, that "community of love" between her and Joseph, was established miraculously.

We too are "pregnant with God" in a manner of speaking. This "pregnancy" is a gift of God himself. He gives us a desire for himself. It is a "seed" within us, leading to our modern-day Nazareth, to dwell in hiddenness and humility. He leads us each day to laborious work, perhaps at little tasks which, if performed with great love, would truly preach the Gospel loudly!

Nazareth is our model and spiritual home. Like the Holy Family, we lead an ordinary life, filled with jobs done with great love for God and neighbor. Through these little daily tasks, we become "witnesses" of God. We must live in such a way that *our lives would not make sense* if God did not exist. In the marketplaces of the world, we must be preachers of the Gospel with our lives as well as (when required) with words. We must be preachers without compromise.

We are people called by God to give him birth in the marketplaces. We are to show him to those who dwell around us, and we do this by how we *live*.

3 | Giving Alms of Loving Words

Almsgiving during this season can be in the form of money, food, or clothing. Not everyone may be able to give these, but we all can give the alms of words, which we all need. We can give the alms of words everywhere.

See that lonely child? Have you a moment to spare to give him the alms of a few little words? They will bring light into a darkness that should not be there. Making friends with a lonely, lost, or unloved child, be he or she poor or rich, is to bring Christ to that little one. Take the child into your heart and you take Christ into your heart! And surely he will reverse the process in eternity by taking *you* into *his* heart!

Like all other alms, words must be given lovingly, gently, thoughtfully, in union with Christ, for alms given without love, compassion, graciousness, or deep understanding bring hurt and pain and do even more damage than indifference and coldness. Without these we prostitute the very act of giving.

Is our love watchful, ready to give the alms of gentle "key" words that may keep a door from closing? A gate may be unlocked and opened, allowing light and love to flood minds beginning to doubt the very existence of love. Do our eyes really see? Are we not blind to the thousands of little signs that exist in our own family? Father is a little grayer, a little more worried, a bit more silent. Mother is more tense, often with eyes that reveal tears. Sister or brother is sharper, thinner, less pleasant, more withdrawn. Do we really see?

4 | Alms for Our Brothers and Sisters

Are we convinced that we are our "brother's keeper"? Do we understand how far this "keeping" goes? Business associates, friends, fellow workers, strangers who cross our paths now and then, our whole work-a-day world—*all are our brothers and sisters,* whom we must cherish in the Lord. A smile and a pleasant word about the weather given to an ill-clad poor person in a public conveyance, or to a stranger, might mean the difference between his hatred of all that we stand for and understanding.

For example, with foreigners, clearly enunciated words, spoken slowly, lovingly, with a smile of encouragement, are rich "alms." The sick may be tiresome sometimes in their self-centeredness, pain and loneliness, their repetitious speech. They too need our alms of words. The forgotten, the unwanted, the lost, the rambling alcoholic, the neurotic, the borderline "psychos"—would they be where they are if someone had given them the alms of words when they so desperately needed them? Such words of love, compassion, and patience soothe the burning wounds of exhausted minds.

Words are so easy to give, yet so often withheld. They assuage the loneliness of the elderly, bring peace and joy, make crooked ways straight and people feel wanted and loved again. Let us lovingly show Christ to our brothers and sisters in the thousand ways of love's ingenuity, but especially in the alms of loving words!

5 Awaiting the Desired One

I want to discuss with you this wondrous season of Advent, the days of expectation, of awaiting the desired one. I ask myself, do we really desire the Lord? To desire something is to be constantly absorbed in that desire. This Advent we should go deeply into our hearts, minds, and souls. Let us clean house, and make a loving manger for the Christ Child into which he can be born in all his splendor.

One thing that can prevent this is looking at the world from the narrow cell of self. I suggest that for this Advent we remove from our vocabularies, from our conversations, our thoughts (and, if possible, from our dreams) the sentences: "I feel," "I want," and "I would like." Let us replace them with: "What does *God* want of me?"

Let us bury the word "I." Take a big shovel, make a big hole, stick the word "I" in there, and put a cross on top. Because the word "I" is the greatest enemy of *he, she,* and *we.* Remember that; it's very important. So try not to use the word "I," especially, "Oh *I* need this... Oh, *I* need that." No!

If this change of attitude takes place, our life would really take a giant leap toward peace and love, and hence toward happiness and joy. So do this for Advent, and do little things with great love for Christ. Then our minds, hearts, and souls will become a lovely manger in which the Lord can be born and grow to his full stature within us. When he does, we shall know happiness supreme.

6 | *St. Nicholas, Bishop*
The Messenger of the Little Infant

When I was a little girl in Russia, St. Nick was a mammoth gingerbread, all decked out with pink, green, and white decorations. Sometimes he was as big as a real baby. Only one St. Nick was baked in any household, so you had to be *very* good all through the year to get St. Nick. You worked hard for him all through the year. Yes, siree, you certainly did! You had to be the best child in the family, the most deserving, to get St. Nick.

Everyone knows, of course, about St. Nicholas. For wasn't he commissioned by the Christ Child himself, and his darling mother, and his good foster father, to come to earth every Christmas until the end of time, to tell the children of all the world the story of the Holy Night, and to bring them gifts of faith, hope, and charity, and such other gifts as they in their littleness and simplicity desired, and had asked of the holy baby?

Yes, in many countries today St. Nicholas is the "giver of gifts" at the side of Christ. St. Nicholas, shortened to "Santa Claus," is really the messenger of the little infant. The Christ Child, being too small at the moment, cannot deliver the presents himself. So he has commissioned St. Nicholas, now "Santa Claus," to do it in his stead.

7 Music of Love for the Little Child

I see you today—I see you as musical instruments, perfectly attuned to the will of God, and becoming a beautiful symphony. This music penetrates places where the only other sounds are the voices of angry, frightened people who do not know God and couldn't care less about him.

I think of you as minstrels, learning to sing lullabies to the Christ Child. I think of you as notes in this beautiful melody of the Holy Spirit. I listen to these notes, one by one, hoping and praying that each will be clear and true. The notes of your songs are your daily work and your attitudes. I pray that no sour notes ever enter your songs to the Christ Child.

I think of you as young trees and bushes adorned as brides and bridegrooms for a wedding feast, adorned as only God can clothe nature and the people who love him. I see you attuned to the Holy Spirit, the great wind, the ineffable composer of the right songs that the Holy Child likes to hear.

I see you cherished by his mother, who waits for you to come and share not only her Christmas joy in the stable of Bethlehem, but her whole life, so hidden and wonderful. It is she who has called us to imitate the lives of the Holy Family in Nazareth. Theirs was a humble and hidden life, composed of ordinary little things, but oh, how well done, and with great love!

8 *The Immaculate Conception* Litany of Loreto: Holy Virgin of Virgins

Virgin of Virgins, cool as the snow on the heights, untouched and unscaled... warm, glowing like fire, whose heat can consume without consuming, a fire that draws with its glow and its warmth all who behold it.

Virgin of Virgins, simple and humble, unnoticed by others.

In her are reflected old faces and young, and all between. She is all virgins, and yet there is none to compare with this simple and humble maiden of Israel.

Virgin of Virgins, woman of earth, resting in peace in the awesome and terrible hands of the Lord. At home in all the houses of earth; at home in the essence of the triune and infinite God.

Virgin of Virgins, slender, small... so fragile and young to the onlooker's eyes... riding her donkey defenseless through plains, hastening to the help of her cousin in pain.

Virgin of Virgins, all dressed in shimmering gold, spanning the height between heaven and earth; majestic, incredible, more powerful than all the power of humanity and nature combined; bidding the stars and sun as a child bids her pets. Behold, angels lie prostrate at her tiny feet.

Virgin of Virgins, friend of the poor, confidante of sinners. Lady demure, whose smile is benediction, whose touch is light. Virgin of Virgins, you are the gate of Christ.

9 | The Sound of the Donkey's Bells

When Russian mothers prepare their children for Christmas, the little ones especially, they say: "If you are a good girl, a good boy, you will hear the donkey's bells. Because Our Lady is going to travel on a donkey to Bethlehem to give birth to the infant, you will hear so very faintly the donkey's bells. But as it comes closer to Christmas, you will hear them clearly and well. But *only* if you are good." So my brother and I used to listen and my mother would wear little bells, first around her wrist and then around her knee too, then more bells as it got closer to Christmas. We were really excited about those bells.

Today it is very quiet. Are you listening? If you are listening, you can hear the faint sound of tinkling bells. He who is pure of heart and childlike shall hear the bell of the donkey ring in his life.

I pray that your hearts and souls and ears will hear very clearly the bells of the donkey, not only in Advent but throughout the year. I wish to give you the sound of a donkey's bells so that you might hear it all your life, for then you shall also ride with the holy one and hear the first church bells, which were the donkey's bells when he was carrying Our Lady and our Lord.

10 | A Modern Bethlehem

The world is a Bethlehem where all the inns have no room for him. The canyons of modern cities are caveless, skyscrapers having shuttered their entrances. The music of the donkey's hoofs is lost in the *swoosh* of our endless traffic. Where, then, shall the woman give birth to the wonderful One, in this caveless world, in this Bethlehem with inns that have no room for him?

Stop the noise of the traffic! Pause in your goalless rush. Stop, you organization man or woman, drunk with the pride of technological madness that makes you a slave of machines! See your skyscrapers tremble and dissolve in an avalanche of tears before the voice of the Father. He can make the world a cave that will hold your broken mechanical dreams, smashing your silly idols, your spaceships, your robots, your homes, like they were the fragile works of potters' wheels.

Stop your noise and listen to the music of the donkey's hoofs bearing the weight of the woman whose hour has come.

Hasten! Make warm the caves of your souls so that the holy anointed one may be born in them—or read the writing of destruction on the eternal walls.

11 | Our Hearts— Childlike Mangers for Christ

Christ desires to be born in the manger of our hearts. Are the doors of those hearts of ours wide open to receive the shepherds, the Magi, the stray visitors... in a word, humanity? Are they open to receive one another as Christ would receive each one of us? Are they open to receive those around us in our daily life? Or do we think it enough to make a manger of our hearts so that we might hold Christ unto ourselves exclusively? If so, that was not what he was born for, and he might bypass the manger of our hearts.

Christ told us that unless we *became like a child* we would not enter the kingdom of heaven. We tend to associate children and Christmas in a very sentimental fashion: a newborn baby is "cute," children are "lovable" creatures. So they are, but that is not what Christ meant. I think he wanted us to have the *heart* of a child. What does it mean to have the heart of a child? A child is utterly trusting, totally open, uninhibited, simple, direct, and unafraid. A child believes without reservation.

Every morning, after Communion, I go to pray to the Infant of Prague. I say, "Give me the heart of a child. Give me the awesome courage to live what it demands." That's what Christmas means to me too.

So, this Christmas, let us go together to kneel at the crib of a child, to receive the heart of a child, and to live accordingly.

12 | *Our Lady of Guadalupe*
The Lady Who Carries the Child

This is really the season of Our Lady. She carries the child, so there is a particular concentration on, a contemplation of Mary during this time. In Advent the heart moves in rhythm with her life. God bent to a woman and the world heard the words: "Hail Mary, full of grace!" She was going to be the Mother of God. A little girl, beholding the vision of an angel, spoke the truth. In doing so, she gave us a lesson in humility, for humility is truth that begs any other kind of lesson. "How can this happen to me? I do not know man." There she was. And she accepted. "May it be done to me according to your word."

We rejoice in Mary because she *always* brings us her Son.

Into the corridors of her heart we go, and different doors open; for she has an innumerable number of doors in those corridors that we call discernment. Think of her life. Think of her silence before Joseph, pregnant as she was. Our Lady wrapped herself in the fantastic silence of contemplation, prayer, and, perhaps, even the mantle of God. It is incomprehensible. Right now we are preparing for Christmas. Behold! Look down the road of a thousand corridors and you will see a young women wrapped in ordinary clothing. If she is worthy to be chosen the Mother of God, I think she is worthy to be chosen by us as our mother. Today we honor her as Our Lady of Guadalupe, patroness of the Americas and especially of Mexico.

13 | *St. Lucy, Martyr* A Vocation of Light

Your vocation as a Christian is luminous, full of light! The only thing that can make it dark is yourself—if you do your own will and not the will of God.

In everyday life, as you trudge through this vale of tears, you will constantly be looking for the promised land. But you love God so much that you are not concerned that he will call you home. A time will come when you will wish to die, simply because living is so difficult. But even then you will say to God, "Okay." You will be more interested in his will than in going to heaven, for it may not be his will that you be in heaven now.

Your goal is to love as God wants you to love so as to be fearless. For the battle in which you are engaged demands courage. Perfect love alone casts out fear. Nothing else can cast it out. So you must learn to love perfectly!

Love is a person; Love is God. You will possess God in proportion as you love. And then, because God is never outdone in generosity, you will possess him because he wishes to be possessed. He comes to you in your deserts and dark nights, and they are no more. Then you will know the Light.

14 St. John of the Cross and Anniversary of the Death of Catherine Doherty
Death: A Door to Life

Father Eddie and I discussed death quite often—death in general, and our own deaths in particular. We were always peaceful about it, for both of us felt that "death was but a door to life."

I have always believed in the resurrection of our Lord Jesus Christ. Jesus was born for us, he suffered for us, he was crucified for us, and he died for us. *And he resurrected!* Because he did, I have this utter sense of faith within me. It is a deep, immovable, definite faith that began to make the waiting easy and the journey light. I have faced death and I know her to be a friend who, someday, would take me by the hand and lead me into the heart of the Father. I know her to be a "smiling child" waiting to bring me to the Christ Child. I know her to be beautiful because she isn't really death but life—life renewed, life exploding, life lived in the heart of the Trinity!

If you are afraid of death, stop it. Stop being afraid. Enter into faith. If your faith seems small, cry out to the Lord that it might increase! Then you, too, will see death for who and what she really is—someone conquered by Christ on the day of his resurrection, and delighted with being conquered!

* Catherine Doherty died on December 14, 1985.

15 Poverty and Prayer

We should start realizing that true poverty is first and foremost a realization of *who we are*. We are created by God; we are creatures of God who are totally dependent on him. We are the poor people of God, the *anawim*—the "little ones" who know that they are totally dependent—who "lean" on God, knowing that without God they can do nothing.

This is the first step to prayer—to know who we are—saved

sinners, entirely dependent on God. We are *dependent.*

To the proud, this is anathema. We look at ourselves and we say, "I depend on no one," and suddenly, in the very saying, we realize that we do. This is the beginning of prayer: we become beggars before God, knowing that even the steps we take are given to us by God.

To begin to pray then is to first cleanse our souls of arrogance and pride. In grave humility and as beggars, we come to him who alone can make us princes and princesses and kings and queens, not of earthly kingdoms, but of the kingdom of God.

When we are thus poor and realize our total poverty, then we can go to Bethlehem and meet the child who became poor for us.

Is there any human being who does not respond to the cry of a child? Did you ever consider the first cry of the Child Jesus? That was his first message of love to us. When we know that we are poor, we can easily enter Bethlehem and answer that cry.

16 A Season of Atonement

He whose birthday we are about to celebrate was born in poverty. *He who was God was born naked.* He was naked in a cave, and he died naked on a cross for love. For the love of us all!

Today the same scene reenacts itself in underprivileged and wealthy countries, in its "caves," where children are born naked (as all babies are), but whose parents have nothing to put on their newborn infants. Jesus, at least, was wrapped in swaddling clothes.

I needn't go into the specifics of the great poverty in today's world; it is already brought to us in all its gory details by the media. Because God loves us, he uses these incredible and forceful pictures to draw the world's attention to what the poor are suffering. Do you see, dearly beloved, why I wish you poverty this Christmas season?

Let us then offer this season in atonement. Let us fast for

those who have nothing to eat. Let us pray for those who don't pray. Let us cry out to God with an ever greater faith so that those all around us can "catch the fire" of faith.

This season, fasting and feasting must go together. Yes, tears and joy must mingle to make an offering for the infant, an offering of diamonds and pearls and other jewels—all kinds of atonement! For today's infant is every child who is born in shacks and in streets, or discarded in garbage cans or sewers; and we must take the place of the three kings.

17 | Spiritual Bulldozing

I feel that there is a great deal of noise in our hearts. We have to learn to reduce it to a gentle silence that listens to God. We need to do what the Gospel says: "Make straight the paths of the Lord" in our own hearts. To do this, we need to pray to the Lord for a "bulldozer" to push away the rockfall and debris. God will do this for us if we stop the swirling dust of our own mutterings, the constant using of the pronoun "I," our thinking that we are always right and someone else is wrong, our non-listening to our own brothers and sisters.

The weight of listening is heavy. That is why we need to pray for a spiritual bulldozer to make straight the ways of the Lord in our hearts. Then God himself might walk these paths, unencumbered. He can come into our hearts and do the listening there. He can listen to others through us, talk through us, understand through us, help through us. He can console those who come to us. If the paths of our hearts are made straight, he would "come running!" He wants to be with us until the end of time, as he said in the Gospel, and he still desires to serve. And what better service could there be than to have a listening ear of God in our hearts?

It is time, dearly beloved, time to pray so that we might listen to the hunger of others. Usually people don't want us to do too much for them. They want us to listen because *listening means love and friendship*, for which there is such a great hunger today.

18 | The Tenderness of God

Listen with your heart. It takes listening, a special kind of listening, to hear the tenderness of God; and that is what you are going to hear this Christmas. If you let yourself enter into the immense sea of his tenderness, you will understand even better why we are a family of God—why we have been gathered together by him.

His tenderness will beget in us a tenderness for our brothers and sisters; and the circle of love which he has come to bring this day, this strange mysterious day of his birth, will slowly embrace the whole earth as he desires it to do.

We might not see that we are embraced so tenderly. On the contrary, before us will be catastrophes, tragedies, a blaspheming of the light of Christ, and what-have-you. But listen, listen with your heart... listen with your mind... listen with all of your being, and you will hear the tenderness of God! Strange as this might seem, tenderness is usually not heard but felt. However, you will experience it in both ways.

But in order to do so, my dearly beloved, we must place into his cupped infant hands our own dispossession, our own poverty. We will give it joyfully, tied up with Christmas ribbon and fancy paper, this total surrender of ourselves, give it into the hands of the great King, into the hands of the Son born to redeem us, so that he, in turn, can carry it to the Father, the Father who loves us so much!

19 | The Meaning of Strannik

To make the idea of *strannik*—which is the Russian word for pilgrim—known to the West, I think that perhaps you should read *The Story of the Other Wise Man* by Henry Van Dyke. It is a short book, a very lovely one.

A *strannik* is a pilgrim who "stops everywhere" to do good, not one who is hell-bent to get to some holy shrine and who ignores the intervening steps. Rather, a *strannik* is one who takes time during a journey to be alert to the "opportunities of grace" that lie along the pathway, to be on the lookout for God and to meet him in another person's eyes.

While I was in Vermont once, it rained and there was an elderly lady who couldn't get her raincoat organized. The sleeves wouldn't fall into place, and she couldn't find the hood. So I stopped the procession that was following me and helped her. She smiled at me and said, "Thank you!" The woman next to me said, "Do you always stop to do good?" I said, "No. I stop to be of service to my brethren, which I do not consider *being good,* but *being normal.*" And I went on. That's what I mean—that sort of thing. For some people, it could be an apostolate in itself... entering the terrible loneliness of the world, experiencing that loneliness, sharing that loneliness, and becoming wiser for it.

20 | Growing in Faith

Lately I have been possessed by a holy impatience. As I always do in Advent, I've been praying frequently to the infant, asking him over and over again for one grace: growth in faith for us all! Growth in faith means growth in love, humility, obedience, patience, and joy. Growth in faith means growth in openness and trust with each other. Oh, it means so much—this request of mine! It means that our work and our homes become a *hallway of heaven,* another Bethlehem, another Nazareth.

For this to happen, however, all of us must go through Golgotha. So I pray that we may each joyously accept the cross that God has prepared for us on the hills of love. Growth in faith means that we will understand the mystery of God's words: "He who loses his life will save it." So, on the threshold of another year, let us try to begin anew. Let us carry our crosses on our backs. Let us really begin to live in Christ, for him and through him. Truly he is worthy of our love. Nothing on earth or in heaven matters except God. See how he comes to us in a wooden manger, proclaiming his love even before he can speak our language. Notice the wood in the manger. How he loves wood! He chose it as a crib, and then he chose to work with it as a carpenter. Finally, he died on wood. All this for love of us!

21 | *First Day of Winter*
The Stillness of the Season

My outdoor Russian shrine here in Combermere stands peaceful and quiet, its roof covered with snow. The Virgin of Kiev is reflected in the vigil light that always burns before her face. It looks especially beautiful in the dark of the winter nights. Squirrels and raccoons scamper around, leaving tracks in the snow, as does my doe who comes to drink at the river where the current is too swift to freeze. Once in a while, bear tracks are also seen in the snow!

In such an environment, winter comes to greet me and leads me, slowly and gently, further into Advent, to the expected one—the child in the cave—the child who is God. It isn't difficult for me to imagine that snow and ice, trees and animals, share in my expectation. In December the island where I live sings of the coming of the Prince of Peace. My island is bare now. And there is a stillness, a holy stillness that makes very real to me the words of the Christmas antiphons, "When the night was still, our Almighty Word leapt down from heaven."

My mind turns to that Holy Night which is always so close, though it happened almost two thousand years ago. I cannot help meditating on this beautiful antiphon. My mind spins a cradle of silence into which the Word who leapt from heaven comes to rest.

22 | The Gurgle of a Baby

Listen! Do you hear the gurgle of a baby? Almost none of us can resist the gurgle-song of a baby, or a baby's smile. Yes, listen! It is his gurgle!

He is in the manger and he is happy to have become a man —a human being. Consider the incredible nature of what happened. God entered the womb of a human! God stayed there as every child stays—nine months! Then he was born. That, my friend, my dearly beloved, is the incarnation!

And he was happy to be incarnated because he loves us. Hence that funny little gurgle is the song, the smile of a child.

Come, let us arise and go together to Bethlehem. We shall be all one around his crib, though seemingly divided by time and space. But when we love, neither time nor space matters. So we shall all be together and we shall behold his gurgle, his song, his smile.

Let us remember it forever, until we meet him face to face. For it will assuage our depressions, our anxieties, our tensions. From his smile we are going to learn to smile and to sing ourselves, no matter where we are and what we have to do, because we shall know that our life is an eternal pilgrimage to Bethlehem.

23 | Is Your Heart Ready for Christmas?

What kind of birthplace are you providing for the Christ Child? Is the straw shiny and golden and clean? Is the manger solid, and will it hold up under the weight of the child? Are the animals quiet, scrubbed, brushed? Have you made the door of the stable of your heart secure against the cold winds of apathy, selfishness, indifference, so that these cannot penetrate? Is the dry wood of your sacrifices, your penances, your prayers, ready to be lit to provide warmth in that cold stable?

Are you ready for the coming of Love? Behold, he comes in the womb of a woman. You will catch your first glimpse of Love on the straw of a stable. There he is, emptying himself, the Lord of Hosts; out of love he became a child.

This child who lies in the manger possesses all power and glory! He has dominion over life and death. Nothing escapes his dominion. He made all the laws which brought the universe into existence—they were created by him and are subject to him. Yet it is the same child, the same humble Carpenter of Nazareth, the same man who died naked on a cross, who possesses all power and glory.

This Christmas will be a very special one, because I will put this child into your arms, and I ask you to care for him as if he were your very own baby. Turn to Our Lady, and she will teach you how to care for him.

24 | Christmas Eve
A Night of Splendor

This is a night of splendor, a night of expectancy and joy all tender. There is in it the scent of a thousand opening flowers and of spring.

How strange, for snow and ice still hold the earth imprisoned. How strange; in the forests trees are still asleep. Nowhere can be seen the smallest green bud.

This is a night of splendor with music in the air. How strange, for beneath the soft light of a moon, all is quiet, white-quilted with snow.

This is a night of splendor, for somewhere it seems a lily regal, slim, is shedding its perfume. How strange, for it is winter. Lilies do not bloom in the snow.

It is a night of splendor, filled with the sound of a donkey's hoofs that walk with a strange, joyful cadence that speaks of glory hidden and other awesome things.

This is a night of splendor, a night of expectancy and joy all tender. Why is it then that my heart wonders if it is ready to be a cradle for a child?

25 | *Christmas Day*
A Feast for Little Children

Christmas. The familiar story—a stable, a manger, the baby, the Virgin Mother, shepherds, carols, presents, Christmas trees, good will to all men and women. But is Jesus' warm and healing infant smile lost, wasted, on a cold indifferent world that would reject its very source, and, anew with every generation, crucify it with cruel mockery and wanton jest? It seems like it. Does it not? Behold in our century the cold hearts, the empty souls, the days spent in worship of self, in worrying about the altars of hideous idols we have created: security, power, wealth, health, beauty of body. These idols, our own distorted images, are what we really worship.

Babe of Bethlehem, have mercy on us! Send your angels to call us to your feet. Send us your graces to open our blind eyes, so that, prostrating ourselves before your utter destitution, we may find in its infinite richness a laver of our sins. Help us to become as little children, who alone shall enter heaven. As little children we shall see easily through the tinsel of wealth, power, security. And we shall reject all of them for your sake, embracing only your love. Sear us with the sparks of your fire. We can then indeed bring the true message of your birth to a world that has forgotten its very meaning, and thus restore it, and all that dwell therein, to your Father in heaven who so loved us as to send you to redeem us.

26 | *St. Stephen, First Martyr*
The Incarnation and Martyrdom

It has been said that the blood of martyrs is the seed of faith. Yet, it's not necessary that we shed blood; if we give ourselves, it's the same thing. Look at the very depths. We're all martyrs to ourselves. The battle is with ourselves. That's martyrdom.

The moment we engage ourselves in following Christ, we enter into the land of pain. When we enter into his pain, he is incarnated. As we enter into the incarnation, we enter into the terrible pain of humanity and our own pain in surrendering to the incarnation. First, we don't understand that we are surrendering to the incarnation, but eventually it comes about by the grace of God, and then the faith that surrenders to the incarnation must surrender to the crucifixion.

As we grow older, the pain grows in a different way. We already accept the incarnation and we have surrendered to the incarnation. But we also must surrender to the idea of the crucifixion, because deep down in our souls we really look forward to the resurrection. The inevitable, the inescapable, is the fact that we must pass through the crucifixion; otherwise, there will be no resurrection.

27 | St. John the Beloved, Apostle
The Heartbeats of God

Long ago, an ordinary man called John laid his head on the breast of Christ and listened to the heartbeats of the Lord. Who can venture to guess what that man felt as he heard the beat of that mighty heart? None of us can ever be in his place, but all of us could hear, if we would but listen, the heartbeats of God, the song of love he sings to us whom he has loved so much. If we meditated on the most holy Sacrament of the Eucharist we would not only hear his heartbeats, we would hear our hearts beating in unison with his; would be united with our Lord and our God.

God's heart is the only true resting place for all of us, the real oasis to which God calls us. But the key to his heart is identification with him and with all those he calls his little ones. Don't you see how simple it is!

This deep love of humanity requires an enlargement of heart that is so great that we could not aspire to it unless God showed us the way. We must pray for that enlargement of heart. This means touching God with one hand and touching our fellow human being with the other—and we become cruciform. We enter into a new dimension of faith and prayer and that helps the Lord to enlarge our heart.

28 | *Holy Innocents, Martyrs*
Do You Love Him?

As I kneel before the crib, I ask the Lord of Hosts, the King of power and glory who lies before me—a little child—that you might meet and know him as the child *and* the King, the man *and* the God in one person. I ask that you might know him who has called you so specially to himself, who changes himself into a tremendous lover, and desires of you but one thing: that you might love him back by surrendering totally and completely to him.

If, by some miracle of God's grace, you were to find yourself transported to Bethlehem, and the Christ Child were to ask you by name, as he did to Peter, "Do you love me, Sally, Dick, JoAnne, Joe?" What would you answer him? Could you answer like Peter, "Lord, you know that I love you"? Or would you have to say, "Yes, I love you, Lord, thus far, but no further!" Or, "I love you, Lord, so much—and no more."

Let us implore Emmanuel, the child, who is King of love, to teach us the one virtue which will bring us to our knees before his face—the virtue of humility, which is only another word for truth. In this humility we can tell him that we love him and that we want to be his completely; we can also humbly and truthfully beg him for the grace to do so.

I wish that the coming new year be a year of growth in faith; for as you grow in faith, you will grow in love and surrender, and that is really all that matters!

29 | Being Christ-Centered in Charity

Throughout this beautiful Christmas season I have prayed very ardently for you that the Infant Christ might touch your hearts, minds, and souls with his tiny hand, and open them to his own beauty, and to the realizaton of his need for you in his Mystical Body! I have prayed that you might begin to be Christ-centered, instead of self-centered. Yes, this is my prayer for you. To be Christ-centered is to be Love-centered.

Regarding this love, this charity, don't you see, dearly beloved, that you not only wound charity but cut it into pieces and crucify charity when you are rude in your manners, rude in your speech, rude in tone of voice? You do it when you snap at each other. You do it when you use smart and sarcastic techniques on one another, like disdainful silences which wound and shout louder than words. Refusal to reply to a simple question is like a slap in the face of another. Do you consider this as promoting charity, or crucifying it?

If you crucify charity, then remember charity is love, and Love is God, and you are guilty of crucifying God. May he have mercy on your soul!

This might seem a little negative to you. But for all the words that I use, all the seemingly new angles that I present to you, when all is said and done, come back to this sentence of John the Beloved: "Little children, let us love one another." I have nothing else to say, really for this is the very essence of our religion, our faith.

30 | A Family Story

Our Lady's dress is gingham, in simple lines, like housewives wear. An apron is over it, and her long black hair is neatly tied at the nape of her neck. She comes down from heaven sure and demure, as if she were a modern housewife descending to make the family breakfast. She is alone and goes in and out from house to house with a shopping basket.

What does she see? From some she comes out quite sad, from others glad. It seems she prefers the houses with lots of kids and things not quite so tidy because of them. There she stays a long time and as she comes out, her basket bulges. She bypasses certain homes—nice ones and comfortable, but a little cold. She goes everywhere across the world and soon her shopping bag is really bulging! Up she goes to heaven in the twilight in her ordinary house dress, and there she is in front of her Son.

Now we shall see what is in the basket. She smiles happily and lifts the top. And what do we see? Why hearts! Lots of them! Beating merrily, happily. They are strange hearts—two in one, beating in unison, encircled by a crown of little hearts that beat the same. Why that's simple! Why didn't I guess? She brings to Christ little churches—families! Families that live with him through her. And Mary kneels at his feet and talks to him about this family or that. Each of these hearts beat in unison with her heart. They are hearts of families that pray together, and so stay together—with Jesus, Mary, and Joseph, in heaven.

31 | *New Year's Eve* On the Threshold of the New Year

Enter the new year with hope, knowing that you can do nothing of yourself. Walk in faith, and that faith will grow and grow! And you will begin to understand that *he can do all things in you.* So in total simplicity and childlikeness, in a faith that sings of your desire for him, in a love that celebrates with an untarnished hope, face this new year without fear! Why should you be afraid when the Lord is with you? We live in the resurrected Christ. Together, upholding each other in love and joy and faith, we shall restore that which needs restoring in the church.

Love, as I look at it, is mine to have—and to give—so it is yours for the taking. I give you, in the midst of all the Christmas decorations, my love. And I ask the Lord to give you peace. I pray passionately that you become "at peace"—first with God, then with yourself, and then with everyone. May you be gifted this coming year with understanding, tenderness, compassion, forgiveness, reconciliation, faith, hope, and love.

I pray that your heart may become more and more like that of the Christ Child, and that you will pray with me, "Give me the heart of a child, and the awesome courage to live it out as an adult." I pray that, through all your years, you will walk close to Our Lady, for the child came through her and through her you can go to him.

Other Writings by
Catherine de Hueck Doherty

Apostolic Farming
Dearly Beloved — 3 volumes
Dear Father
Dear Seminarian
Doubts, Loneliness, Rejection
Fragments of My Life
The Gospel of a Poor Woman
The Gospel Without Compromise
Journey Inward
Lubov
Molchanie
My Heart and I
My Russian Yesterdays
Not Without Parables
Our Lady's Unknown Mysteries
The People of the Towel and the Water
Poustinia
Re-entry into Faith
Sobornost
Soul of My Soul
Stations of the Cross
Strannik
Urodivoi
Welcome, Pilgrim

Available from: Madonna House Publications
Combermere, Ontario, Canada
K0J 1L0